REEDS
MARINA GUIDE
202[...]

The source dir[...]
all sail & pov[...]
owne[...]

© Adlard Coles Na[...]

Adlard Coles N[...]
50 Bedford Square, Lor[...]
29 Earlsfort Terrace, D[...]

Tel: 01865 41[...]
e-mail: info@reedsal[...]
www.reedsalman[...]

Cover pho[...]
Poole Quay Boat Ha[...]
Port of Poole[...]
Poole Town Qua[...]
Tel: 01202 64[...]
www.poolequayboat[...]

Section 1

The Marinas and Serv[...]
has been fully update[...]
2023 season. These u[...]
provide chartlets and[...]
details for some 200 r[...]
around the shores of[...]
Ireland, including the[...]
Islands, the perfect co[...]
any Reeds Nautical Al[...]

Section 2

The Marine Supplies &[...]
section lists more that[...]
services at coastal and[...]
locations around the [...]
It provides a quick an[...]
reference to manufac[...]
retailers of equipmen[...]
and supplies both nat[...]
and locally together v[...]
emergency services.

Advertisement[...]
Enquiries about adver[...]
should be addres[...]
adlardcoles@bloom[...]

Printed by Bell and Bain[...]

C000046904

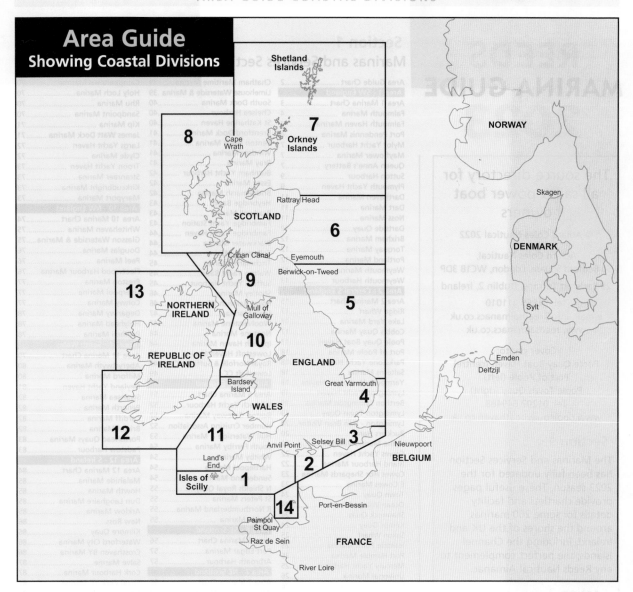

Area Guide
Showing Coastal Divisions

Area 1 .....**South West England** .... Isles of Scilly to Anvil Point

Area 2 .....**Central Southern England** .... Anvil Point to Selsey Bill

Area 3 .....**South East England** .... Selsey Bill to North Foreland

Area 4 .....**East England** .... North Foreland to Great Yarmouth

Area 5 .....**North East England** .... Great Yarmouth to Berwick-upon-Tweed

Area 6 .....**South East Scotland** .... Eymouth to Rattray Head

Area 7 .....**North East Scotland** .... Rattray Head to Cape Wrath including Orkney & Shetland Is

Area 8 .....**North West Scotland** .... Cape Wrath to Crinan Canal

Area 9 .....**South West Scotland** .... Crinan Canal to Mull of Galloway

Area 10 ...**North West England** .... Isle of Man & N Wales, Mull of Galloway to Bardsey Is

Area 11 ...**South Wales & Bristol Channel** .... Bardsey Island to Land's End

Area 12 ...**South Ireland** .... Malahide, clockwise to Liscannor Bay

Area 13 ...**North Ireland** .... Liscannor Bay, clockwise to Lambay Island

Area 14 ...**Channel Islands** .... Guernsey and Jersey

SOUTH WEST ENGLAND – Isles of Scilly to Anvil Point

Key to Marina Plans symbols

Bottled gas		P	Parking
Chandler		✗	Pub/Restaurant
Disabled facilities			Pump out
Electrical supply			Rigging service
Electrical repairs			Sail repairs
Engine repairs			Shipwright
First Aid			Shop/Supermarket
Fresh Water			Showers
Fuel - Diesel			Slipway
Fuel - Petrol		WC	Toilets
Hardstanding/boatyard			Telephone
@ Internet Café			Trolleys
Laundry facilities		V	Visitors berths
Lift-out facilities			Wi-Fi

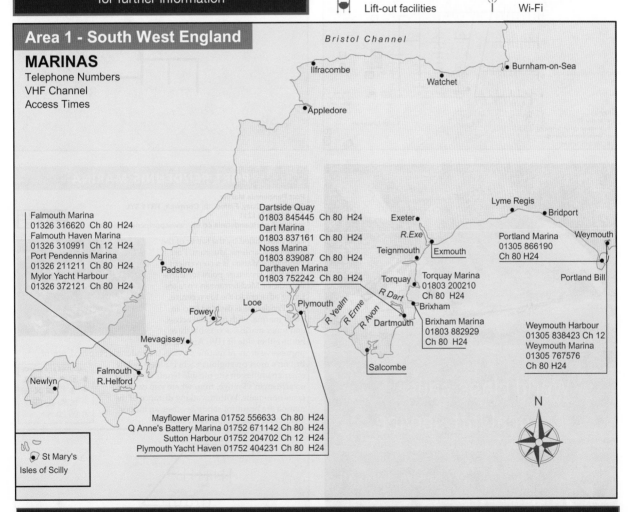

Area 1 - South West England

MARINAS
Telephone Numbers
VHF Channel
Access Times

Bristol Channel

Ilfracombe

Watchet

Burnham-on-Sea

Appledore

Falmouth Marina
01326 316620 Ch 80 H24
Falmouth Haven Marina
01326 310991 Ch 12 H24
Port Pendennis Marina
01326 211211 Ch 80 H24
Mylor Yacht Harbour
01326 372121 Ch 80 H24

Padstow

Dartside Quay
01803 845445 Ch 80 H24
Dart Marina
01803 837161 Ch 80 H24
Noss Marina
01803 839087 Ch 80 H24
Darthaven Marina
01803 752242 Ch 80 H24

Exeter

R.Exe

Teignmouth

Exmouth

Torquay

Torquay Marina
01803 200210
Ch 80 H24

R Dart

Brixham

Lyme Regis

Bridport

Portland Marina
01305 866190
Ch 80 H24

Weymouth

Portland Bill

Fowey

Looe

Plymouth

R Yealm *R Erme* *R Avon*

Dartmouth

Brixham Marina
01803 882929
Ch 80 H24

Weymouth Harbour
01305 838423 Ch 12
Weymouth Marina
01305 767576
Ch 80 H24

Mevagissey

Newlyn

Falmouth
R.Helford

Salcombe

Mayflower Marina 01752 556633 Ch 80 H24
Q Anne's Battery Marina 01752 671142 Ch 80 H24
Sutton Harbour 01752 204702 Ch 12 H24
Plymouth Yacht Haven 01752 404231 Ch 80 H24

N

St Mary's
Isles of Scilly

FALMOUTH MARINA

Falmouth Marina
North Parade, Falmouth, Cornwall, TR11 2TD
Tel: 01326 316620
Email: falmouth@premiermarinas.com
www.premiermarinas.com

VHF	Ch 80
ACCESS	H24

Falmouth Marina sits within the safe and sheltered waters and outstanding natural beauty of the Fal Estuary, with 24/7 access to the glorious cruising grounds and countryside of Cornwall.

The marina is family-friendly and ideal for boaters of all abilities, with both secure wet and dry stack berthing options. Falmouth provides first-class facilities, along with an array of marine and hospitality services, including a chandlery, brokerage, fully serviced boatyard, bar/restaurant and an onsite hairdresser.

FACILITIES AT A GLANCE

Key
a   Marina office
b   Waste oil and bin compound
c   Under cover boat storage
d   Dry stack facilities

FALMOUTH HAVEN MARINA

Falmouth Haven Marina
44 Arwenack Street
Tel: 01326 310991
Email: welcome@falmouthhaven.co.uk

VHF	Ch 12
ACCESS	H24

Run by Falmouth Harbour Commissioners (FHC), Falmouth Haven Marina has become increasingly popular since its opening in 1982, enjoying close proximity to the amenities and entertainments of Falmouth town centre. Sheltered by a breakwater, Falmouth Haven caters for 50 boats and offers petrol and diesel supplies as well as good shower and laundry facilities.

Falmouth Harbour is considered by some to be the cruising capital of Cornwall and its deep water combined with easily navigable entrance – even in the severest conditions – makes it a favoured destination for visiting yachtsmen.

FACILITIES AT A GLANCE

PORT PENDENNIS MARINA

Port Pendennis Marina
Challenger Quay, Falmouth, Cornwall, TR11 3YL
Tel: 01326 211211
marina@.portpendennis.co.uk   www.portpendennis.co.uk

VHF	Ch 80
ACCESS	H24

Easily identified by the tower of the National Maritime Museum, Port Pendennis Marina is a convenient arrival or departure point for trans-Atlantic or Mediterranean voyages. Lying adjacent to the town centre, Port Pendennis is divided into an outer marina, with full tidal access, and inner marina, accessible three hours either side of HW. Among its impressive array of marine services is Pendennis Shipyard, one of Britain's most prestigious yacht builders, while other amenities on site include tennis court and a yachtsman's lounge, from where you can send faxes or e-mails. Within walking distance of the marina are beautiful sandy beaches, an indoor swimming pool complex and castle.

FACILITIES AT A GLANCE

The friendly marina in the heart of
Falmouth, Cornwall

Fronting Marina Square, with a choice of restaurants overlooking the harbour

Adjacent to the Maritime Museum, in the centre of town

Berthing for yachts to over 80m l.o.a & 4m draft

Luxury shower facilities

Laundry

Yachtsmans lounge

Free WiFi

Tennis court

Port

Pendennis

" The perfect stopover for **Transatlantic & Biscay** passages.

Falmouth, Cornwall, TR11 3YL
Tel: 01326 211211 | Fax: 01326 311116
Email: marina@portpendennis.com
VHF Channel 80

www.portpendennis.com

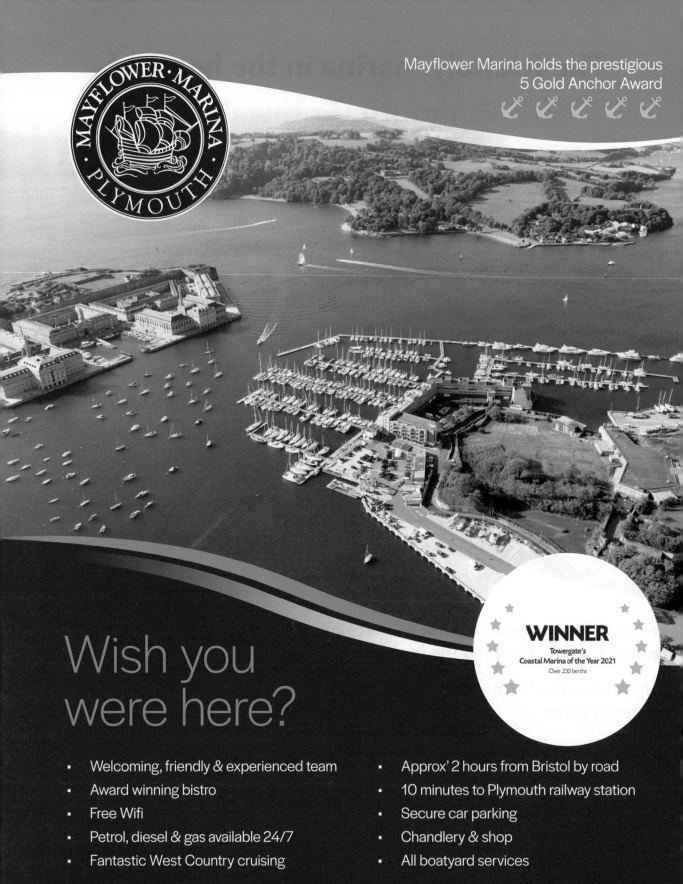

MYLOR YACHT HARBOUR

Mylor Yacht Harbour Marina
Mylor, Falmouth, Cornwall, TR11 5UF
Tel: 01326 372121
Email: enquiries@mylor.com

VHF Ch M, 80
ACCESS H24

Nestled on the western shore of the beautiful Fal Estuary, Mylor Yacht Harbour's stunning marina has 180 berths and is surrounded by 240 swinging moorings. A large dedicated visitor pontoon, easy H24 access and excellent shore-side facilities set within an Area of Outstanding Natural Beauty combine to make Mylor a must-visit cruising destination.

The historic site was founded in 1805 as the Navy's smallest dockyard but is now a thriving yacht harbour and full service boatyard. Superb on site café, restaurant and yacht club all overlook the harbour and scenic coastal footpaths run from the top of the gangway. Falmouth is just 10 minutes away.

FACILITIES AT A GLANCE

Not Dredged

34

B Dredged to 2m below CD

A

C

D

E

P

30

g

60

38

i

N

Key
a Harbour cafe and shops
b Showers/toilets
c Kingsmoor Cottage and Castaways Wine Bar
d Marina office
e Rigging pontoon
f New public slipway
g Fueling pontoon
h Marine services and Harbour office
i Water taxi pick up
j Yacht club/laundry
k Holiday accommodation

P

Destination Mylor

A welcoming yacht harbour anchored by the country's finest sailing waters.

Image © Aerial Cornwall

1

- Contemporary marina & safe moorings
- One of the largest visitor pontoons in the south west
- Full service boatyard
- Boat lifting & shore storage
- 1st class shore side facilities
- All tides access & prime sailing location

VHF ch. 37/80

Mylor
Yacht Harbour

mylor.com
01326 372 121
enquiries@mylor.com

MAYFLOWER MARINA

Mayflower Marina
Richmond Walk, Plymouth, PL1 4LS
Tel: 01752 556633
Email: info@mayflowermarina.co.uk

⚓⚓⚓⚓

VHF Ch 80
ACCESS H24

Sitting on the famous Plymouth Hoe, with the Devon coast to the left and the Cornish coast to the right, Mayflower Marina is a friendly, well-run marina. Facilities include 24 hour access to fuel, gas and a launderette, full repair and maintenance services as well as an on site bar and brasserie. The marina is located only a short distance from Plymouth's town centre, where there are regular train services to and from several major towns and cities.

FACILITIES AT A GLANCE

Northern approach Breakwater

J

K

WC

WC

P

P

N

A

H

L

G

B

E

D

C

F

Southern approach

Key
a Marina office
b Brokerage, chandlery
c Cafe
d Bar
e Brasserie
f Berth holders toilets and showers
g Ocean Court Flats

NB Arrows denote direction of numbers low to high. Even numbers on port side, odd to starboard

QUEEN ANNE'S BATTERY

Queen Anne's Battery
Plymouth, Devon, PL4 OLP
Tel: 01752 671142
Email: qab@mdlmarinas.co.uk www.queenannesbattery.co.uk

VHF Ch 80
ACCESS H24

Plymouth, a vibrant and fast growing city, is home to Queen Anne's Battery, a 235 resident berth marina with outstanding facilities for yachtsmen and motor cruisers alike. Located just south of Sutton Harbour, QAB promises a welcoming stay with alongside pontoon berthing protected by the surrounding breakwater. While on the city's doorstep, the marina is a short walk away from the historical Barbican, providing peace and tranquility to visitors.

The marina is often frequented by crowds of people marveling the many prestigious international yacht and powerboat races Plymouth Sound facilitates.

QAB is an exposed treasure along a beautiful historic coastline, at times resembling a mini 'Cowes' with its vibrancy.

FACILITIES AT A GLANCE

F

E

D

C

B

A

P

P

P

P

P

P

P

N

Key
a Toilets and showers
b Royal Western Yacht Club
c Marina office and provisions shop
d Bar/restaurant
e Cafe

PLYMOUTH YACHT HAVEN

Plymouth Yacht Haven Ltd
Shaw Way, Mount Batten, Plymouth, PL9 9XH
Tel: 01752 404231 www.yachthavens.com
Email: enquiries@plymouthyachthaven.com

VHF	Ch 80
ACCESS	H24

Situated minutes from Plymouth Sound, Plymouth Yacht Haven enjoys a tranquil setting, yet is just a five minute water taxi ride from the bustling Barbican with all its restaurants and attractions. The Yacht Haven offers excellent protection from the prevailing SW winds and is within easy reach of some of the most fantastic cruising grounds.

This 450-berth marina can accommodate vessels up to 45m in length and 7m in draught. Members of staff are on site 24/7 to welcome you as a visitor and to serve diesel. With an on site 75T travel hoist and storage, a restaurant, chandlery, and extensive range of marine service, Plymouth Yacht Haven has plenty to offer both on and off the water.

FACILITIES AT A GLANCE

Key
a	Houses	e	Snacks and takeaway
b	Berth holders car park	f	Mountbatten Watersports Centre and bar/restaurant
c	Washdown area	g	Main reception - toilets, showers, phones,launderette and disabled facilities
d	Shipwright, etc	h	The Bridge restaurant

SUTTON HARBOUR

Sutton Harbour
The Jetty, Sutton Harbour, Plymouth, PL4 0DW
Tel: 01752 204702 Fax: 01752 204693
Email: marina@sutton-harbour.co.uk
www.suttonharbourmarina.com

VHF	Ch 12
ACCESS	H24

Sutton Harbour Marina, located in the heart of Plymouth's historic Barbican area and a short stroll from the city centre, offers 5-star facilities in a sheltered location, surrounded by boutique waterfront bars and restau a minimum 3.5m depth, the harbour has 24hr lock access on request with free flow approx 3hrs either side of high tide. The marina of choice for international yacht races such as The Transat and Fastnet. Visitors are invited to come and enjoy the unrivalled shelter, facilities, atmosphere and location that Sutton harbour offers.

FACILITIES AT A GLANCE

Key
a	Fish market
b	National Marine Aquarium
c	Customs House
d	The Cove
e	Marina office
f	Lock tower

DARTHAVEN MARINA

Darthaven Marina
Brixham Road, Kingswear, Devon, TQ6 0SG
Tel: 01803 752242
Email: admin@darthaven.co.uk
www.darthaven.co.uk

VHF Ch 80
ACCESS H24

Darthaven Marina is a family run business situated in the village of Kingswear on the east side of the River Dart. Within half a mile from Start Bay and the mouth of the river, it is the first marina you come to from seaward and is accessible at all states of the tide. Darthaven prides itself on being more than just a marina, offering a high standard of marine services with both electronic and engineering experts plus wood and GRP repairs on site. A shop, post office and three pubs are within a walking distance of the marina, while a frequent ferry service takes passengers across the river to Dartmouth.

FACILITIES AT A GLANCE

Key
a Main office
   Chandlery
   Electricians
b Shipwrights
c Engineers
d Yacht taxi pontoon
e Berthing office
f Welding workshop

DART MARINA

Dart Marina
Sandquay Road, Dartmouth, Devon, TQ6 9PH
Tel: 01803 837161 Fax: 01803 835040
Email: yachtharbour@dartmarina.com
www.dartmarinayachtharbour.com

VHF Ch 80
ACCESS H24

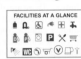

Dart Marina Yacht Harbour, in one of the most stunning locations on the UK coastline, is a peaceful spot for simply sitting on deck relaxing and perfectly positioned for day sailing or more ambitious cruising. With visitor berths, 110 annual berths, all accessible at any tide, the Yacht Harbour is sought after for its intimate atmosphere and stylish setting.

Professional, knowledgeable and helpful, the marina team is on-site all year round and there are impeccable facilities including showers, bathrooms and laundry.

In Dartmouth there are restaurants, bistros, cafes, delis, independent shops, galleries, a cinema, chandlers, antique and lifestyle shops in abundance.

FACILITIES AT A GLANCE

NOSS ON DART MARINA

Noss on Dart Marina
Bridge Road, Kingswear, Devon, TQ6 0EA
Tel: 01803 839087
Email: noss@premiermarinas.com
www.premiermarinas.com

VHF Ch 80
ACCESS H24

Set on the eastern bank of the River Dart, in a secluded area of outstanding natural beauty, Noss on Dart Marina offers easy access to some of the most beautiful anchorages and ports in Devon. Located close to astounding woodland walks along the Dart Valley Trail, for wildlife spotting and a hotspot for local festivals and regattas.

Noss on Dart is currently undergoing a £75m development, with the 232-berth floating marina, fully serviced boatyard, dry-stack and first commercial building to accommodate marine tenants now complete and operational. The next stage of the redevelopment will be the construction of a hotel, café and residential apartments.

FACILITIES AT A GLANCE

Key
a Marina office
b Hotel, bar, restaurant
c Commercial building

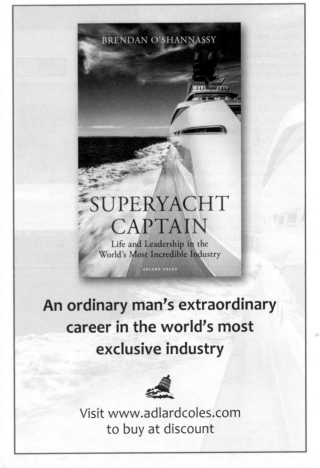

DARTSIDE QUAY

Dartside Quay
Galmpton Creek, Brixham, Devon, TQ5 0EH
Tel: 01803 845445
Email: dartsidequay@mdlmarinas.co.uk
www.dartsidequay.co.uk

VHF | Ch 80
ACCESS | HW±2

Located at the head of Galmpton Creek, Dartside Quay lies three miles upriver from Dartmouth. In a sheltered position and with beautiful views across to Dittisham, it offers extensive boatyard facilities. The seven-acre dry boat storage area has space for over 300 boats and is serviced by a 65-ton hoist operating from a purpose-built dock, plus a 20-ton trailer hoist operating on a slipway. There are also a number of overnight/monthly moorings available (dry out) in the summer months. You will also find various specialist marine tenants on site able to assist with boat repairs and maintenance.

FACILITIES AT A GLANCE

Key
a Commercial unit
b Lower main quarry
c Middle quarry
d Top quarry
e Upper main quarry
f Cottage
g Battery, hazardous waste and oil disposal
h Admin/yard office

BRIXHAM MARINA

Brixham Marina
Berry Head Road, Brixham, Devon, TQ5 9BW
Tel: 01803 882929
Email: brixham@mdlmarinas.co.uk
www.brixhammarina.co.uk

VHF | Ch 80
ACCESS | H24

Home to one of Britain's largest fishing fleets, Brixham Harbour is located on the southern shore of Torbay, which is well sheltered from westerly winds and where tidal streams are weak. Brixham Marina, housed in a separate basin to the work boats, provides easy access in all weather conditions and at all states of the tide. Provisions and diesel are available and there is a bar and restaurant, ideal for when you've worked up an appetite out on the water. Local attractions include Berry Head Nature Reserve and a visit to the replica of Francis Drake's *Golden Hind*.

FACILITIES AT A GLANCE

Key
a Dock manager's office
b Information centre
c Boat sales and Sea School

TORQUAY MARINA

Torquay Marina
Torquay, Devon, TQ2 5EQ
Tel: 01803 200210
Email: torquaymarina@mdlmarinas.co.uk
www.torquaymarina.co.uk

VHF | Ch 80
ACCESS | H24

Tucked away in the north east corner of Torbay, Torquay Marina is well sheltered from the prevailing SW'ly winds, providing safe entry in all conditions and at any state of the tide. Located in the centre of Torquay, the marina boasts a sea school, stand-up paddleboarding/watersports centre and artisan café, and also offers easy access to the town's numerous stores, bars and restaurants.

Torquay is ideally situated for either exploring Tor Bay itself, with its many delightful anchorages, or else for heading west to experience several other scenic harbours such as Dartmouth and Salcombe. It also provides a good starting point for crossing to Brittany, Normandy or the Channel Islands.

FACILITIES AT A GLANCE

Key
a Dock manager's office
b Dockmaster offices
c Restaurant, cafe and newsagents

PORTLAND MARINA

Portland Marina
Osprey Quay, Portland, Dorset, DT5 1DX
Tel: 01305 866190
Email: portland@boatfolk.co.uk
www.boatfolk.co.uk/portlandmarina

VHF | Ch 80
ACCESS | H24

Portland Marina is an ideal location for both annual berthing and weekend stopovers. The marina offers first class facilities including washrooms, on-site bar and restaurant, lift out and storage up to 50T, dry stacking up to 9m, 24-hour manned security, fuel berth, sewage pump out, extensive car parking and a full range of marine services including a chandlery.

The marina is within walking distance of local pubs and restaurants on Portland with Weymouth's bustling town centre and mainline railway station just a short bus or ferry ride away.

FACILITIES AT A GLANCE

Key
a Admin Office, washrooms, showers and laundry
b Bar and Restaurant
c Business/retail units
d Refuse and recycling bins
e Commercial units
f Dry stack storage building
g Sunseeker

Berthing guide
From low at hammerheads
Odds outside
Evens inside

WEYMOUTH HARBOUR

Harbour Office
13 Custom House Quay, Weymouth, Dorset, DT4 8BG
Tel: 01305 838423
Email: weymouthharbour@dorsetcouncil.gov.uk
www.weymouth-harbour.co.uk

VHF Ch 12
ACCESS H24

Weymouth Harbour, situated on the Jurassic Coast, lays N of Portland in the protected waters of Weymouth Bay. Located in the heart of the old town and accessible at any state of tide, the Georgian harbour has numerous overnight berths. Pontoons on both quays have electricity and fresh water, as well as modern shower facilities. Restaurants and shops abound within walking distance and visitors are also welcome in the Royal Dorset YC and Weymouth SC, both situated on the quayside.

Vessels are advised to call *Weymouth Harbour* on Ch12 on approach, and vessels over 15m are recommended to give prior notification of intended arrival.

FACILITIES AT A GLANCE

Key
a Waiting pontoon for bridge
b Lifeboat
c Weymouth Sailing Club
d Royal Dorset Yacht Club

WEYMOUTH MARINA

Weymouth Marina
70 Commercial Road, Dorset, DT4 8NA
Tel: 01305 767576 Fax: 01305 767575
Email: weymouth@boatfolk.co.uk
www.boatfolk.co.uk/weymouthmarina

VHF Ch 80
ACCESS H24

With more than 280 permanent and visitors' berths, Weymouth is a modern, purpose-built marina ideally situated for yachtsmen cruising between the West Country and the Solent. It is also conveniently placed for sailing to France or the Channel Islands. Accessed via the town's historic lifting bridge, which opens every even hour 0800–2000 (plus 2100 Jun–Aug), the marina is dredged to 2.5m below chart datum. It provides easy access to the town centre, with its abundance of shops, pubs and restaurants, as well as to the traditional seafront where an impressive sandy beach is overlooked by an esplanade of hotels.

FACILITIES AT A GLANCE

Explore.

Just one Premier Advantage

VISITOR NIGHTS 42

SWANWICK MARINA

The freedom to explore our ten first class marinas with **42 visitor nights***, and **easy marina transfers** are just two of the benefits our annual berth holders enjoy. Premier Advantage is our unrivalled benefits package also offering storage ashore, fuel at cost, Sea Start breakdown support, Loyalty Reward credits and more. **Upgrade to Premier - the finest marinas, quality boatyards, and exceptional service.**

*Subject to availability

EASTBOURNE

BRIGHTON

CHICHESTER

SOUTHSEA

PORT SOLENT

GOSPORT

UNIVERSAL MARINA

SWANWICK

NOSS ON DART

FALMOUTH

Call **01489 884 060**
Visit **premiermarinas.com/premieradvantage**

PREMIER MARINAS

CENTRAL SOUTHERN ENGLAND – Anvil Point to Selsey Bill

2

Key to Marina Plans symbols

🛢	Bottled gas	P	Parking
	Chandler	✗	Pub/Restaurant
♿	Disabled facilities		Pump out
	Electrical supply		Rigging service
	Electrical repairs		Sail repairs
	Engine repairs	✗	Shipwright
✚	First Aid	🛒	Shop/Supermarket
	Fresh Water		Showers
D	Fuel - Diesel		Slipway
P	Fuel - Petrol	WC	Toilets
	Hardstanding/boatyard	✆	Telephone
@	Internet Café		Trolleys
	Laundry facilities	V	Visitors berths
	Lift-out facilities		Wi-Fi

Area 2 - Central Southern England

MARINAS
Telephone Numbers
VHF Channel
Access Times

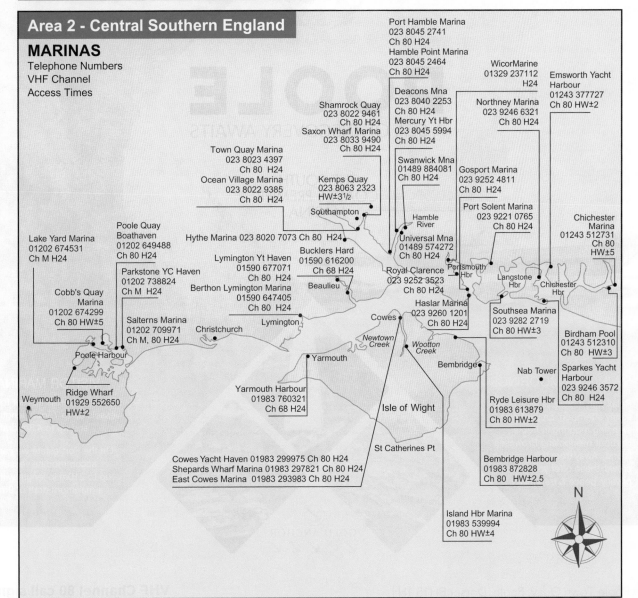

Port Hamble Marina
023 8045 2741
Ch 80 H24

Hamble Point Marina
023 8045 2464
Ch 80 H24

WicorMarine
01329 237112
H24

Emsworth Yacht Harbour
01243 377727
Ch 80 HW±2

Deacons Mna
023 8040 2253
Ch 80 H24

Mercury Yt Hbr
023 8045 5994
Ch 80 H24

Northney Marina
023 9246 6321
Ch 80 H24

Shamrock Quay
023 8022 9461
Ch 80 H24

Saxon Wharf Marina
023 8033 9490
Ch 80 H24

Swanwick Mna
01489 884081
Ch 80 H24

Gosport Marina
023 9252 4811
Ch 80 H24

Town Quay Marina
023 8023 4397
Ch 80 H24

Ocean Village Marina
023 8022 9385
Ch 80 H24

Kemps Quay
023 8063 2323
HW±3½

Port Solent Marina
023 9221 0765
Ch 80 H24

Chichester Marina
01243 512731
Ch 80 HW±5

Southampton

Hamble River

Lake Yard Marina
01202 674531
Ch M H24

Poole Quay Boathaven
01202 649488
Ch 80 H24

Hythe Marina 023 8020 7073 Ch 80 H24

Bucklers Hard
01590 616200
Ch 68 H24

Universal Mna
01489 574272
Ch 80 H24

Portsmouth Hbr

Langstone Hbr

Chichester Hbr

Parkstone YC Haven
01202 738824
Ch M H24

Lymington Yt Haven
01590 677071
Ch 80 H24

Beaulieu

Royal Clarence
023 9252 3523
Ch 80 H24

Cobb's Quay Marina
01202 674299
Ch 80 HW±5

Berthon Lymington Marina
01590 647405
Ch 80 H24

Haslar Marina
023 9260 1201
Ch 80 H24

Southsea Marina
023 9282 2719
Ch 80 HW±3

Birdham Pool
01243 512310
Ch 80 HW±3

Salterns Marina
01202 709971
Ch M, 80 H24

Christchurch

Lymington

Cowes

Newtown Creek

Wootton Creek

Bembridge

Nab Tower

Sparkes Yacht Harbour
023 9246 3572
Ch 80 H24

Poole Harbour

Yarmouth

Ryde Leisure Hbr
01983 613879
Ch 80 HW±2

Weymouth

Ridge Wharf
01929 552650
HW±2

Yarmouth Harbour
01983 760321
Ch 68 H24

Isle of Wight

St Catherines Pt

Cowes Yacht Haven 01983 299975 Ch 80 H24
Shepards Wharf Marina 01983 297821 Ch 80 H24
East Cowes Marina 01983 293983 Ch 80 H24

Bembridge Harbour
01983 872828
Ch 80 HW±2.5

Island Hbr Marina
01983 539994
Ch 80 HW±4

N

2

RIDGE WHARF YACHT CENTRE

Ridge Wharf Yacht Centre
Ridge, Wareham, Dorset BH20 5BG
Tel: 01929 552650 Fax: 01929 554434
Email: office@ridgewharf.co.uk www.ridgewharf.co.uk

VHF
ACCESS HW±2

On the south bank of the River Frome, which acts as the boundary to the North of the Isle of Purbeck, is Ridge Wharf Yacht Centre. Access for a 1.5m draught is between one and two hours either side of HW, with berths drying out to soft mud. The Yacht Centre cannot be contacted on VHF, so it is best to phone up ahead of time to inquire about berthing availability.

A trip upstream to the ancient market town of Wareham is well worth while, although owners of deep-draughted yachts may prefer to go by dinghy. Tucked between the Rivers Frome and Trent, it is packed full of cafés, restaurants and shops.

FACILITIES AT A GLANCE

LAKE YARD MARINA

Lake Yard Marina
Lake Drive, Hamworthy, Poole, Dorset BH15 4DT
Tel: 01202 674531
Email: office@lakeyard.com www.lakeyard.com

VHF Ch M
ACCESS H24

Lake Yard is situated towards the NW end of Poole Harbour, just beyond the SHM No 73. The entrance can be easily identified by 2FR (vert) and 2FG (vert) lights. Enjoying 24 hour access, the marina has no designated visitors' berths, but will accommodate visiting yachtsmen if resident berth holders are away. Its on site facilities include full maintenance and repair services as well as hard standing and a 50 ton boat hoist, although for the nearest fuel go to Corralls (Tel 01202 674551), opposite the Town Quay. Lake Yard's Waterfront Club, offering spectacular views across the harbour, opens 7/7 for breakfast, lunch and evening meals.

FACILITIES AT A GLANCE

COBB'S QUAY MARINA

Cobb's Quay Marina
Hamworthy, Poole, Dorset, BH15 4EL
Tel: 01202 674299
Email: cobbsquay@mdlmarinas.co.uk
www.cobbsquaymarina.co.uk

VHF Ch 80
ACCESS H24

Lying on the west side of Holes Bay in Poole Harbour, Cobb's Quay is accessed via two lifting bridges. The hourly lifting schedule which runs from 0530 to 2330 (except for weekday rush hours) makes the entrance into Holes Bay accessible 24/7. With fully serviced pontoons for yachts up to 20m LOA, visitors can enjoy the facilities including Cobbs Bar & Restaurant. The marina also offers a 280-berth dry stack area for motorboats up to 10m. With increased security and lower maintenance costs, the service can be utilised by pre-booking launches. There is also a 40-ton hoist, fully serviced boatyard, and on-site self-storage. Poole Harbour is the second largest natural harbour in the world and is rich in wildlife, water sports and secret hideaways.

FACILITIES AT A GLANCE

Key
a Marina office
b Convenience store
c Bar & Restaurant

POOLE QUAY BOAT HAVEN

Poole Quay Boat Haven
Poole Town Quay, Poole, Dorset, BH15 1HJ
Tel: 01202 649488
Email: info@poolequayboathaven.co.uk
www.poolequayboathaven.co.uk

VHF Ch 80
ACCESS H24

Once inside the Poole Harbour entrance small yachts heading for Poole Quay Boat Haven should use the Boat Channel running parallel south of the dredged Middle Ship Channel, which is primarily used by ferries sailing to and from the Hamworthy terminal. The marina can be accessed via the Little Channel and is easily identified by the large breakwater alongside the Quay. With deep water at all states of the tide the marina has berthing available for 125 yachts up to 60m, but due to its central location the marina can get busy so it is best to reserve a berth.

There is easy access to all of Poole Quay's facilities including restaurants, bars, Poole Pottery and the Waterfront Museum.

FACILITIES AT A GLANCE

Key
a Berthing office
b Showers/Toilets
c The Quay Hotel
d Fish landing area

PORT OF POOLE MARINA

Port of Poole Marina
Poole Town Quay, Poole, Dorset, BH15 1HJ
Tel: 01202 649488
Email: info@poolequayboathaven.co.uk

VHF	Ch 80
ACCESS	H24

Beware of the chain ferry operating at the entrance to Poole harbour. Once inside small yachts heading for the marina should use the Boat Channel running parallel south of the Middle Ship Channel. The marina is to the east of the main ferry terminals and can be identified by a large floating breakwater at the entrance.

The marina has deep water at all tides and berthing for 60 permanent vessels. It is also used as an overflow for visitors from Poole Quay Boat Haven, subject to availability.

A water taxi is available during daylight hours to access the quay for restaurants and shops, also accessible with a 10–15min walk round the quays.

FACILITIES AT A GLANCE

NB All green lights are 2FG(vert)   2FR(vert)

PARKSTONE YACHT HAVEN

Parkstone Yacht Club
Pearce Avenue, Parkstone, Poole, Dorset, BH14 8EH
Tel: 01202 738824 Fax: 01202 716394
Email: office@parkstoneyc.co.uk

VHF	Ch M
ACCESS	H24

Situated on the north side of Poole Harbour between Salterns Marina and Poole Quay Boat Haven, Parkstone Yacht Haven can be entered at all states of the tides. Its approach channel has been dredged to 2.0m and is clearly marked by buoys. Run by the Parkstone Yacht Club, the Haven provides 200 deep water berths for members and visitors' berths. Other services include a new office facility with laundry and WCs, bar, restaurant, shower/changing rooms and wi-fi. With a busy sailing programme for over 2,500 members, the Yacht Club plays host to a variety of events including Poole Week, which is held towards the end of August. Please phone for availability.

FACILITIES AT A GLANCE

SALTERNS MARINA

Salterns Marina
40 Salterns Way, Lilliput, Poole
Dorset, BH14 8JR
Tel: 01202 709971
Email: marina@salterns.co.uk www.salterns.co.uk

VHF	Ch M, 80
ACCESS	H24

Salterns Marina provides a service which is second to none. Located off the North Channel, it is approached from the No 31 SHM and benefits from deep water at all states of the tide. Facilities include 275 alongside pontoon berths as well as 75 swinging moorings with a free launch service. However, with very few designated visitors' berths, it is best to contact the marina ahead of time for availability.

Fuel, diesel and gas can all be obtained 24/7 and the well-stocked chandlery, incorporating a coffee shop, stays open seven days a week.

FACILITIES AT A GLANCE

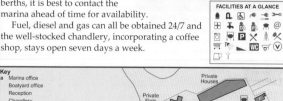

Key
a Marina office
   Boatyard office
   Reception
   Chandlery
   Salterns Brokerage
   Coffee shop
   Toilets/Showers
   Marine Sales
   Laundry
   Sales offices

b Fuel pumps
   Yacht hoist
d Admin
   Dinghy racks
e Toilets & showers
f Salterns Hotel
g Boatyard workshop
h 45 tonne travel hoist
i Boatyard

YARMOUTH HARBOUR

Yarmouth Harbour
Yarmouth, Isle of Wight, PO41 0NT
Tel: 01983 760321
info@yarmouth-harbour.co.uk
www.yarmouth-harbour.co.uk

VHF	Ch 68
ACCESS	H24

Yarmouth is the most westerly harbour on the Isle of Wight's NW coastline, a convenient passage stopover with all tide access, as well as a key tourism destination and gateway to West Wight's Area of Outstanding Natural Beauty. The harbour and town offer plenty of amenities, cafés, restaurants and pubs. There are two boatyards, the River Yar, and Harold Hayles.

The harbour has 150+ visitor moorings available daily from walk ashore pontoons providing direct access to Yarmouth town to non-walk ashore pontoons and moorings buoys just outside the harbour. Call *Yarmouth Harbour* on Ch68 prior to entering the harbour. Berthing Masters patrol the entrance and will direct vessels for overnight and short stay berths, fuel and loading/unloading.

FACILITIES AT A GLANCE

Key
a Royal Solent Yacht Club
b Harbour office
c Yarmouth Sailing Club
d Harold Hayles Boatyard

2

LYMINGTON YACHT HAVEN

Lymington Yacht Haven
King's Saltern Road, Lymington, S041 3QD
Tel: 01590 677071 www.yachthavens.com
Email: havenmasters@lymingtonyachthaven.com

⚓⚓⚓⚓
VHF Ch 80
ACCESS H24

Lymington Yacht Haven has the enviable position of being the first marina that comes into sight on your port hand side as you make your way up the well-marked Lymington river channel. Nestled between the 500 acre Lymington to Keyhaven nature reserve and the famous Georgian market town of Lymington, there is something for everyone.

Lymington Yacht Haven is manned 24/7 for fuel and berthing and boasts the most modern luxury shore side facilities you will find in the UK. Bike and electric bike hire are available through the marina office to explore the beautiful New Forest.

FACILITIES AT A GLANCE

Key
a Royal Lymington Yacht Club
b Lymington Town Sailing Club
c Owners store
d LYH office, brokerage, showers and laundry
e Haven Bar Bistro
f Yacht charter and sales
g Rigger
h Power boat sales
i Electronics

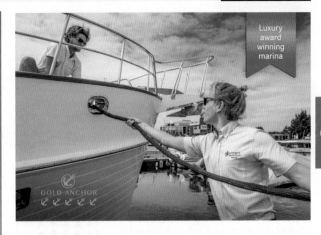

BERTHON LYMINGTON MARINA

Berthon Lymington Marina Ltd
The Shipyard, Lymington, Hampshire, SO41 3YL
Tel: 01590 647405
www.berthon.co.uk Email: marina@berthon.co.uk

VHF Ch 80
ACCESS H24

Situated approximately half a mile up river of Lymington Yacht Haven, on the port hand side, is Lymington Marina. Easily accessible at all states of the tide, it offers between 60 to 70 visitors' berths, with probably the best washrooms in the Solent. Its close proximity to the town centre and first rate services mean that booking is essential on busy weekends. Lymington Marina's parent, Berthon Boat Co, has state of the art facilities and a highly skilled work force of 100+ to deal with any repair, maintenance or refit.

Lymington benefits from having the New Forest on its doorstep and the Solent Way footpath provides an invigorating walk to and from Hurst Castle.

FACILITIES AT A GLANCE

Key
a Dockmaster's office
b Berthon International
c Yacht maintenance & repair
d Building refit shed
e Anchor House
f Seaforth House
g Refueller

LYMINGTON TOWN QUAY

Lymington Harbour Commissioners
Bath Road, Lymington, S041 3SE
Tel: 01590 672014
Email: info@lymingtonharbour.co.uk

VHF Ch 66
ACCESS H24

In 2020, the Town Quay pontoon was extended to provide 46 walk ashore berths for visiting boats, including 26 finger berths. All have power, water and free wi-fi. The Town Quay also has 32 fore and aft visitor moorings.

The Quay provides easy access to the historic cobbles and the attractive Georgian high street with its bars, restaurants and shops. The facilities of the town are close by with the historic Saturday market in the High Street. The New Forest is easily accessible by bus train and bicycle.

FACILITIES AT A GLANCE

LYMINGTON – DAN BRAN VISITOR PONTOON

Lymington Harbour Commissioners
Bath Road, Lymington, S041 3SE
Tel: 01590 672014
Email: info@lymingtonharbour.co.uk

VHF	Ch 66
ACCESS	H24

Lymington Harbour Commission provides dedicated walk ashore visitor berths at the Lymington Town Quay and at the Dan Bran pontoon which comes ashore adjacent to the Royal Lymington YC and Lymington Town SC. Dan Bran is accessible at all states of the tide inside the wave screen. Power is available along its 650' length with use of the facilities at Lymington Town SC and walk ashore access to the town and nearby nature reserves on the salt marsh. Sited between the marinas a short walk from Town Quay, it is ideal for club rallies/events and can accommodate up to 50 boats together. The sea water swimming bath adjacent to the pontoon is a popular venue for children and families.

FACILITIES AT A GLANCE

Key
a Royal Lymington Yacht Club
b Lymington Town Sailing Club
c Yacht charter and sales
d Power boat sales

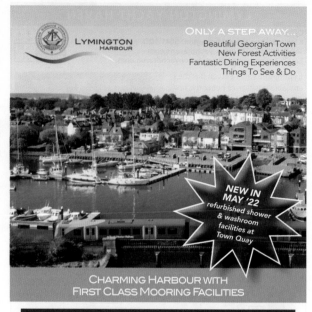

BUCKLERS HARD MARINA

Bucklers Hard
Beaulieu, New Forest, Hampshire, SO42 7XB
Tel: 01590 616200
www.beaulieuriver.co.uk harbour.office@beaulieu.co.uk

⚓⚓⚓⚓⚓

VHF	Ch 68
ACCESS	H24

Situated on the Beaulieu River, Buckler's Hard Yacht Harbour is the ideal location from which to sail in the Solent or visit for a short stay to explore the surrounding New Forest. Recent investment in the TYHA 5 Gold Anchor marina offers improved facilities and technology to keep pace with modern demands, while preserving the unique character and charm of the unspoilt natural haven.

Both permanent marina berths and river moorings are available. Visiting boats are welcome and advised to book in advance or radio Beaulieu River Radio on CH68 before entering the river

FACILITIES AT A GLANCE

NB
Pontoon numbering runs from low inside with even numbers on the north side of pontoons and odd on the south.

COWES

THE PERFECT BOATING DESTINATION

© Paul Wyeth   © Martin Allen/CWL   © Smoking Lobster, Cowes

HYTHE MARINA VILLAGE

Hythe Marina Village
Shamrock Way, Hythe, Southampton, SO45 6DY
Tel: 023 8020 7073
Email: hythe@mdlmarinas.co.uk
www.hythemarinavillage.co.uk

VHF Ch 80
ACCESS H24

Situated on the western shores of Southampton Water, Hythe Marina Village is approached by a dredged channel leading to a lock basin. The lock gates are controlled H24 throughout the year with a waiting pontoon south of the approach basin.

Hythe Marina Village incorporates full marine services as well as on-site restaurants and a selection of shops can be found in the town centre, a 5 minute walk away. Forming an integral part of the New Forest Waterside, Hythe is the perfect base from which to explore Hampshire's pretty inland villages and towns, or alternatively you can catch the ferry to Southampton's Town Quay.

FACILITIES AT A GLANCE

Key
a Restaurants and bars
b Lock building
c Boat storage and Trailer park

COWES YACHT HAVEN

Cowes Yacht Haven
Vectis Yard, Cowes, Isle of Wight, PO31 7BD
Tel: 01983 299975
www.cowesyachthaven.com
Email: info@cowesyachthaven.com

VHF Ch 80
ACCESS H24

Situated virtually at the centre of the Solent, Cowes is best known as Britain's premier yachting centre and offers all types of facilities to yachtsmen. Cowes Yacht Haven, operating 24 hours a day, has very few permanent moorings and is dedicated to catering for visitors and events. At peak times it can become very crowded and for occasions such as Cowes Week or Round the Island Race you need to book up in advance.

FACILITIES AT A GLANCE

ISLAND HARBOUR MARINA

Island Harbour Marina
Mill Lane, Binfield, Newport, Isle of Wight, PO30 2LA
Tel: 01983 539994 Fax: 01983 523401
Email: info@island-harbour.co.uk

VHF Ch 80
ACCESS HW±4

Situated in beautiful rolling farmland about half a mile south of Folly Inn, Island Harbour Marina provides around 200 visitors' berths. Protected by a lock that is operated daily from 0800 – 2100 during the summer and from 0800 – 1730 during the winter, the marina is accessible for about three hours either side of HW for draughts of 1.5m.

Due to its secluded setting, the marina's on site chandlery also sells essential provisions and newspapers. A half hour walk along the river brings you to Newport, the capital and county town of the Isle of Wight.

FACILITIES AT A GLANCE

Key
a Control tower
b Bin store
c Chandlery
d Restaurant

COWES HARBOUR SHEPARDS MARINA

Cowes Harbour Shepards Marina
Medina Road, Cowes, Isle of Wight, PO31 7HT
Tel: 01983 297821 Email: shepards.chc@cowes.co.uk
www.cowesharbourshepardsmarina.co.uk

VHF	Ch 80
ACCESS	H24

Shepards Marina is one of Cowes Harbour's main marina facilities offering services and amenities for yacht racing events, rallies, and catering also to the cruising sailor and powerboater. The marina has capacity for 130 visiting boats, and 40 resident berth holders.

Visitor berths can be booked in advance, subject to availability. All berths benefit from water and electricity, free Wi-Fi, inclusive showers, and site-wide CCTV. Discounted rates are available for rallies of six or more boats, sailing schools, and winter berthing.

On site are The Basque Kitchen, Salty Sailing, Island Divers, and Solent Sails.

Fuel can be obtained from the Cowes Harbour Services Fuel Berth, 200m south of the Chain Ferry.

FACILITIES AT A GLANCE

Key
a   Marina office
b   Sugar Store Events Centre
c   Solent Sails
d   Salty Sailing
e   Island Divers
f   The Basque Kitchen

EAST COWES MARINA

East Cowes Marina
Britannia Way, East Cowes, Isle of Wight, PO32 6UB
Tel: 01983 293983
Email: eastcowes@boatfolk.co.uk
www.boatfolk.co.uk/eastcowesmarina

VHF	Ch 80
ACCESS	H24

Accommodating around 235 residential yachts and 150 visiting boats at all states of the tide, East Cowes Marina is situated on the quiet and protected east bank of the Medina River, about a quarter mile above the chain ferry. A small convenience store is just five minutes walk away. The new centrally heated shower and toilet facilities ensure the visitor a warm welcome at any time of the year, as does the on-site pub and restaurant.

Several water taxis provide a return service to Cowes, ensuring a quick and easy way of getting to West Cowes.

FACILITIES AT A GLANCE

Key
a   Marina office
b   Showers, toilets & laundry
c   Pub and restaurant
d   RNLI, Inshore Lifeboat Centre
e   Yacht stores

TOWN QUAY

Associated British Ports
Town Quay, Southampton, SO14 2AQ
Tel: 02380 234397 Mobile: 07764 293588
Email: info@townquay.com www.townquay.com

VHF | Ch 80
ACCESS | H24

In the heart of Southampton, Town Quay is walking distance from the City's cultural quarter, West Quay Shopping Centre and a variety of restaurants, bars and theatres making the marina a vibrant place to stay all year round.

The marina is accessible at all states of the tide and the reception is open 24 hours a day with free drinks and wi-fi. Free cycle hire and use of a gas BBQ on the 'chill out' deck is available.

Located on the eastern shores of Southampton Water, Town Quay offers unrivalled views of Southampton's busy maritime activity and direct access to the world famous cruising and racing waters of the Solent.

FACILITIES AT A GLANCE

01–18 →
01–23 →
01–28 →
01–25 →
01–26 →
01–08 →

A
B
C
D
E
F

Visitor pontoon
Reception & facilities
Wave break

OCEAN VILLAGE MARINA

Ocean Village Marina
2 Channel Way, Southampton, SO14 3TG
Tel: 023 8022 9385
Email: oceanvillage@mdlmarinas.co.uk
www.oceanvillagemarina.co.uk

VHF | Ch 80
ACCESS | H24

The entrance to Ocean Village Marina lies on the port side of the River Itchen, just before the Itchen Bridge. With the capacity to accommodate large yachts and tall ships, the marina, accessible 24 hours a day, is a renowned home for international yacht races.

Situated at the heart of an exciting new waterside development incorporating shops, a cinema, restaurants, a multi-storey car park and a £50m luxury spa hotel complex, Ocean Village offers a vibrant atmosphere for all visitors.

FACILITIES AT A GLANCE

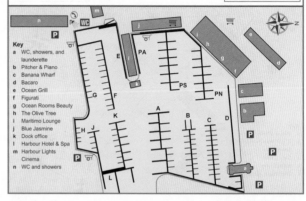

Key
a WC, showers, and launderette
b Pitcher & Piano
c Banana Wharf
d Bacaro
e Ocean Grill
f Figurati
g Ocean Rooms Beauty
h The Olive Tree
i Maritimo Lounge
j Blue Jasmine
k Dock office
l Harbour Hotel & Spa
m Harbour Lights Cinema
n WC and showers

SHAMROCK QUAY

Shamrock Quay
William Street, Northam, Southampton, Hants, SO14 5QL
Tel: 023 8022 9461
Email: shamrockquay@mdlmarinas.co.uk
www.shamrockquay.co.uk

VHF | Ch 80
ACCESS | H24

Shamrock Quay, lying upstream of the Itchen Bridge on the port hand side, offers excellent facilities to yachtsmen. It also benefits from being accessible and manned 24/7 a day. On-site there is a 75-ton travel hoist and a 47-ton boat mover, and for dining out a fully licenced restaurant/bar and a café.

The city centre is about two miles away, where among the numerous attractions are the Medieval Merchant's House in French Street, the Southampton City Art Gallery and the SeaCity Museum in the Civic Centre.

FACILITIES AT A GLANCE

Key
a Offices and shops
b Marina office
c Café

KEMPS QUAY

Kemp's Shipyard Ltd
Quayside Road, Southampton, SO18 1BZ
Tel: 023 8063 2323 Fax: 023 8022 6002
Email: enquiries@kempsquay.com

VHF
ACCESS | HW±3.5

At the head of the River Itchen on the starboard side is Kemps Quay, a family-run marina with a friendly, old-fashioned feel. Accessible only 3½ hrs either side of HW, it has a limited number of deep water berths, the rest being half tide, drying out to soft mud. Its restricted access is, however, reflected in the lower prices.

Although situated on the outskirts of Southampton, a short bus or taxi ride will soon get you to the city centre. Besides a nearby BP Garage selling bread and milk, the closest supermarkets can be found in Bitterne Shopping Centre, which is five minutes away by bus.

FACILITIES AT A GLANCE

2

SAXON WHARF

Saxon Wharf
Lower York Street, Northam, Southampton, SO14 5QF
Tel: 023 8033 9490
Email: saxonwharf@mdlmarinas.co.uk
www.saxonwharfmarina.co.uk

VHF Ch 80
ACCESS H24

Placed on the River Itchen in Southampton, Saxon Wharf is a marine service centre specifically designed for the superyacht market. With a 200-ton boat hoist and heavy duty pontoons, Saxon Wharf is the ideal location for large vessels in need of secure, quick turnaround lift-outs, repair work or even full-scale refits.

With a Dry Stack facility boasting the largest capacity forklift truck in the UK, Saxon Wharf can now dry stack boats of up to 13m LOA. There is also ample storage ashore and 24-hour security. Shamrock Quay, where there are bars and restaurants, is within 300 metres of this location.

FACILITIES AT A GLANCE

Key
a   Office
b   Security gate
c   Oyster Yacht Services
d   Offices

HAMBLE POINT MARINA

Hamble Point Marina
School Lane, Hamble, Southampton, SO31 4NB
Tel: 023 8045 2464
Email: hamblepoint@mdlmarinas.co.uk
www.hamblepointmarina.co.uk

VHF Ch 80
ACCESS H24

Situated virtually opposite Warsash, this is the first marina you will come to on the western bank of the Hamble. Accommodating yachts and power boats up to 30m in length, it offers easy access to the Solent.

The marina boasts extensive facilities including 137 dry stack berths for motorboats up to 10m and over 50 tenants who provide boat-owners with a wide range of marine services from boat repairs to electrical work. Hamble Point is within a 20-minute walk of Hamble Village, where there are a plethora of pubs and restaurants on offer.

FACILITIES AT A GLANCE

Key
a   Information
b   First aid point
c   Marina office
d   Administration office
e   Ketch Rigger Bar and Restaurant
f   Sailmakers

PORT HAMBLE MARINA

Port Hamble Marina
Satchell Lane, Hamble, Southampton, SO31 4QD
Tel: 023 8045 2741
Email: porthamble@mdlmarinas.co.uk
www.porthamblemarina.co.uk

VHF Ch 80
ACCESS H24

Port Hamble Marina is situated on the River Hamble right in the heart of the South Coast's sailing scene. With thousands of visitors every year, this busy marina is popular with racing enthusiasts and cruising vessels looking for a vibrant atmosphere. The picturesque Hamble village, with its inviting pubs and restaurants, is only a few minutes walk away.

On site, Port Hamble also offers excellent amenities including luxurious male and female facilities and boutique style shower rooms for members. Banana Wharf bar and restaurant provides the perfect spot to socialise by the water, whilst petrol and diesel is available 7/7. Locally there are several companies catering for every boating need.

FACILITIES AT A GLANCE

Key
a   Dock manager's office
b   Boat sales
c   Royal Air Force YC
d   Banana Wharf Bar & Restaurant

MERCURY YACHT HARBOUR

Mercury Yacht Harbour and Holiday Park
Satchell Lane, Hamble, Southampton, SO31 4HQ
Tel: 023 8045 5994
Email: mercury@mdlmarinas.co.uk
www.mercuryyachtharbour.co.uk

VHF Ch 80
ACCESS H24

Mercury Yacht Harbour is set in a picturesque and sheltered wooded site where the shallow waters of Badnam Creek join the River Hamble. Enjoying deep water at all states of the tide, it accommodates yachts up to 24m LOA and boasts an array of facilities.

For a good meal look no further than the Gaff Rigger bar and restaurant, whose roof terrace offers striking views over the water. The adjoining holiday park offers self-catering accommodation, a campsite, bell tents for glamping, touring pitches and floating marine lodges in the marina itself. Hamble Village, with plenty of pubs, restaurants and shops, is only a 20-minute walk away.

FACILITIES AT A GLANCE

Key
a   Toilets and showers
b   Launderette
c   TBS Boats
d   Gaff Rigger Bar & Restaurant
e   Dockmaster, marina manager's office
f   Waste disposal
g   Recycling area

UNIVERSAL MARINA

Universal Marina
Crableck Lane, Sarisbury Green, Southampton, SO31 7ZN
Tel: 01489 574272
Email: universal@premiermarinas.co.uk

VHF	Ch 80
ACCESS	H24

Beautifully located on the east bank of the River Hamble and surrounded by natural wildlife and marshlands, Universal Marina is the newest addition to the Premier Marinas family.

Offering 24/7 access to explore the Solent cruising grounds, the visitor can enjoy tranquil riverside walks or simply relax and soak up the vibrant, friendly marina atmosphere. A fully serviced boatyard and the river's largest drystack facility are onsite, together with a restaurant, café, and an array of marine service tenants including a chandlery.

FACILITIES AT A GLANCE

Key
a Marina reception
b Berth holder facilities
c Cafe
d Restaurant
e Marine tenants and workshops
f Berth holder facilities and chandlery
g Boatyard
i Drystack facilities

SWANWICK MARINA

Swanwick Marina
Swanwick, Southampton, Hampshire, SO31 1ZL
Tel: 01489 884081
Email: swanwick@premiermarinas.com
www.premiermarinas.com

VHF	Ch 80
ACCESS	H24

Nestling on the picturesque eastern bank of the River Hamble, Swanwick Marina offers 24/7 access to the Solent, with excellent access by road and a variety of walks, pubs and restaurants to explore close by.

Welcoming to boats of all sizes, Swanwick has over 320 berths on with a choice of water-berthing and dry-stack. There is a café, secure berth holder parking and the almost complete on Pavilion building, which will house boat sales and marine businesses; Swanwick also boasts a quality fully-serviced boatyard, a self-store and an outstanding mix of tenant marine services, including a chandlery.

FACILITIES AT A GLANCE

Key
a Marina office
b The Boat House Cafe
c Chandlery
d Boat sales offices
e Boatyard office
f Drystack holding
g Pavilion Building

Jolly Sailor

Hamble River

DEACONS MARINA & BOATYARD

Deacons Marina & Boatyard
Bridge Road, Bursledon, Hampshire, SO31 8AZ
Tel: 02380 402253
Email: deacons@boatfolk.co.uk
www.boatfolk.co.uk/deaconsmarina

VHF	Ch 80
ACCESS	H24

Deacons Marina and Boatyard is situated on a sheltered bank of the Hamble River, a stones throw from Bursledon, with 130 berths afloat and space for 160 boats ashore.

The marina boasts friendly and knowledgeable staff, skilled in boat repair and maintenance and offers craneage facilities for lifting boats up to 20t and 45ft in length. All supported by marine on-site businesses to provide a fully serviced one stop facility for boat owners.

FACILITIES AT A GLANCE

Key
a Marine Power
b Marina office
c Marine Services
d Alexandra's Bistro
e Offices
f Force 4 Chandlery
g Why Boats brokerage and boat sales

HAMBLE RIVER

RYDE LEISURE HARBOUR

Ryde Harbour
The Esplanade, Ryde, Isle of Wight, PO33 1JA
Tel: 01983 613879 Fax: 01983 613903
www.rydeharbour.com Email: ryde.harbour@iow.gov.uk

VHF	Ch 80
ACCESS	HW±2

Known as the 'gateway to the Island', Ryde, with its elegant houses and abundant shops, is among the Isle of Wight's most popular resorts. Its well-protected harbour is conveniently close to the exceptional beaches as well as to the town's restaurants and amusements.

Drying to 2.5m and therefore only accessible to yachts that can take the ground, the harbour accommodates 90 resident boats as well as up to 75 visiting yachts. Fin keel yachts may dry out on the harbour wall.

Ideal for family cruising, Ryde offers a wealth of activities, ranging from ten pin bowling and ice skating to crazy golf and tennis.

FACILITIES AT A GLANCE

Ice rink and ten pin bowling complex

BEMBRIDGE HARBOUR

Bembridge Harbour
Harbour Office, The Duver, St Helens, Ryde
Isle of Wight, PO33 1YB
Tel: 01983 872828 Fax: 01983 872922
Email: thorpemalcolm@btconnect.com
www.bembridgeharbour.co.uk

| VHF | Ch 80 |
| ACCESS | HW±2.5 |

Bembridge is a compact, pretty harbour whose entrance, although restricted by the tides (recommended entry for a 1.5m draught is 2½hrs before HW), is well sheltered in all but north north easterly gales. Offering excellent sailing clubs, beautiful beaches and fine restaurants, this Isle of Wight port is a first class haven with plenty of charm. With approximately 120 new visitors' berths on the Duver Marina pontoons, which can now be booked online, the marina at St Helen's Quay at the western end of the harbour is now allocated to annual berth holders only.

FACILITIES AT A GLANCE

HASLAR MARINA

Haslar Marina
Haslar Road, Gosport, Hampshire, PO12 1NU
Tel: 023 9260 1201
Email: haslar@boatfolk.co.uk
www.boatfolk.co.uk/haslarmarina

| VHF | Ch 80 |
| ACCESS | H24 |

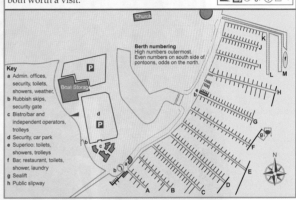

This purpose-built marina lies to port on the western side of Portsmouth Harbour entrance and is easily recognised by its prominent lightship incorporating a bar and restaurant. Accessible at all states of the tide, Haslar's extensive facilities do not however include fuel, the nearest is at the Gosport Marina only a few cables north. Within close proximity is the Royal Navy Submarine Museum and the Museum of Naval Firepower 'Explosion' both worth a visit.

FACILITIES AT A GLANCE

Key
a Admin. offices, security, toilets, showers, weather,
b Rubbish skips, security gate
c Bistro/bar and independent operators, trolleys
d Security, car park
e Superloo: toilets, showers, trolleys
f Bar, restaurant, toilets, shower, laundry
g Sealift
h Public slipway

Berth numbering
High numbers outermost. Even numbers on south side of pontoons, odds on the north.

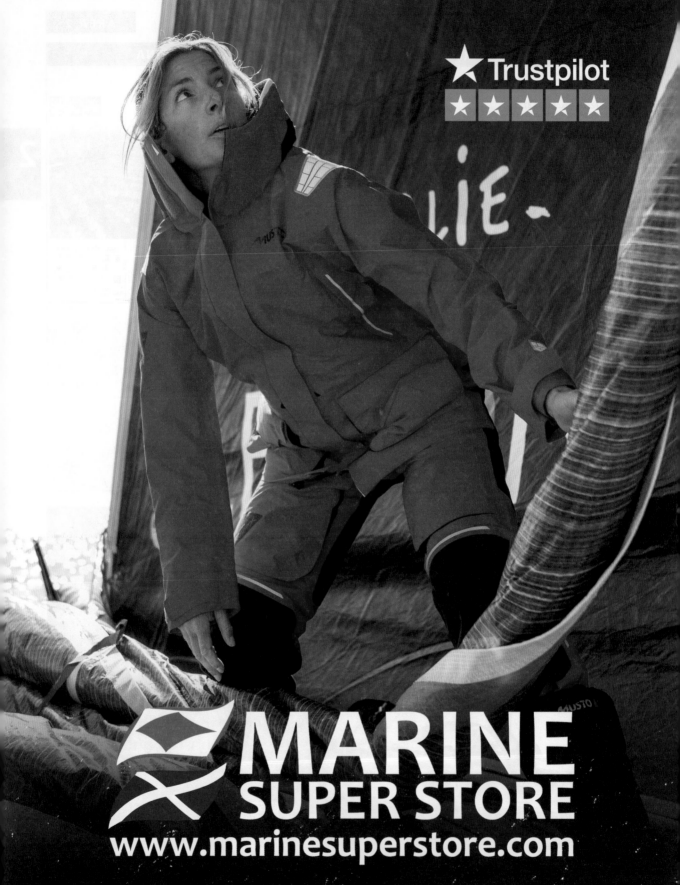

2

GOSPORT MARINA

Gosport Marina
Mumby Road, Gosport, Hampshire, PO12 1AH
Tel: 023 9252 4811
Email: gosport@premiermarinas.com
www.premiermarinas.com

VHF Ch 80
ACCESS H24

Gosport Marina is located at the mouth of Portsmouth Harbour, just minutes from the eastern edge of the cruising grounds of the Solent. Family-friendly and popular with cruisers and racers alike, Gosport offers 24/7 access to open water and a choice of both traditional wet-berth and dry-stack, plus luxury facilities and a self-store. Gosport Marina's specialist boatyard, Endeavour Quay, is fully-equipped to lift and service boats up to 40m, with three large boatsheds and a wide variety of marine service tenants, including a dedicated chandlery. When it is time to relax, The Deck at the Boat House is the perfect spot to unwind.

FACILITIES AT A GLANCE

Key
a Gosport reception and berth holder facilities
b Apartment buildings
c The Deck and Boat House
d Berth holder facilities
e Boat sheds and marine tenants

ROYAL CLARENCE MARINA

Royal Clarence Marina, Royal Clarence Yard
Weevil Lane, Gosport, Hampshire PO12 1AX
Tel: 02392 523523
Email: info@royalclarencemarina.org
www.royalclarencemarina.org

VHF Ch 80
ACCESS H24

Royal Clarence Marina enjoys a unique setting, with the former Royal Navy victualling yard as its backdrop. Only five minutes from the entrance of Portsmouth Harbour, this Transeurope marina lies within a deep-water basin giving 24/7 access for a draft of up to 4.5m. This remarkably peaceful and calm marina has wide pontoon spacing, little tidal flow, and exceptional protection from the swell produced in Portsmouth Harbour. The new facilities, now just opposite the marina, have been described as the best on the South Coast and with two popular restaurants onsite, makes a great location for visitors.

FACILITIES AT A GLANCE

PORT SOLENT MARINA

Port Solent Marina
South Lockside, Portsmouth, PO6 4TJ
Tel: 023 9221 0765
Email: portsolent@premiermarinas.com
www.premiermarinas.com

VHF Ch 80
ACCESS H24

Port Solent Marina is located to the northeast of Portsmouth Harbour, just minutes away from the cruising grounds of the Solent. Accessible via a 24/7 lock, this purpose-built marina offers a secure and sheltered berthing for yachts and motorboats alike, with a complete range of facilities including a fully serviced boatyard with a sizable boatshed, a self-store and a array of onsite marine tenants. Onsite leisure complex, The Boardwalk offers choices shops, bars and restaurants, with a gym and a large cinema multiplex also close by.

FACILITIES AT A GLANCE

Key
a Laundry, berth holders showers, toilets and baby change
b Port Solent YC
c Chandlery, marine engineers
d Boat shed and self-store
e Berth holders showers, toilets and public toilets, baby change
f David Lloyd Health and Fitness Club
g The Boardwalk - bars/restaurants
h Odeon cinema
i Marina control and Port Solent reception
j Residential building

WICORMARINE YACHT HAVEN

WicorMarine Yacht Haven
Cranleigh Road, Portchester, Hampshire, PO16 9DR
Tel: 01329 237112
Email: inbox@wicormarine.co.uk www.wicormarine.co.uk

VHF
ACCESS H24

WicorMarine Yacht Haven is situated in the picturesque upper reaches of Portsmouth Harbour away from the hustle and bustle. The walk-ashore pontoons and traditional mid-river berths offer an affordable alternative to busy marinas and are only 30 mins from the harbour entrance.

An excellent range of boatyard facilities including a 12T boat hoist, undercover storage, H24 showers and toilets, diesel, fresh water, on site repair services and a chandlery complete with Calor Gas and Campingaz exchange.

The popular, licensed Salt Cafe is open to visitors all year round where you can take in the stunning views of the harbour from the waterfront deck.

FACILITIES AT A GLANCE

Key
a Causeway
b Dinghy pontoon
c End pontoon
d West link
e Slip
– Moorings
l Pontoon moorings

SOUTHSEA MARINA

Southsea Marina
Fort Cumberland Road, PO4 9RJ
Tel: 02392 822719
Email: southsea@premiermarinas.com
www.premiermarinas.com

VHF	Ch 80
ACCESS	HW±3

Nestling on the Eastney Peninsula, in the quieter reaches of Langstone Harbour, Southsea Marina is perfectly located for exploring the Solent. A family-friendly, working marina, ideal for sailing and motor cruisers alike; Southsea offers outstanding value, first-class facilities and a personal service that includes a 24/7 manned reception. Access to and from the marina is gained via a tidal cill gate ±3HW. With a quality full-service boatyard, ample storage ashore and a great mix of onsite tenant marine services. When it's time to relax, the marina's two onsite restaurants offer a choice of delicious Indian and home-style cuisine.

FACILITIES AT A GLANCE

NAVIGATORS MARINE SERVICE CENTRE

SPARKES MARINA

Sparkes Marina
38 Wittering Road, Hayling Island, Hampshire, PO11 9SR
Tel: 023 9246 3572
Email: sparkes@mdlmarinas.co.uk   www.sparkesmarina.co.uk

VHF	Ch 80
ACCESS	H24

Just inside the entrance to Chichester Harbour, on the eastern shores of Hayling Island, lies Sparkes Marina. Its facilities include 24-hour showers and toilets, a laundry room, an office/reception, and Drift: Hayling Island bar and restaurant.

In addition to its berthing and marina services, Sparkes has many skilled professionals on site, including specialists in engineering, outboard engines, glass fibre repairs, rigging, sails and covers, marine carpentry, electrical, boat management and valeting. There is storage ashore for over 200 boats, 24/7 staff cover and wi-fi, whilst petrol and diesel are also available.

FACILITIES AT A GLANCE

Key
a	Waterside Boat Sales	d	Hayling Glass Fibre Repairs	f	Toilets/showers
b	Drift: Hayling Island		Hayling Rigging Services	g	Laundry room
c	Harbour office	e	Disabled toilets/showers	h	Sail Style
				i	AD Marine Services

NORTHNEY MARINA

Northney Marina
Northney Road, Hayling Island, Hampshire, PO11 0NH
Tel: 023 9246 6321
Email: northney@mdlmarinas.co.uk
www.northneymarina.co.uk

VHF	Ch 80
ACCESS	H24

Situated in Chichester Harbour, Northney Marina is set on the northern shore of Hayling Island in the well-marked Sweare Deep Channel, which branches off to port almost at the end of Emsworth Channel. This 228-berth marina offers excellent boatyard facilities, a chandlery, provisions store and laundry area, diesel, a slipway, Salt Shack Café, wi-fi and 24/7 staff cover. There is also an events area for rallies.

FACILITIES AT A GLANCE

Key
a Marina office and provisions store
b Recycling facilities

2

EMSWORTH YACHT HARBOUR

Emsworth Yacht Harbour Ltd
Thorney Road, Emsworth, Hants, PO10 8BP
Tel: 01243 377727 Fax: 01243 373432
Email: info@emsworth-marina.co.uk
www.emsworth-marina.co.uk

VHF
ACCESS HW±2

Accessible about one and a half to two hours either side of high water, Emsworth Yacht Harbour is a sheltered site, offering good facilities to yachtsmen.

Created in 1964 from a log pond, the marina is within easy walking distance of the pretty little town of Emsworth, which boasts at least 10 pubs, several high quality restaurants and two well-stocked convenience stores.

FACILITIES AT A GLANCE

Key
a Ground floor - toilets and showers
  1st floor - harbour office
b Home Marine -
  outboard engine repairs

CHICHESTER MARINA

Chichester Marina
Birdham, Chichester, West Sussex, PO20 7EJ
Tel: 01243 512731
Email: chichester@premiermarinas.com
www.premiermarinas.com

VHF Ch 80
ACCESS HW±5

A first-class marina set in the beauty of a natural harbour and picturesque countryside makes Chichester Marina a wonderful destination and ideal to explore on foot or by boat.

This locked, family-friendly, marina is home to over 1000 berths and combines luxury facilities with serene surroundings. It is also home to a friendly yacht club and The Boat House Café, which offers bistro dining. The marina also boasts a fully-serviced boatyard, which includes two boat hoists, a slipway and ample boat storage, plus a wide variety of tenant marine services.

FACILITIES AT A GLANCE

Key
a Salterns Apartments
b Toilets, showers, baby change
c Trailer sailer storage
d Marine Services/boatshed
e Launderette
f Toilets, showers, baby change,
   telephone, disabled facilities
g Restaurant/bar, chandlery, shop
h Berth holder car park
i dinghy park
j Marina control building

BIRDHAM POOL MARINA

Birdham Pool Marina
Birdham Pool, Chichester, Sussex
Tel: 01243 512310 Fax: 01243 513163
Email: mikebraidley@castlemarinas.co.uk

VHF Ch 80
ACCESS HW±3.5

Birdham Pool is the UK's oldest marina, with a charm not found elsewhere. A recent programme of improvements sees 28 new berths, a new 30-ton crane to lift out boats up to 50ft long and 2m draft, brand new facilities block and new Marine Trades Centre showcasing traditional skilled craftsmen. Visitors will not be disappointed by the unique and picturesque setting, with views across the South Downs as well as Chichester Harbour. Access is HW±3·5, via a dredged channel marked by starboard hand piles.

FACILITIES AT A GLANCE

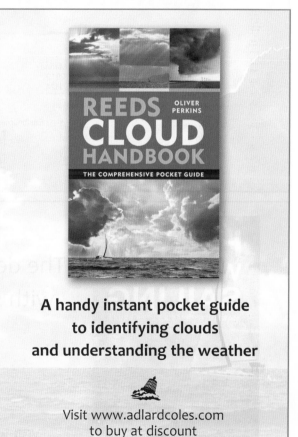

SOUTH EAST ENGLAND – Selsey Bill to North Foreland

Key to Marina Plans symbols

Symbol		Symbol	
	Bottled gas	**P**	Parking
	Chandler		Pub/Restaurant
	Disabled facilities		Pump out
	Electrical supply		Rigging service
	Electrical repairs		Sail repairs
	Engine repairs		Shipwright
	First Aid		Shop/Supermarket
	Fresh Water		Showers
	Fuel - Diesel		Slipway
	Fuel - Petrol	**WC**	Toilets
	Hardstanding/boatyard		Telephone
@	Internet Café		Trolleys
	Laundry facilities	**V**	Visitors berths
	Lift-out facilities		Wi-Fi

Area 3 - South East England

MARINAS
Telephone Numbers
VHF Channel
Access Times

N. Foreland

Margate

Ramsgate

Ramsgate Royal Harbour Marina
01843 572100
Ch 14, 80 H24

S. Foreland

Dover

Folkestone

Dover Marina
01304 241663
Ch 80 H24

Lady Bee Marina
01273 593801
Ch 14 H24

Brighton Marina
01273 819919
Ch M, 80 H24

Rye

Shoreham

Brighton

Harbour of Rye
01797 225225
Ch 14 HW±2

Littlehampton

Littlehampton Marina
01903 713553
Ch 80
HW-3 to +2.5
Hillyards
01903 713327
HW-3 to +2.5

Newhaven
Newhaven Marina
01273 513881
Ch 80 H24

Eastbourne

Sovereign Harbour Marina
01323 470099
Ch 17 H24

N

LITTLEHAMPTON MARINA

Littlehampton Marina
Ferry Road, Littlehampton, W Sussex
Tel: 01903 713553 Fax: 01903 732264
Email: sales@littlehamptonmarina.co.uk

VHF	Ch 80
ACCESS	HW-3 to +2.5

A typical English seaside town with funfair, promenade and fine sandy beaches, Littlehampton lies roughly midway between Brighton and Chichester at the mouth of the River Arun. It affords a convenient stopover for yachts either east or west bound, providing you have the right tidal conditions to cross the entrance bar with its charted depth of 0.7m. The marina lies about three cables above Town Quay and Fisherman's Quay, both of which are on the starboard side of the River Arun, and is accessed via a retractable footbridge that opens on request to the HM (note that you should contact him by 1630 the day before you require entry).

FACILITIES AT A GLANCE

Key
a Marina offices
b Cafe

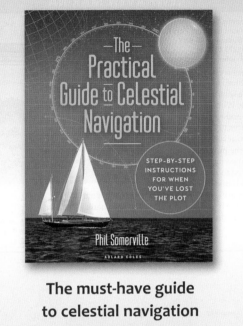
3

LADY BEE MARINA

Lady Bee Marina
138-140 Albion Street, Southwick
West Sussex, BN42 4EG
Tel: 01273 593801 Fax: 01273 870349

VHF	Ch 14
ACCESS	H24

Shoreham, only five miles west of Brighton, is one of the South Coast's major commercial ports handling, among other products, steel, grain, tarmac and timber. On first impressions it may seem that Shoreham has little to offer the visiting yachtsman, but once through the lock and into the eastern arm of the River Adur, the quiet Lady Bee Marina, with its Spanish waterside restaurant, can make this harbour an interesting alternative to the lively atmosphere of Brighton Marina. Run by the Harbour Office, the marina meets all the usual requirements, although fuel is available in cans from Southwick garage or from Corral's diesel pump situated in the western arm.

FACILITIES AT A GLANCE

Key
a Sussex Yacht Club
b Riverside Boatyard

BRIGHTON MARINA

Brighton Marina
West Jetty, Brighton, East Sussex, BN2 5UP
Tel: 01273 819919
Email: brighton@premiermarinas.com
www.premiermarinas.com

VHF	Ch M, 80
ACCESS	H24

Perfect for yachts and motorboats alike, Brighton is the UK's largest marina with over 1300 berths and offers easy access to open water and a great starting point for exploring the South Coast or a trip to France.

Brighton Marina also boasts a modern and friendly yacht club that warmly welcomes members and visiting yachtsman. With a fully serviced, quality boatyard, storage ashore, luxury facilities and a comprehensive mix of tenant marine services including a chandlery, together these make Brighton Marina a great place to berth, relax and carry out major or routine boat repairs on the South Coast.

FACILITIES AT A GLANCE

Key
a David Lloyd Heath & Fitness Club
b Bowling alley
c Casino/night club
d Multiplex cinema
e Yacht club
f Petrol station
g Mariners Quay
h Marina reception
i Boatyard reception

NEWHAVEN MARINA

Newhaven Marina
The Yacht Harbour, Fort Road, Newhaven
East Sussex, BN9 9BY
Tel: 01273 513881
Email: john.stirling@newhavenmarina.co.uk

VHF	Ch 80
ACCESS	H24

Some seven miles from Brighton, Newhaven lies at the mouth of the River Ouse. With its large fishing fleet and regular ferry services to Dieppe, the harbour has over the years become progressively commercial, therefore care is needed to keep clear of large vessels under manoeuvre.

The marina lies approximately quarter of a mile from the harbour entrance on the west bank and was recently dredged to allow full tidal access except on LWS.

FACILITIES AT A GLANCE

SOVEREIGN HARBOUR MARINA

Sovereign Harbour Marina
Pacific Drive, Eastbourne, East Sussex, BN23 5BJ
Tel: 01323 470099
Email: eastbourne@premiermarinas.com
www.premiermarinas.com

VHF	Ch 17
ACCESS	H24

Sovereign Harbour is Eastbourne's best kept secret, made up of four private and tranquil berthing harbours that offer over 800 quality berths. The marina is entered via one of two 24/7 high-capacity locks that are safe and easy to navigate. Sovereign Harbour offers outstanding facilities, including a fully serviced boatyard, chandlery and self-store, plus a friendly Yacht Club and Berth Holder's Association. Onshore, 'The Waterfront' leisure area boasts a mix of bars, restaurants and cafés, adding to the laid-back ambiance of the marina and offers a rich annual events programme.

FACILITIES AT A GLANCE

Key

a The Waterfront, shops, restaurants, pubs and offices
b Harbour office - weather information and visitor's information
c Cinema
d Retail park - supermarket and post office
e Restaurant
f 24 hr fuel pontoon (diesel, petrol and holding tank pump out)
g Boatyard, boatpark, marine engineers, riggers and electricians
NB Berth numbering runs from low outer to high inner

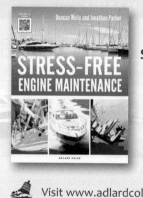

HARBOUR OF RYE

Harbour of Rye
New Lydd Road, Camber, E Sussex, TN31 7QS
Tel: 01797 225225
Email: rye.harbour@environment-agency.gov.uk
www.environment-agency.gov.uk/harbourofrye

VHF	Ch 14
ACCESS	HW±2

The Strand Quay moorings are located in the centre of the historic town of Rye with all of its amenities a short walk away. The town caters for a wide variety of interests with the nearby Rye Harbour Nature Reserve, a museum, numerous antique shops and plentiful pubs, bars and restaurants. Vessels, up to a length of 15 metres, wishing to berth in the soft mud in or near the town of Rye should time their arrival at the entrance for not later than one hour after high water. Larger vessels should make prior arrangements with the Harbour Master. Fresh water, electricity, shower and toilet facilities are available.

FACILITIES AT A GLANCE

DOVER MARINA

Dover Harbour Board
Harbour House, Dover, Kent, CT17 9TF
Tel: 01304 241663 Fax: 01304 242549
Email: marina@doverport.co.uk www.doverport.co.uk/marina

VHF Ch 80
ACCESS H24

Nestling under the famous White Cliffs, Dover sits between South Foreland to the NE and Folkestone to the SW. Boasting a maritime history stretching back as far as the Bronze Age, Dover is today one of Britain's busiest commercial ports, with a continuous stream of ferries and cruise liners plying to and from their European destinations. However, over the past years the harbour has made itself more attractive to the cruising yachtsman, with the marina, set well away from the busy ferry terminal, offering three sheltered berthing options in the Tidal Harbour, Granville Dock and Wellington Dock.

FACILITIES AT A GLANCE

Key
a Marina office
b Storage
c Waste oil disposal
d Scrubbing berth (tidal)

ROYAL HARBOUR MARINA

Royal Harbour Marina, Ramsgate
Harbour Office, Military Road, Ramsgate, Kent, CT11 9LQ
Tel: 01843 572100
Email: portoframsgate@thanet.gov.uk
www.portoframsgate.co.uk

VHF Ch 14, 80
ACCESS H24

Steeped in maritime history, Ramsgate was awarded 'Royal' status in 1821 by George IV in recognition of the warm welcome he received when sailing from Ramsgate. Offering good shelter and modern facilities, including both red and white diesel, the Royal Harbour comprises an outer marina accessible H24 and an inner marina, entered approximately HW±2. Permission to enter or leave the Royal Harbour must be obtained from Port Control on channel 14 and berthing instructions can be obtained from the Dockmaster on channel 80. Full information may be found on the website.

FACILITIES AT A GLANCE

Key
a Harbour office
b Port Control (VHF 14)
c Dock office
d Showers/toilets laundry
e RNLI
f Dockmasters office
g Fuel barge (VHF 14)
h Museum

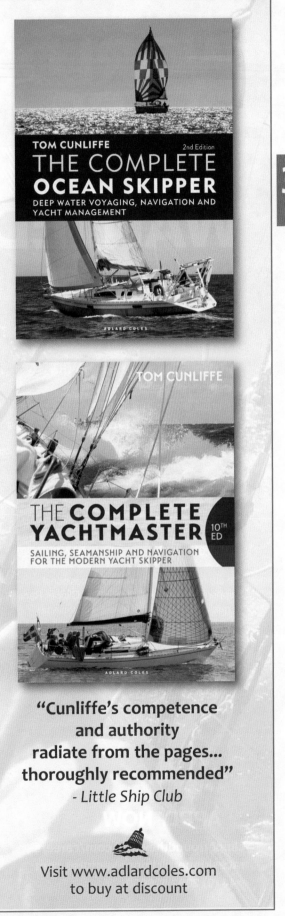
3

EAST ENGLAND – North Foreland to Great Yarmouth

Key to Marina Plans symbols

🛢	Bottled gas	P	Parking
	Chandler	✗	Pub/Restaurant
♿	Disabled facilities		Pump out
	Electrical supply		Rigging service
	Electrical repairs		Sail repairs
	Engine repairs	✗	Shipwright
✚	First Aid	🛒	Shop/Supermarket
	Fresh Water		Showers
D	Fuel - Diesel	◤	Slipway
P	Fuel - Petrol	WC	Toilets
	Hardstanding/boatyard	◔	Telephone
@	Internet Café		Trolleys
☐	Laundry facilities	V	Visitors berths
	Lift-out facilities		Wi-Fi

4

Area 4 - East England

MARINAS
Telephone Numbers, VHF Channel, Access Times

Gt Yarmouth

Lowestoft
Royal Norfolk & Suffolk YC 01520 566726 Ch 14, 80 H24
Lowestoft Haven Marina 01520 580300 Ch M, 80 H24
Lowestoft Cruising Club 07810 522515 H24

Southwold

Suffolk Yacht Hbr 01473 659240 Ch 80 H24
Royal Harwich YC Marina 01473 780319 Ch 77 H24
Woolverstone Marina 01473 780206 Ch 80 H24
Fox's Marina 01473 689111 Ch 80 H24
Neptune Marina 01473 215204 Ch M, 80 H24
Ipswich Haven Marina 01473 236644 Ch M, 80 H24

Orford

Shotley Marina 01473 788982 Ch 80 H24

South Dock Marina 020 7252 2244 Ch M HW-2½ to +1½
Poplar Dock Marina 020 7308 9930 Ch 13 HW±1
St Katharine Haven 020 7264 5312 Ch 80 HW-2 to +1½
Chelsea Harbour 07770 542783 Ch 80 HW±1½
Brentford Dock Marina 020 8232 8941 HW±2½
Penton Hook Marina 01932 568681 Ch 80 H24
Windsor Marina 01753 853911 Ch 80 H24
Bray Marina 01628 623654 Ch 80 H24

Ipswich

Harwich

Titchmarsh Marina 01255 672185 Ch 80 HW±5

Walton Yacht Basin 01255 675873 Ch 80 HW-¾ to +¼

Burnham Yacht Harbour 01621 782150 Ch 80 H24
Essex Marina 01702 258531 Ch 80 H24
Bridgemarsh Marina 01621 740414 Ch 80 HW±4
Fambridge Yacht Haven 01621 740370 Ch 80 H24
Fambridge Yacht Station 01621 742911 Ch 80 H24

Limehouse Marina 020 7308 9930 Ch 80 HW±3

R Thames

Bradwell Marina 01621 776235 Ch M, 80 HW±4½
Blackwater Marina 01621 740264 Ch M HW±2
Tollesbury Marina 01621 869202 Ch 80 HW±2
Heybridge Basin 07712 079764 Ch 80 HW±1

N

N. Foreland

Chatham Maritime Marina 01634 899200

Gillingham Marina 01634 280022 Ch 80 HW±4½

Ramsgate

GILLINGHAM MARINA

Gillingham Marina
173 Pier Road, Gillingham, Kent, ME7 1UB
Tel: 01634 280022 Fax: 01634 280164
Email: berthing@gillingham-marina.co.uk
www.gillingham-marina.co.uk

VHF Ch 80
ACCESS HW±4.5

Gillingham Marina comprises a locked basin, accessible four and a half hours either side of high water, and a tidal basin upstream which can be entered approximately two hours either side of high water. Deep water moorings in the river cater for yachts arriving at other times.

Visiting yachts are usually accommodated in the locked basin, although it is best to contact the marina ahead of time. Lying on the south bank of the River Medway, the marina is approximately eight miles from Sheerness, at the mouth of the river, and five miles downstream of Rochester Bridge. Facilities include a well-stocked chandlery, brokerage and an extensive workshop.

FACILITIES AT A GLANCE

Key
a Workshop
b Showers & toilets
c Shop
d Laundry
e Play area
f Reception & club
g Tender storage
h Lead in pontoon
i Petrol & diesel
j Leisure centre

PORT WERBURGH

Port Werburgh
Vicarage Lane, Hoo, Rochester, Kent, ME3 9TW
Tel: 01634 252107 Fax: 01634 253477
Email: jillswann@wanttoliveafloat.com

VHF Ch 80
ACCESS HW±3

Hoo Marina has been purchased by Residential Marine Ltd and is now incorporated into Port Werburgh. The port, some eight miles upriver from Sheerness, can be approached either straight across the mud flats at HW or via the creek, which has access HW±3 for shallow draught boats. The path of the creek is marked by withies, which must be kept to port.

The port accommodates residential and leisure boats from 20–200ft and has a lifting service available for craft up to 17 tons; a dry dock is available for larger boats. There are no workshop facilities but boat owners are encouraged to work on their own boats. Security is provided by H24 CCTV coverage.

All berths are supplied with water and electricity and the onsite amenity block has showers, toilets and a laundry room. There is a grocery store adjacent and shops in Hoo village approximately half a mile distant. There is a frequent bus service to nearby Rochester.

FACILITIES AT A GLANCE

CHATHAM MARITIME MARINA

Chatham Maritime Marina, The Lock Building,
Leviathan Way, Chatham Maritime, Chatham, Medway, ME4 4LP
Tel: 01634 899200
Email: chatham@mdlmarinas.co.uk
www.chathammaritimemarina.co.uk

VHF **Ch 80**
ACCESS **H24**

Chatham Maritime Marina
is situated on the banks
of the River Medway in Kent,
providing an ideal location
from which to explore the
surrounding area. There are
plenty of secluded anchorages
in the lower reaches of the
Medway Estuary, while the
river is navigable for some
13 miles from its mouth at
Sheerness right up to Rochester, and even beyond
for those yachts drawing less than 2m. Only 45
minutes from London by road, the marina is part of a
multi-million pound leisure and retail development,
accommodating 412 boats up to 24m LOA.

FACILITIES AT A GLANCE

Key
a Fuel berth
b Pontoon access gate
c Lifting pontoon
d Boat storage
e Facilities building
f Events berthing
g Waiting pontoon
h Lock control building
i Pump House No.5
j Pub, restaurant, hotel and
  convenience store
k Floating quay

LIMEHOUSE WATERSIDE & MARINA

Limehouse Waterside & Marina
46 Goodhart Place, London, E14 8EG
Tel: 020 7308 9930
Email: limehouse@aquavista.com www.aquavista.com

VHF **Ch 80**
ACCESS **HW±3**

Limehouse Marina, situated
where the canal system
meets the Thames, is now
considered the 'Jewel in the
Crown' of the British inland
waterways network. With
complete access to 2,000
miles of inland waterway
systems and with access to
the Thames at most stages of
the tide except around low
water, the marina provides
a superb location for river,
canal and sea-going pleasure craft alike. Boasting a
wide range of facilities and 137 berths, Limehouse
Marina is housed in the old Regent's Canal Dock.

FACILITIES AT A GLANCE

Key
a Cruising Association
b Chemical toilet disposal

4

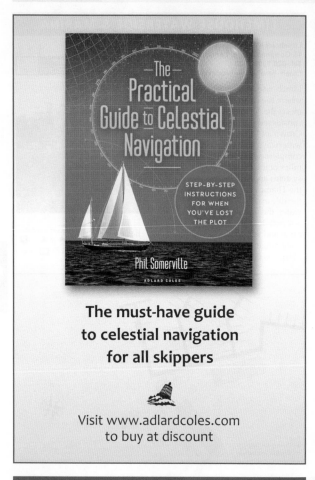
SOUTH DOCK MARINA

South Dock Marina
Rope Street, Off Plough Way
London, SE16 7SZ
Tel: 020 7252 2244 Fax: 020 7237 3806
Email: christopher.magro@southwark.gov.uk

VHF	Ch M
ACCESS	HW-2.5 to +1.5

South Dock Marina is housed in part of the old Surrey Dock complex on the south bank of the River Thames. Its locked entrance is immediately downstream of Greenland Pier, just a few miles down river of Tower Bridge. For yachts with a 2m draught, the lock can be entered HW-2½ to HW+1½ London Bridge, although if you arrive early there is a holding pontoon on the pier. The marina can be easily identified by the conspicuous arched rooftops of Baltic Quay, a luxury waterside apartment block. Once inside this secure, 200-berth marina, you can take full advantage of all its facilities as well as enjoy a range of restaurants and bars close by or visit historic maritime Greenwich.

FACILITIES AT A GLANCE

Key
a Marina office
b Conspic building

CHELSEA HARBOUR MARINA

Chelsea Harbour Marina
Estate Managements Office
C2-3 The Chambers, London, SW10 0XF
Tel: 07770 542783 Fax: 020 7352 7868
Email: harboumaster@chelsea-harbour.co.uk

VHF	
ACCESS	HW±1.5

Chelsea Harbour is widely thought of as one of London's most significant maritime sites. It is located in the heart of SW London, therefore enjoying easy access to the amenities of Chelsea and the West End. On site is the Chelsea Harbour Design Centre, where 80 showrooms exhibit the best in British and International interior design, offering superb waterside views along with excellent cuisine in the Wyndham Grand.

The harbour lies approximately 48 miles up river from Sea Reach No 1 buoy in the Thames Estuary and is accessed via the Thames Flood Barrier in Woolwich Reach. With its basin gate operating one and a half hours either side of HW (+ 20 minutes at London Bridge), the marina welcomes visiting yachtsmen.

FACILITIES AT A GLANCE

Key
a Belvedere Tower
b Harbour Yard
c Wyndham Grand Hotel
d Kings Quay
e Chelsea Crescent
f Thames Quay
   Showers, toilets & laundry

ST KATHARINE DOCKS

St Katharine Docks Marina
50 St Katharine's Way, London, E1W 1LA
Tel: 020 7264 5312
Email: ptetlow@skdocks.co.uk
www.skdocks.co.uk/marina

VHF	Ch 80
ACCESS	HW -2 to +1.5

IGY Destination, St Katharine Docks Marina offers 185 berths equipped for boats up to 40m in three separate, secure and calm basins. The historic docks are located next to Tower Bridge.

This is a unique marina benefiting from waterside dining, boutique shops and excellent transport links to the West End. Visitors are welcomed all year round and the marina provides its own calendar of events details of which can be found on the website and social media pages.

The marina is ideally situated for visiting the Tower of London, Tower Bridge, *HMS Belfast* and the City of London all of which can be reached on foot. A short river bus service away is Greenwich and the Cutty Sark and to the west the Shard and London Eye.

FACILITIES AT A GLANCE

Key
a Ivory House
b Dickens Inn
c Marina reception
d Tower Hotel
e Floating event pontoon

BRENTFORD DOCK MARINA

Brentford Dock Marina
2 Justin Close, Brentford, Middlesex, TW8 8QE
Tel: 020 8232 8941 Mob: 07970 143 987
E-mail: brentforddockmarina@gmail.com

VHF
ACCESS HW±2.5

Brentford Dock Marina is situated on the River Thames at the junction with the Grand Union Canal. Its hydraulic lock is accessible for up to two and a half hours either side of high water, although boats over 9.5m LOA enter on high water by prior arrangement. There is a grocery store on site. The main attractions within the area are the Royal Botanic Gardens at Kew and the Kew Bridge Steam Museum at Brentford.

FACILITIES AT A GLANCE

Key
a Shop
b Rubbish disposal
c Recycling bins
d Marina office and first aid
e Toilets, showers and slop out facilities

PENTON HOOK MARINA

Penton Hook Marina
Staines Road, Chertsey, Surrey, KT16 8PY
Tel: 01932 568681
Email: pentonhook@mdlmarinas.co.uk
www.pentonhookmarina.co.uk

VHF
ACCESS H24

Penton Hook, the largest inland marina in Europe, is situated on what is considered to be one of the most attractive reaches of the River Thames; close to the vibrant town of Staines-on-Thames and about a mile downstream from Runnymede.

Providing unrestricted access to the River Thames through a deep water channel below Penton Hook Lock, the marina can accommodate ocean-going craft of up to 30m LOA and is ideally placed for a visit to Thorpe Park, reputedly one of the country's most popular family leisure attractions.

FACILITIES AT A GLANCE

Key
a Information point
b Dock manager's office
c Yacht club
d Repairs and engineering
e Boat sales office

WINDSOR MARINA

Windsor Marina
Maidenhead Road, Windsor
Berkshire, SL4 5TZ
Tel: 01753 853911
Email: windsor@mdlmarinas.co.uk www.windsormarina.co.uk

VHF
ACCESS H24

Situated on the outskirts of Windsor town on the south bank of the River Thames, Windsor Marina enjoys a peaceful garden setting. On site is the Windsor Yacht Club, a small chandlery and fuel (diesel and petrol), enabling you to fill up as and when you need.

A trip to the town of Windsor, comprising beautiful Georgian and Victorian buildings, would not be complete without a visit to Windsor Castle. With its construction inaugurated over 900 years ago by William the Conqueror, it is the oldest inhabited castle in the world and accommodates a priceless art and furniture collection.

FACILITIES AT A GLANCE

Key
a Boat sales & engineers
b Recycling bins
c Marina office
d Trimmers
e Yacht club

BRAY MARINA

Bray Marina
Monkey Island Lane, Bray
Berkshire, SL6 2EB
Tel: 01628 623654
Email: bray@mdlmarinas.co.uk www.braymarina.co.uk

VHF
ACCESS H24

Bray Marina is situated in a country park setting among shady trees, providing berth holders with a tranquil mooring. From the marina there is direct access to the Thames and there are extensive well-maintained facilities available for all boat owners. The 400-berth marina boasts a Mediterranean-themed bar and restaurant, an active club, which holds social functions and boat training lessons, a small chandlery, fuel (diesel and petrol), and engineering services.

Upstream is Cliveden House, with its extensive gardens and woodlands. Cookham is home of the Queen's Swan Keeper, who can sometimes be seen in traditional costume. Further on still is Hambledon Mill; from here the river is navigable as far as Lechlade.

FACILITIES AT A GLANCE

Key
a Boat storage
b Boat sales office
c Marina office, toilets/showers restaurant
d Battery, hazardous waste, oil and fuel disposal
e Repairs and engineering

BURNHAM YACHT HARBOUR MARINA

Burnham Yacht Harbour Marina Ltd
Burnham-on-Crouch, Essex, CM0 8BL
Tel: 01621 782150 HM: 01621 786832
Email: admin@burnhamyachtharbour.co.uk

VHF	Ch 80
ACCESS	H24

Burnham Yacht Harbour is situated in the pretty town of Burnham-on-Crouch with its quaint shops, elegant quayside and riverside walks. The train station, with direct train links to London Liverpool Street Station, is within walking. There is provision of all facilities you would expect

to find from a modern secure marina with H24 tidal access, 350 fully serviced berths, the popular Swallowtail Restaurant and Bar, friendly staff, engineers, shipwrights, workshop, friendly staff, chandlery and yacht brokerage. The entrance is easily identified by a yellow pillar buoy with an 'X' topmark.

FACILITIES AT A GLANCE

Key
a Workshop
b Yacht sales
c Marina office
d Shower block
e The Swallowtail
f RNLI shore station
g Country park

Visiting Burnham Yacht Harbour?
Please call our Harbourmaster on
01621 786832
or call up on **VHF Channel 80**
for visitor berth allocation.

– 350 fully serviced berths
– Safe and secure moorings
– 24 hour tidal access
– Restaurant, bar and conference room
– Heated workshop
– Shipwrights, engineers and outfitters
– Yacht brokerage
– Refurbished shower and toilet block
– Free Wifi
– Direct rail links to London

For a full list of incentives and deals please visit our website www.burnhamyachtharbour.co.uk
or call 01621 782150
or email us admin@burnhamyachtharbour.co.uk

ESSEX MARINA

Essex Marina
Wallasea Island, Essex, SS4 2HF
Tel: 01702 258531 Fax: 01702 258227
Email: info@essexmarina.co.uk
www.essexmarina.co.uk

VHF	Ch 80
ACCESS	H24

Surrounded by beautiful countryside, Essex Marina is situated in Wallasea Bay, about half a mile up river of Burnham on Crouch. Boasting 500 deep water berths, including 50 swinging moorings, the marina can be accessed at all states of the tide. On site are a 70 ton boat hoist, a chandlery and brokerage service as well as the Essex Marina Yacht Club.

Essex Marina is the home of Boats.co.uk. There is a ferry service which runs from Easter until the end of September, taking passengers across the river 6 days a week to Burnham, where you will find numerous shops and restaurants.

FACILITIES AT A GLANCE

Key
a Marina office & chandlery
b Essex Marina Yacht Club
c Brokerage & boat sales
d Licenced bar & restaurant

BRIDGEMARSH MARINA

Bridgemarsh Marine
Fairholme, Bridge Marsh Lane, Althorne, Essex
Tel: 01621 740414 Mobile: 07968 696815 Fax: 01621 742216

VHF	Ch 80
ACCESS	HW±4

On the north side of Bridgemarsh Island, just beyond Essex Marina on the River Crouch, lies Althorne Creek. Here Bridgemarsh Marine accommodates over 100 boats berthed alongside pontoons supplied with water and electricity. A red beacon marks the entrance to the

creek, with red can buoys identifying the approach channel into the marina. Accessible four hours either side of high water, the marina has an on site yard with two docks, a slipway and crane. The village of Althorne is just a short walk away, from where there are direct train services (taking approximately one hour) to London.

FACILITIES AT A GLANCE

HEYBRIDGE BASIN

Heybridge Basin
Lock Hill, Heybridge Basin, Maldon, Essex, CM9 4RY
Tel: 07712 079764
Email: paul.hindley@waterways.org.uk
www.essexwaterways.com

VHF	Ch 80
ACCESS	HW±1

Towards the head of the River Blackwater and not far from Maldon, lies Heybridge Basin sea lock. It is situated at the lower end of the 14M Chelmer and Blackwater Navigation Canal and can be entered approximately 1-1.5hrs before HW for vessels drawing up to 2m. There is good holding ground in the river just outside the lock. There are in excess of 300 permanent moorings along the navigation and room for up to 20 rafting visiting vessels in the Basin, which has a range of facilities, including shower and laundry. Please book at least 24hrs in advance especially during the summer months. The manned lock is operational for tides between 0600 and 2000 during summer months (0800–1700 Apr–Oct).

FACILITIES AT A GLANCE

Daisy Meadow Car Park

Lockhouse

BRADWELL MARINA

Bradwell Marina, Port Flair Ltd, Waterside
Bradwell-on-Sea, Essex, CM0 7RB
Tel: 01621 776235
Email: info@bradwellmarina.com
www.bradwellmarina.com

VHF	Ch M, 80
ACCESS	HW±4.5

Opened in 1984, Bradwell is a privately-owned marina situated in the mouth of the River Blackwater, serving as a convenient base from which to explore the Essex coastline or as a departure point for cruising further afield to Holland and Belgium.

The yacht basin can be accessed four and a half hours either side of HW and offers plenty of protection from all wind directions. With a total of 350 fully serviced berths, generous space has been allocated for manoeuvring between pontoons. Overlooking the marina is Bradwell Club House, incorporating a bar, restaurant, launderette and ablution facilities.

FACILITIES AT A GLANCE

Key
a Clubhouse
b Tower office

4

FAMBRIDGE YACHT STATION

Fambridge Yacht Station
Church Road, North Fambridge, Essex, CM3 6LU
Tel: 01621 742911 www.yachthavens.com
Email: fambridge@yachthavens.com

VHF	Ch 80
ACCESS	H24

The Yacht Station is located just under a mile downstream of Fambridge Yacht Haven and is set within the sheltered River Crouch directly between the rural villages of North and South Fambridge. Home to the North Fambridge Yacht Club, the Yacht Station has a 120m visitor pontoon providing deep water berthing alongside and foot access to mud berths and the North Fambridge. There are also 120 deep water swinging moorings in 4 straight E/W trots just off the visitor pontoon. A launch service operates 7 days a week during the summer, call in advance for times. As with the marina, excellent repair facilities can be found ashore for vessels with a maximum weight of 25t.

FACILITIES AT A GLANCE

Key
a Yacht Station reception
b Crane dock
c N Fambridge YC
d Floating dinghy storage
e IBS Boat Supplies

Mud berths

Fl(3)G.4s   Fl(3)G.4s

Swinging moorings

FAMBRIDGE YACHT HAVEN

Fambridge Yacht Haven
Church Road, North Fambridge, Essex, CM3 6LU
Tel: 01621 740370 www.yachthavens.com
Email: fambridge@yachthavens.com

VHF Ch 80
ACCESS H24

The Haven is split over two sites in the village of North Fambridge. The marina is located just under a mile upstream of its 'Yacht Station' facility with access via Stow Creek, which branches N off the R Crouch. The channel is straight and clearly marked to the ent of the Yacht Haven. Home to the West Wick Yacht Club, the marina has 220 berths to accommodate vessels up to 20m LOA. North Fambridge features the 500 year-old Ferry Boat Inn, a favourite haunt with the sailing fraternity. Burnham-on-Crouch is six miles down river, while the Essex and Kent coasts are within easy sailing distance. Excellent repair facilities can be found ashore together with undercover storage for vessels up to 19m LOA with a maximum weight of 40 tons.

FACILITIES AT A GLANCE

Visitors welcome

Key
a Marina reception
b Waste
c West Wick YC
d Boat Shed Essex
e Marina maintenance, workshop & stores
f Under cover storage
g Chandler

Leading lights white on white

Stow Creek

Fambridge Yacht Haven
Family-friendly marina

– 220 sheltered & fully serviced pontoon berths
– 120 deepwater swinging moorings
– 120m visitor pontoon with full tidal access
– A TransEurope Marina
– FREE Wi-Fi for berth holders & visitors
– On-site Children's Adventure Play Park
– Walking distance from the famous Ferry Boat Inn
– Hassle-free Park & Ride Service
– Modern 25t & 18t slipway hoists & 30t mobile crane

Call **01621 740370** or **VHF Ch 80**
or visit **yachthavens.com**

Fambridge Yacht Haven

BLACKWATER MARINA

Blackwater Marina
Marine Parade, Maylandsea, Essex
Tel: 01621 740264
Email: info@blackwater-marina.co.uk

VHF Ch M
ACCESS HW±2

Blackwater Marina is a place where families in day boats mix with Smack owners and yacht crews; here seals, avocets and porpoises roam beneath the big, sheltering East Coast skies and here the area's rich heritage of working Thames Barges and Smacks remains part of daily life today.
But it isn't just classic sailing boats that thrive on the Blackwater. An eclectic mix of motor cruisers, open boats and modern yachts enjoy the advantages of a marina sheltered by its natural habitat, where the absence of harbour walls allows uninterrupted views of some of Britain's rarest wildlife and where the 21st century shoreside facilities are looked after by experienced professionals, who are often found sailing on their days off.

FACILITIES AT A GLANCE

Key
a Maylandsea Bay YC
b Harlow (Blackwater) Sailing Club
c Marina office

Flag Station

Marina Bar

TOLLESBURY MARINA

Tollesbury Marina
The Yacht Harbour, Tollesbury, Essex, CM9 8SE
Tel: 01621 869202 Fax: 01621 868489
email: harbourmaster@tollesburymarina.com

VHF Ch 80
ACCESS HW±2

Tollesbury Marina lies at the mouth of the River Blackwater in the heart of the Essex countryside. Within easy access from London and the Home Counties, it has been designed as a leisure centre for the whole family, with on-site activities comprising tennis courts and a covered heated swimming pool as well as a convivial bar and restaurant. Accommodating over 240 boats, the marina can be accessed two hours either side of HW and is ideally situated for those wishing to explore the River Crouch to the south and the Rivers Colne, Orwell and Deben to the north.

FACILITIES AT A GLANCE

Waste oil container

Waste bin

Scrubbing posts

Waste bin

Tollesbury Cruising Club

Key
a Brokerage and Chandlery
b Workshop
c Covered Heated Pool and Tennis

TITCHMARSH MARINA

Titchmarsh Marina Ltd
Coles Lane, Walton on the Naze, Essex, CO14 8SL
Tel: 01255 672185 Fax: 01255 851901
Email: info@titchmarshmarina.co.uk
www.titchmarshmarina.co.uk

| VHF | Ch 80 |
| ACCESS | HW±5 |

Titchmarsh Marina sits on the south side of The Twizzle in the heart of the Walton Backwaters. As the area is designated a 'wetland of international importance', the marina has been designed and developed to function as a natural harbour. The 420 berths are well-sheltered by the high-grassed clay banks, offering good protection in all conditions. The marina entrance has a depth of 1.3m at LWS but once inside the basin this increases to around 2m; there is a tide gauge at the fuel berth. Among the excellent facilities onsite are the well-stocked chandlery and the Harbour Lights restaurant and bar serving food daily.

FACILITIES AT A GLANCE

Key
a Harbour master, chandlery (+ cycle hire) marine engineers, marine electronics
b Hardstanding
c Harbour Lights - restaurant and bar

4

WALTON YACHT BASIN

Walton and Frinton Yacht Trust
Mill Lane, Walton on the Naze, CO14 8PF
Managed by Bedwell & Co Tel: 01255 675873
Mobile: 07957 848031

| VHF | Ch 80 |
| ACCESS | HW-0.75,HW+0.25 |

Walton Yacht Basin lies at the head of Walton Creek, an area made famous in Arthur Ransome's *Swallows & Amazons* and *Secret Waters*. The creek can only be navigated HW±2, although yachts heading for the Yacht Basin should arrive on a rising tide as the entrance gate is kept shut once the tide turns in order to retain the water inside. Before entering the gate, moor up against the Club Quay to enquire about berthing availability.

A short walk away is the popular seaside town of Walton, full of shops, pubs and restaurants. Its focal point is the pier which, overlooking superb sandy beaches, offers various attractions. Slightly further out of town, the Naze affords pleasant coastal walks with striking panoramic views.

FACILITIES AT A GLANCE

SUFFOLK YACHT HARBOUR

Suffolk Yacht Harbour Ltd
Levington, Ipswich, Suffolk, IP10 0LN
Tel: 01473 659240
Email: enquiries@syharbour.co.uk
www.syharbour.co.uk

| VHF | Ch 80 |
| ACCESS | H24 |

A friendly, independently-run marina on the East Coast of England, Suffolk Yacht Harbour enjoys a beautiful rural setting on the River Orwell, yet is within easy access of Ipswich, Woodbridge and Felixstowe. With approximately 550 berths, the marina offers extensive facilities while the Haven Ports Yacht Club provides a bar and restaurant.

FACILITIES AT A GLANCE

SHOTLEY MARINA

Shotley Marina Ltd
Shotley Gate, Ipswich, Suffolk, IP9 1QJ
Tel: 01473 788982 Fax: 01473 788868
Email: sales@shotleymarina.co.uk
www.shotleymarina.co.uk

VHF	Ch 80
ACCESS	H24

Based in the well protected Harwich Harbour where the River Stour joins the River Orwell, Shotley Marina is only eight miles from the county town of Ipswich. Entered via a lock at all states of the tide, its first class facilities include extensive boat repair and maintenance services as well as a well-stocked chandlery and on site bar and restaurant. The marina is strategically placed for sailing up the Stour to Manningtree, up the Orwell to Pin Mill or exploring the Rivers Deben, Crouch and Blackwater as well as the Walton Backwaters.

FACILITIES AT A GLANCE

Key
a   Shotley Marine Services
b   Lock control
c   Lock waiting pontoons
d   SPYC
e   Mariners Bar and function rooms
f   Baths, showers and toilets
g   Launderette
h   Shipwreck bar and restaurant
i   Shotley Point YC
j   HMS Ganges Museum

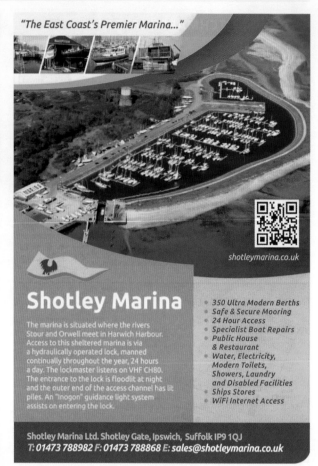
ROYAL HARWICH YACHT CLUB MARINA

Royal Harwich Yacht Club Marina
Marina Road, Woolverstone, Suffolk, IP9 1AT
Tel: 01473 780319 Fax: 01473 780919 Berths: 07742 145994
www.royalharwichyachtclub.co.uk
Email: office.manager@royalharwich.co.uk

VHF	Ch 77
ACCESS	H24

This 54 berth marina is ideally situated at a mid point on the Orwell between Levington and Ipswich. The facility is owned and run by the Royal Harwich Yacht Club and enjoys a full catering and bar service in the Clubhouse. The marina benefits from full tidal access, and can accommodate yachts up to 14.5m on the hammerhead. Within the immediate surrounds, there are boat repair services, and a well stocked chandlery. The marina is situated a mile's walk from the world famous Pin Mill and is a favoured destination with visitors from Holland, Belgium and Germany. The marina welcomes racing yachts and cruisers, and is able to accommodate multiple bookings.

FACILITIES AT A GLANCE

FOX'S MARINA

Fox's Marina & Boatyard
The Strand, Ipswich, Suffolk, IP2 8SA
Tel: 01473 689111
Email: foxs@foxsmarina.com www.foxsmarina.com

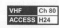 VHF Ch 80
ACCESS H24

Located on the picturesque River Orwell, Fox's provides good shelter in all conditions and access at all states of tide with 100 pontoon berths and ashore storage for 200 vessels. A 70T hoist is able to handle boats up to 80ft in length.

Fox's Marina & Boatyard offers a full range of in-house services and, with 10,000 sq ft of heated workshop space, are specialists in repairs and refits of sailing/motor yachts and commercial craft. Specific services include coppercoat and osmosis treatment, specialist GRP and gelcoat repairs, spray painting and varnishing, and custom stainless fabrication. Also on-site, Fox's Chandlery and Marine Store, is the largest stockist of marine chandlery and equipment, sailing, leisure and country clothing in East Anglia.

FACILITIES AT A GLANCE

Key
a Workshops, rigging and electronics
b Harbourmaster office
c Yacht Club
d Outlook Cafe, Bar & Bistro

WOOLVERSTONE MARINA

Woolverstone Marina and Lodge Park
Woolverstone, Ipswich, Suffolk, IP9 1AS
Tel: 01473 780206
Email: woolverstone@mdlmarinas.co.uk
www.woolverstonemarina.co.uk

 VHF Ch 80
ACCESS H24

Woolverstone Marina is set in 22 acres of glorious parkland on the picturesque River Orwell. Within easy reach of the sea and a multitude of scenic destinations, this is a great base to start cruising. Walton Backwaters and the River Deben are only a short distance away. If you prefer longer distance cruising then Belgium and Holland are directly across the North Sea.

Besides boat repair services and ablution facilities, the marina also incorporates a lodge park with luxurious lodges, yacht brokerage and an on-site restaurant/bar, which overlooks the river.

FACILITIES AT A GLANCE

Key
a Marina office, toilets, showers, and launderette
b Restaurant and Bar

NEPTUNE MARINA

Neptune Marina Ltd
Neptune Quay, Ipswich, IP4 1QJ
Tel: 01473 215204
Email: enquiries@neptune-marina.com

VHF	Ch M, 80
ACCESS	H24

Neptune Marina is situated at Neptune Quay on the historic waterfront, and ever-increasing shoreside developments. This 26-acre dock is accessible through a H24 lock gate, with a waiting pontoon outside. Onsite facilities include boatyard and lift-out facilities plus wifi for boat owners.

The Neptune Marina building occupies an imposing position in the NE corner of the dock with quality coffee shop and associated retail units. There are a number of excellent restaurants along the quayside and adjacent to the marina.

The modern town centre catering for all needs is just a 10-minute walk away.

FACILITIES AT A GLANCE

Key
a Old Custom House
b Conference centre
c Floating French restaurant
d Bistro
e Bellway apartments
f Neptune Marina office & facilities
g Marina storage yard

IPSWICH HAVEN MARINA

Ipswich Haven Marina
Associated British Ports
New Cut East, Ipswich, Suffolk, IP3 0EA
Tel: 01473 236644 Fax: 01473 236645
Email: ipswichhaven@abports.co.uk

VHF	Ch M, 80
ACCESS	H24

Lying at the heart of Ipswich, the Haven Marina enjoys close proximity to all the bustling shopping centres, restaurants, cinemas and museums that this County Town of Suffolk has to offer. The main railway station is only a 10-minute walk away, where there are regular connections to London, Cambridge and Norwich, all taking just over an hour to get to.

Within easy reach of Holland, Belgium and Germany, East Anglia is proving an increasingly popular cruising ground. The River Orwell, displaying breathtaking scenery, was voted one of the most beautiful rivers in Britain by the RYA.

FACILITIES AT A GLANCE

Key
a Toilets, showers, laundry, office
b Licensed bistro
c R&J Marine Electronics
d Boat sales
e Fairline PDI Shed
f Future restaurant retail
g Burton Waters Repair Shop

LOWESTOFT HAVEN MARINA

Lowestoft Haven Marina
School Road, Lowestoft, Suffolk, NR33 9NB
Tel: 01502 580300
Email: lowestofhaven@abports.co.uk
www.lowestofthavenmarina.co.uk

⚓⚓⚓

| VHF | Ch M, 80 |
| ACCESS | H24 |

Lowestoft Haven Marina is based on Lake Lothing with easy access to both the open sea and the Norfolk Broads. The town centres of both Lowestoft and Oulton Broad are within a short distance of the marina.

The marina's 140 berths can accommodate vessels from 7–20m. Offering a full range of modern facilities the marina welcomes all visitors.

FACILITIES AT A GLANCE

Key
a Boat storage
b Marina office

ROYAL NORFOLK & SUFFOLK YACHT CLUB

Royal Norfolk and Suffolk Yacht Club
Royal Plain, Lowestoft, Suffolk, NR33 0AQ
Tel: 01502 566726
Email: admin@rnsyc.org.uk   www.rnsyc.net

| VHF | Ch 14, 80 |
| ACCESS | H24 |

With its entrance at the inner end of the South Pier, opposite the Trawl Basin on the north bank, the Royal Norfolk and Suffolk Yacht Club marina occupies a sheltered position in Lowestoft Harbour. Lowestoft has always been an appealing destination to yachtsmen due to the fact that it can be accessed at any state of the tide, 24 hours a day. Note, however, that conditions just outside the entrance can get pretty lively when the wind is against tide. The clubhouse is enclosed in an impressive Grade 2 listed building overlooking the marina and its facilities include a bar and restaurant as well as a formal dining room.

FACILITIES AT A GLANCE

Key
a Showers, toilets including disabled   d Sun lounge
b Restaurant   e Bar
c Reception   f Marina office

RNSYC

4

LOWESTOFT CRUISING CLUB

Lowestoft Cruising Club
Off Harbour Road, Oulton Broad, Lowestoft, Suffolk, NR32 3LY
Tel: 07810 522515
www.lowestoftcruisingclub.co.uk

| VHF | |
| ACCESS | H24 |

Lowestoft Cruising Club welcomes visitors and can offer a friendly atmosphere, some of the finest moorings and at very competitive rates. Whatever the weather, these moorings provide a calm, safe haven for visiting yachts and with the Mutford lock only 250 metres away, easy access onto the Norfolk and Suffolk Broads. Facilities include electricity and water, plus excellent showers, toilets and secure car parking. These moorings are the nearest ones to the railway stations (to Norwich and Ipswich), bus routes, shops, banks, pubs and restaurants in Oulton Broad.

FACILITIES AT A GLANCE

Cruise between a network of marinas across Europe

TransEurope Marinas cardholders benefit from a 50% visitor's berthing discount
in each associated marina for up to five days a year.
For a current list of members and further information, please visit

www.transeuropemarinas.com

UK 🇬🇧

1. Bangor Marina
2. Rhu Marina
3. Troon Yacht Haven
4. Royal Quays Marina
5. Whitehaven Marina
6. Fleetwood Haven Marina
7. Conwy Marina
8. Neyland Yacht Haven
9. Penarth Marina
10. Upton Marina
11. Portishead Marina
12. Mylor Yacht Harbour
13. Mayflower Marina
14. Poole Quay Boat Haven
15. Buckler's Hard Yacht Harbour
16. Town Quay Marina
17. Cowes Yacht Haven
18. Royal Clarence Marin
19. Emsworth Yacht Harboura
20. Birdham Pool Marina
21. Dover Marina
22. Gillingham Marina
23. Fambridge Yacht Haven
24. Tollesbury Marina
25. Fox's Marina
26. Brundall Bay Marina

Italy 🇮🇹

1. Porto Romano
2. Venezia Certosa Marina
3. Marina del Cavallino

Germany ▭

1. Sonwik Marina
2. Ancora Marina
3. Marina Boltenhagen
4. Marina Wiek auf Rügen
5. Naturhafen Krummin
6. Lagunenstadt Ueckermünde

France 🇫🇷

1. Dunkerque
2. Calais
3. Boulogne-sur-mer
4. Saint Valery sur Somme
5. Dieppe
6. Saint Valery en Caux
7. Fécamp
8. Le Havre Plaisance
9. Port-Deauville
10. Dives-Cabourg-Houlgate
11. Ouistreham/Caen
12. Granville
13. Saint-Quay Port d'Armor
14. Perros-Guirec
15. Roscoff
16. Marinas de Brest
17. Douarnenez-Tréboul
18. Loctudy
19. Port la Forêt
20. Concarneau
21. Ports de Nantes

Spain 🇪🇸

1. Marina Combarro
2. Nauta Sanxenxo
3. Puerto Calero
4. Alcaidesa Marina
5. Pobla Marina

Belgium ▭

1. VNZ Blankenberge
2. VY Nieuwpoort

Netherlands ▭

1. Marina Den Oever
2. Jachthaven Waterland
3. Jachthaven Wetterwille
4. Marina Port Zélande
5. Jachthaven Biesbosch
6. Delta Marina Kortgene

Portugal 🇵🇹

1. Douro Marina
2. Quinta do Lorde Marina

Ireland 🇮🇪

1. Malahide Marina

Slovenia 🇸🇮

1. Marina Portorož

Croatia 🇭🇷

1. Marina Punat

Greece 🇬🇷

1. Linariá Marina
2. Kos Marina

NORTH EAST ENGLAND - Great Yarmouth to Berwick-upon-Tweed

Key to Marina Plans symbols

Bottled gas		Parking
Chandler		Pub/Restaurant
Disabled facilities		Pump out
Electrical supply		Rigging service
Electrical repairs		Sail repairs
Engine repairs		Shipwright
First Aid		Shop/Supermarket
Fresh Water		Showers
Fuel - Diesel		Slipway
Fuel - Petrol		Toilets
Hardstanding/boatyard		Telephone
Internet Café		Trolleys
Laundry facilities		Visitors berths
Lift-out facilities		Wi-Fi

Area 5 - North East England

5

MARINAS
Telephone Numbers
VHF Channel
Access Times

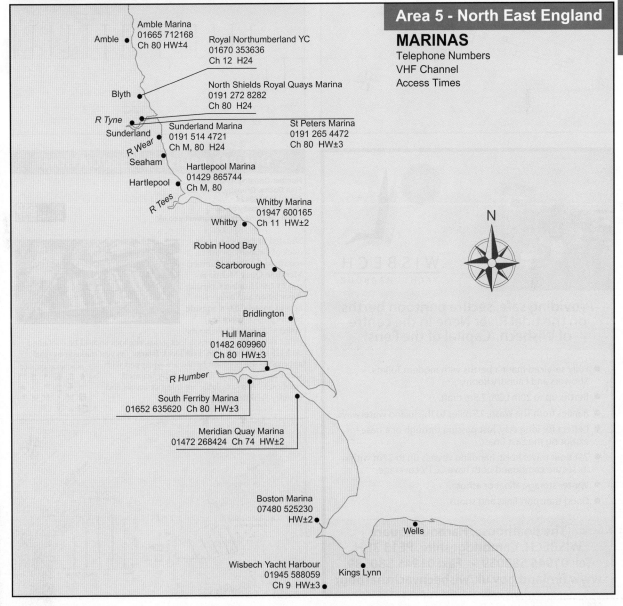

Amble Marina
01665 712168
Ch 80 HW±4

Royal Northumberland YC
01670 353636
Ch 12 H24

North Shields Royal Quays Marina
0191 272 8282
Ch 80 H24

Sunderland Marina
0191 514 4721
Ch M, 80 H24

St Peters Marina
0191 265 4472
Ch 80 HW±3

Hartlepool Marina
01429 865744
Ch M, 80

Whitby Marina
01947 600165
Ch 11 HW±2

Hull Marina
01482 609960
Ch 80 HW±3

South Ferriby Marina
01652 635620 Ch 80 HW±3

Meridian Quay Marina
01472 268424 Ch 74 HW±2

Boston Marina
07480 525230
HW±2

Wisbech Yacht Harbour
01945 588059
Ch 9 HW±3

Amble
Blyth
R Tyne
Sunderland
R Wear
Seaham
Hartlepool
R Tees
Whitby
Robin Hood Bay
Scarborough
Bridlington
R Humber
Wells
Kings Lynn

WISBECH YACHT HARBOUR

Wisbech Yacht Harbour
Harbour Master, Harbour Office, The Boathouse,
Harbour Square, Wisbech, Cambridgeshire PE13 3BH
Tel: 01945 588059 Fax: 01945 580589
Email: afoster@fenland.gov.uk www.fenland.gov.uk

VHF Ch 9
ACCESS HW±3

Regarded as the capital of the English Fens, Wisbech is situated about 25 miles north east of Peterborough and is a market town of considerable character and historical significance. Rows of elegant houses line the banks of the River Nene, with the North and South Brink still deemed two of the finest Georgian streets in England.

Wisbech Yacht Harbour, linking Cambridgeshire with the sea, is proving increasingly popular as a haven for small craft, despite the busy commercial shipping. In recent years the facilities have been developed and improved upon and the HM is always on hand to help with passage planning both up or downstream.

FACILITIES AT A GLANCE

BOSTON GATEWAY MARINA

Boston Gateway Marina
Witham Bank East, Boston, Lincs, PE21 9JU
Tel: 07480 525230
Email: enquiries@bostongatewaymarina.co.uk

VHF
ACCESS H±2

Located near Boston Grand Sluice Lock on the sunny side of the River Witham, the marina is ideally situated for easy access to The Wash and is suitable for both sea-going and river boats. It is a short walk to the centre of the historic town of Boston, Lincolnshire, but retains a tranquil feel. The marina offers visitor, short-term and longer-term moorings to suit each individual customer. Power and water are available for all boats.

The town centre offers the normal variety of facilities within easy walking distance. Local tourist attractions include the 14th century St Botolph's Church – 'The Stump' – the 1390s Boston Guildhall Musuem and a 450-year old market to name but a few.

FACILITIES AT A GLANCE

WISBECH
YACHT HARBOUR

Providing safe, secure pontoon berths on the tidal River Nene in the centre of Wisbech, 'Capital of the Fens'.

- Fully serviced marina berths with modern Toilets, Showers and Laundry Room.
- Berths up to 20m LOA, 2.5m draft.
- 8 miles from The Wash, 15 miles to the inland waterways.
- Perfect for long stay, just passing through or a base for exploring the East Coast.
- 75t boat travel hoist: handling vessels up to 27m within its secure compound both have CCTV coverage.
- Winter storage afloat or ashore.
- Good transport links and shops.

The Boathouse, Harbour Square
WISBECH, Cambridgeshire, PE13 3BH
Tel: 01945 588059 • Fax: 01945 580589.
www.fenland.gov.uk/wisbechyachtharbour

HUMBER CRUISING ASSOCIATION

Humber Cruising Association
Fish Docks, Grimsby, DN31 3SD
Tel: 01472 268424
www.hcagrimsby.co.uk
Email: berthmaster@hcagrimsby.co.uk

VHF Ch 74
ACCESS HW±2

Situated in the locked fish dock of Grimsby, at the mouth of the River Humber, Meridian Quay Marina is run by the Humber Cruising Association and comprises approximately 200 alongside berths plus 30 more for visitors. Accessed two hours either side of high water via lock gates, the lock should be contacted on VHF Ch 74 (call sign 'Fish Dock Island') as you make your final approach. The pontoon berths are equipped with water and electricity; there is a fully licensed clubhouse. Also available are internet access and laundry facilities.

FACILITIES AT A GLANCE

HULL WATERSIDE & MARINA

Hull Waterside & Marina
W 13, Kingston Street, Hull, HU1 2DQ
Tel: 01482 609960 Fax: 01482 224148
Email: hull@aquavista.com
www.aquavista.com

VHF	Ch 80
ACCESS	HW±3

Situated on the River Humber, Hull Marina is literally a stone's throw from the bustling city centre with its array of arts and entertainments. Besides the numerous historic bars and cafés surrounding the marina, there are plenty of traditional taverns to be sampled in the Old Town, while also found here is the Street Life Museum, vividly depicting the history of the city.

Yachtsmen enter the marina via a tidal lock, operating HW±3, and should try to give 15 minutes' notice of arrival via VHF Ch 80. Hull is perfectly positioned for exploring the Trent, Ouse and the Yorkshire coast as well as across the North Sea to Holland or Belgium.

FACILITIES AT A GLANCE

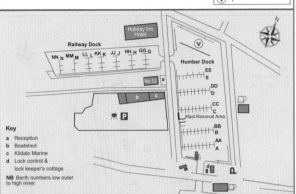

Key
a   Reception
b   Boatshed
c   Kildale Marine
d   Lock control &
    lock keeper's cottage
NB Berth numbers low outer to high inner.

5

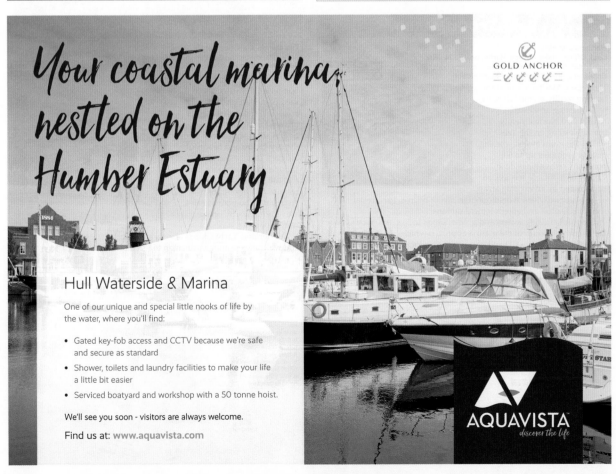

SOUTH FERRIBY MARINA

South Ferriby Marina
Red Lane, South Ferriby, Barton on Humber, Lincs, DN18 6JH
Tel: 01652 635620 (Lock 635219) Mobile: 07828 312071
Email: enquiries@southferribymarina.com

VHF	Ch 74
ACCESS	HW±3

Situated at the entrance to the non-tidal River Ancholme the existing marina has been established since 1966 and is well placed to provide easy access to the River Humber and North Sea. This is a family run business providing a range of services including a boatyard and chandlery. Access is by way of lock at HW±3.

The marina has excellent road and rail services within easy reach, while South Ferriby village has two pubs and a Post Office/Spar Shop just a short walk away.

The picturesque River Ancholme is navigable for about 17 miles; the maximum headroom under bridges is 4.42 metres (14ft 6ins).

FACILITIES AT A GLANCE

Key
a   Chandlery
b   Shipwrights workshop

WHITBY MARINA

Whitby Marina
Whitby Harbour Office, Endeavour Wharf
Whitby, North Yorkshire YO21 1DN
Harbour Office: 01947 602354 Marina: 01947 600165
Email: port.services@scarborough.gov.uk

VHF	Ch 11
ACCESS	HW±2

The only natural harbour between the Tees and the Humber, Whitby lies some 20 miles north of Scarborough on the River Esk. The historic town is said to date back as far as the Roman times, although it is better known for its abbey, which was founded over 1,300 years ago by King Oswy of Northumberland. Another place of interest is the Captain Cook Memorial Museum, a tribute to Whitby's greatest seaman.

A swing bridge divides the harbour into upper and lower sections, with the marina being in the Upper Harbour. The bridge opens on request (VHF Ch 11) each half hour for two hours either side of high water.

FACILITIES AT A GLANCE

Key
a   Marina office
b   Waste oil bin

HARTLEPOOL MARINA

Hartlepool Marina
Lock Office, Slake Terrace, Hartlepool, TS24 0RU
Tel: 01429 865744 www.hartlepool-marina.com
Email: enquiries@hartlepool-marina.com

VHF	Ch M, 80
ACCESS	

Hartlepool Marina is a modern boating facility on the NE coast now boasting an extensively refurbished North amenity block. Nestling on the Tees Valley the multi award winning marina promotes up to 500 pontoon berths alongside a variety of reputable services all surrounded by an exciting array of on water activities, a cosmopolitan mix of bistros, bars, restaurants, shopping, hotels and entertainment options.

Beautiful cruising waters and golden sands to the North and South of the marina approach which is channel dredged to CD and accessible via a lock: vessels wishing to enter should contact the Marina Lock Office on VHF Ch M/80 before arrival.

FACILITIES AT A GLANCE

Key
a   Brittania House - amenity/cafe
b   Neptune House - restaurant & bar
c   Lock office and marina reception
d   220m complex with retail, restaurants and cafes
e   Hartlepool Diving Club and HMS Abdiel sea cadet unit
f   Fisherman's stores & landing area
g   Office units
h   Old West Quay Pub, restaurant and travel inn

SUNDERLAND MARINA

The Marine Activities Centre
Sunderland Marina, Sunderland, SR6 0PW
Tel: 0191 514 4721
Email: info@sunmac.org.uk

VHF	Ch M
ACCESS	H24

Sunderland Marina sits on the the River Wear and is easily accessible through the outer breakwater at all states of tide. A short walk away from the city centre and beautiful beaches, facilities on site include the Snowgoose café and the Marina Vista Italian restaurant. Other pubs, restaurants, hotels and cafes are located nearby on the waterfront.

Sunderland Yacht Club is also located nearby and welcomes visiting yachtsman to its clubhouse.

FACILITIES AT A GLANCE

Key
a.   Marina Reception
b.   RNLI
c.   Snow Goose - Café
d.   Hairdresser
e.   Marina Vista - Restaurant
f.   RNLI Lifeboat station
g.   Hard stand compound
h.   Refuse Compound

ROYAL QUAYS MARINA

Royal Quays Marina
Coble Dene Road, North Shields, NE29 6DU
Tel: 0191 272 8282 Fax: 0191 272 8288
Email: royalquays@boatfolk.co.uk
www.boatfolk.co.uk/royalquays

VHF	Ch 80
ACCESS	H24

Royal Quays Marina enjoys close proximity to the entrance to the River Tyne, allowing easy access to and from the open sea as well as being ideally placed for cruising further up the Tyne. Just over an hour's motoring upstream brings you to the heart of the city of Newcastle, where you can tie up on a security controlled visitors' pontoon right outside the Pitcher and Piano Bar.

With a reputation for a high standard of service, the marina accommodates 300 pontoon berths, all of which are fully serviced. It is accessed via double sector lock gates which operate at all states of the tide and 24 hours a day.

FACILITIES AT A GLANCE

Key
a Marina office
   Toilets/showers
   Laundry
   Payphone
   Lock control
   Brokerage
b Refuse compound
c Chandlery & boat sales
d Access bridge & trolley park
e Boat sales and brokerage
f Bar/restaurant
g Waste oil disposal

ST PETERS MARINA

St Peters Marina, St Peters Basin
Newcastle upon Tyne, NE6 1HX
Tel: 0191 2654472 Fax: 0191 2762618
Email: info@stpetersmarina.co.uk
www.stpetersmarina.co.uk

VHF	Ch 80
ACCESS	HW±3

Nestling on the north bank of the River Tyne, some eight miles upstream of the river entrance, St Peters Marina is a fully serviced, 150-berth marina with the capacity to accommodate large vessels of up to 37m LOA. Situated on site is the Bascule Bar and Bistro, while a few minutes away is the centre of Newcastle. This city, along with its surrounding area, offers an array of interesting sites, among which are Hadrian's Wall, the award winning Gateshead Millennium Bridge and the Baltic Art Centre.

FACILITIES AT A GLANCE

ROYAL NORTHUMBERLAND YACHT CLUB

Royal Northumberland Yacht Club
South Harbour, Blyth, Northumberland, NE24 3PB
Tel: 01670 353636

VHF	Ch 12
ACCESS	H24

The Royal Northumberland Yacht Club is based at Blyth, a well-sheltered port that is accessible at all states of the tide and in all weathers except for when there is a combination of low water and strong south-easterly winds. The yacht club is a private club with some 75 pontoon berths and a further 20 fore and aft moorings.

Visitors usually berth on the north side of the most northerly pontoon and are welcome to use the clubship, HY *Tyne* – a wooden lightship built in 1880 which incorporates a bar, showers and toilet facilities. The club also controls its own boatyard, providing under cover and outside storage space plus a 20 ton boat hoist.

FACILITIES AT A GLANCE

AMBLE MARINA

Amble Marina Ltd
Amble, Northumberland, NE65 0YP
Tel: 01665 712168
Email: marina@amble.co.uk www.amble.co.uk

VHF	Ch 80
ACCESS	HW±4

Amble Marina is a small family run business offering peace, security and a countryside setting at the heart of the small town of Amble. It is located on the banks of the beautiful River Coquet and at the start of the Northumberland coast's area of outstanding natural beauty. Amble Marina has 250 fully serviced berths for residential and visiting yachts. Cafés, bars, restaurants and shops are all within a short walk.

From your berth watch the sun rise at the harbour entrance and set behind Warkworth Castle or walk on wide, empty beaches. There is so much to do or if you prefer simply enjoy the peace, tranquillity and friendliness at Amble Marina.

FACILITIES AT A GLANCE

Key
a Marina office
b Toilets, showers, launderette, telephone and disabled facilities
c Reception pontoon
d Outboard engine sales and service
e Refuse bins and waste oil tank
f Security footgate 200m to town centre shops
g Trailer and cradle storage

SOUTH EAST SCOTLAND – Eyemouth to Rattray Head

Key to Marina Plans symbols

🛢	Bottled gas	P	Parking
	Chandler	✕	Pub/Restaurant
♿	Disabled facilities		Pump out
	Electrical supply		Rigging service
	Electrical repairs		Sail repairs
	Engine repairs		Shipwright
✚	First Aid		Shop/Supermarket
	Fresh Water		Showers
D	Fuel - Diesel		Slipway
P	Fuel - Petrol	WC	Toilets
	Hardstanding/boatyard		Telephone
@	Internet Café		Trolleys
	Laundry facilities	V	Visitors berths
	Lift-out facilities		Wi-Fi

Area 6 - South East Scotland

MARINAS
Telephone Numbers
VHF Channel
Access Times

Aberdeen

Stonehaven

Montrose

Arbroath Harbour
01241 872166
Ch 11, 16   HW±3

Arbroath

Tayport

Port Edgar Marina
0131 3313330
Ch 80   H24

Port Edgar

Granton   Dunbar

Berwick-upon-Tweed

N

PORT EDGAR MARINA

Port Edgar Marina
Shore Road, South Queensferry
West Lothian, EH30 9SQ
Tel: 0131 331 3330 Fax: 0131 331 4878
Email: info@portedgar.co.uk

VHF	Ch 80
ACCESS	H24

Nestled between the iconic Forth Bridges, Edinburgh's 300 berth marina is the ideal base for exploring the Capital and the Forth coastline.

A short walk away is the historic High Street of Queensferry with a great selection of bars and restaurants. Situated 15 minutes away from Edinburgh Airport with easy road access, the secure site provides full boatyard facilities including a 25T slipway hoist, chandlery and café.

FACILITIES AT A GLANCE

Key
a Changing rooms and toilets
b Landing and trolleys
c Port Edgar Yacht Club
d Cafe
e Marina office
f Blue V
g Bosuns Locker

ARBROATH HARBOUR

Arbroath Harbour
Harbour Office, Arbroath, DD11 1PD
Tel: 01241 872166 Fax: 01241 878472
Email: harbourmaster@angus.gov.uk

VHF	Ch 11
ACCESS	HW±3

Arbroath harbour has 59 floating pontoon berths with security entrance which are serviced with electricity and fresh water to accommodate all types of leisure craft. Half height dock gates with walkway are located between the inner and outer harbours, which open and close at half tide, maintaining a minimum of 2.5m of water in the inner harbour.

The town of Arbroath offers a variety of social and sporting amenities to visiting crews and a number of quality pubs, restaurants, the famous twelfth century Abbey and Signal Tower Museum are located close to the harbour. Railway and bus stations are only 1km from the harbour with direct north and south connections.

FACILITIES AT A GLANCE

Key
a Signal Tower Museum
b Tourist Information
c RNLI
d Harbourmaster
e Harbour gates & walkway

"Arbroath Harbour has 59 floating pontoon berths with security entrance which are serviced with electricity and fresh water to accommodate all types of leisure craft. Half height dock gates with a walkway are located between the inner and outer harbours, which open and close at half tide, maintaining a minimum of 2.5m of water in the inner harbour.

Other facilities in the harbour include free parking, toilets and showers, a crew room, fueling facilities, on site laundry facilities and boat builders' yard.

The town of Arbroath also offers a variety of social and sporting amenities to visiting crews and a number of quality pubs, restaurants, the famous twelfth century Abbey and Signal Tower Museum are located close to the harbour. The railway and bus stations are only 1km from the harbour with direct north and south connections."

Arbroath Harbour
Harbour Office Arbroath DD11 1PD

Harbour Master: Bruce Fleming
Tel: 01241 872166
Email: harbourmaster@angus.gov.uk

Reeds PDF ebooks

In response to popular demand, all the Reeds Almanacs are now available as searchable, highlightable PDF ebooks. (All ebooks incorporate the Marina Guide.)

REEDS 2023 NAUTICAL ALMANAC

Visit www.reedsnauticalalmanac.co.uk for further information

Key to Marina Plans symbols

🛢	Bottled gas	P	Parking
	Chandler		Pub/Restaurant
♿	Disabled facilities		Pump out
	Electrical supply		Rigging service
	Electrical repairs		Sail repairs
	Engine repairs		Shipwright
	First Aid		Shop/Supermarket
	Fresh Water		Showers
	Fuel - Diesel		Slipway
	Fuel - Petrol	WC	Toilets
	Hardstanding/boatyard		Telephone
@	Internet Café		Trolleys
	Laundry facilities	V	Visitors berths
	Lift-out facilities		Wi-Fi

Area 7 - North East Scotland

MARINAS
Telephone Numbers
VHF Channel
Access Times

Shetland Islands

Kirkwall Marina
07810 465835
Ch 14 H24

Stromness Marina
07483 366655
Ch 14 H24

Orkney Islands

Scrabster

Wick • Wick Marina
01955 602030
Ch 14 H24

Helmsdale

Ullapool

Whitehills Marina
01261 861291
Ch 14 H4

Banff Harbour Marina
01261 832236
Ch 12 HW±4

Inverness Marina
01463 220501
Ch 12

Buckie Banff Macduff

Inverness

Caley Marina
01463 236539
Ch 74 H24

Findhorn

Peterhead • Peterhead Bay Marina
01779 477868
Ch 14 H24

Lossiemouth 01343 813066
Ch 12 HW±4

Burghead

Seaport Marina
01463 725500
Ch 74 HW±4

Nairn Marina
01667 456008
Ch 10 HW±2

Hopeman

Hopeman

Mallaig

Aberdeen •

N

PETERHEAD BAY MARINA

Peterhead Port Authority
Harbour Office, West Pier, Peterhead, AB42 1DW
Tel: 01779 477868/483600
Email: marina@peterheadport.co.uk
www.peterheadport.co.uk

VHF	Ch 14
ACCESS	H24

Based in the south west corner of Peterhead Bay Harbour, the marina provides one of the finest marine leisure facilities in the east of Scotland. In addition to the services on site, there are plenty of nautical businesses in the vicinity, ranging from ship chandlers and electrical servicing to boat repairs and surveying.

Due to its easterly location, Peterhead affords an ideal stopover for those yachts heading to or from Scandinavia as well as for vessels making for the Caledonian Canal.

FACILITIES AT A GLANCE

BANFF HARBOUR MARINA

Banff Harbour Marina
Harbour Office, Quayside, Banff, Aberdeenshire, AB45 1HQ
Tel: 01261 832236   Mobile: 07920 270360
Email: duncan.mackie@aberdeenshire.gov.uk

VHF	Ch 12
ACCESS	HW±4

A former fishing and cargo port now used as a recreational harbour. Banff offers excellent facilities to both regular and visiting users. The marina now provides 92 berths, of which 76 are serviced pontoon berths and 16 unserviced, traditional moorings, in one of the safest harbours on the NE coast of Scotland.

The outer basin offers adequate berthing for visitors and a tidal area for regulars.

The harbour is tidal with a sandy bottom. Movement during low water neaps is no problem for the shallow drafted boat.

FACILITIES AT A GLANCE

Key
a Harbourmasters Office

NAIRN MARINA

Nairn Marina
Nairn Harbour, Nairnshire, Scotland
Tel: 01667 456008   Fax: 01667 452877
Email: nairn.harbourmaster@virgin.net

VHF	Ch 10
ACCESS	HW±2

Nairn is a small town on the coast of the Moray Firth. Formerly renowned both as a fishing port and as a holiday resort dating back to Victorian times, it boasts miles of award-winning, sandy beaches, famous castles such as Cawdor, Brodie and Castle Stuart, and two championship golf courses. Other recreational activities include horse riding or walking through spectacular countryside.

The marina lies at the mouth of the River Nairn, entry to which should be avoided in strong N to NE winds. The approach is made from the NW at or around high water as the entrance is badly silted and dries out.

FACILITIES AT A GLANCE

Key
a Restaurant
b Yacht Club
c Harbour office

WHITEHILLS MARINA

Whitehills Harbour Commissioners
Whitehills, Banffshire AB45 2NQ
Tel: 01261 861291
www.whitehillsharbour.co.uk
Email: harbourmaster@whitehillsharbour.co.uk

VHF	Ch 14
ACCESS	H24

Built in 1900, Whitehills is a Trust Harbour fully maintained and run by nine commissioners elected from the village. It was a thriving fishing port up until 1999, but due to changes in the fishing industry, was converted into a marina during 2000.

Photo by Colin Heggie

Three miles west of Banff Harbour the marina benefits from good tidal access – although there is just 1.5m at springs – comprising 38 serviced berths, with electricity, as well as eight non-serviced berths.

Whitehills village has a wide range of facilities including a convenience store, a cafe/fish & chip shop, two pubs, a fresh fish shop as well as two good restaurants. It is also a great base for families, with an excellent playpark at Blackpots, just a short walk from the harbour.

FACILITIES AT A GLANCE

Key
a Harbour master
b Fish market
c Galley Restaurant

LOSSIEMOUTH MARINA

Marina Office
Lossiemouth, Moray, IV31 6PB
Tel: 01343 813066
Email: info@lossiemouthmarina.com

VHF	Ch 12
ACCESS	HW±4

Approximately halfway between Inverness and Peterhead, the marina provides over 115 berths. The East Basin and visitor berth area lie just inside the East Basin, providing free water and electricity. Visitor packs can be collected from the marina office (Mon–Fri 9am-4pm), the blue box at the top of the ramp or the the Steamboat Inn. Modern toilet and shower blocks with laundry facilities are located in both basins. Diesel, local shops, restaurants and ATM are all within short walking distance. The marina has excellent undercover workshop facilities, dredging equipment, a 25 tonne sublift, and crane for masting/demasting.

FACILITIES AT A GLANCE

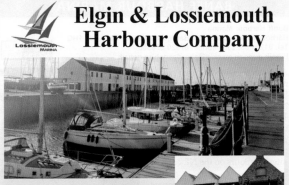

INVERNESS MARINA

Inverness Marina
Longman Drive, Inverness, IV1 1SU
Tel: 01463 220501
Email: info@invernessmarina.com
www.invernessmarina.com

VHF	Ch 12
ACCESS	H24

The marina is situated in the Inverness firth just one mile from the city centre and half a mile from the entrance to the Caledonian Canal. It has a minimum depth of 3m, 24hr access and 150 fully serviced berths. On site are a chandlery and services including rigging, engineering, electronics and boat repair.

Inverness has excellent transport networks to the rest of the UK and Europe and, as the gateway to the Highlands is a great location as a base for a touring golf courses, historic sites and the Whisky Trail. The marina is a perfect base for cruising Orkney, Shetland and Scandinavia.

FACILITIES AT A GLANCE

SEAPORT MARINA

Seaport Marina
Muirtown Wharf, Inverness, IV3 5LE
Tel: 01463 725500
Email: caledonian@scottishcanals.co.uk
www.scottishcanals.co.uk

VHF	Ch 74
ACCESS	HW±4

Seaport Marina is based at Muirtown Basin at the eastern entrance of the Caledonian Canal; a 60 mile coast-to-coast channel slicing through the majestic Great Glen. Only a 15 minute walk

Photo courtesy of D Edes

from the centre of Inverness, the Marina is an ideal base for visiting the Highlands.

There are shops and amenities nearby, as well as chandlers, boat repair services and a slipway. The marina also offers a variety of winter mooring packages and details of transit and short term licences, including the use of the Caledonian Canal can be found on the above website.

FACILITIES AT A GLANCE

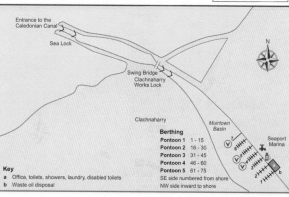

Entrance to the Caledonian Canal

Sea Lock

Swing Bridge
Clachnaharry
Works Lock

Clachnaharry

Muirtown
Basin

Berthing
Pontoon 1 1 - 15
Pontoon 2 16 - 30
Pontoon 3 31 - 45
Pontoon 4 46 - 60
Pontoon 5 61 - 75

Seaport
Marina

Key
a   Office, toilets, showers, laundry, disabled toilets
b   Waste oil disposal

SE side numbered from shore
NW side inward to shore

CALEY MARINA

Caley Marina
Canal Road, Inverness, IV3 8NF
Tel: 01463 236539 Fax: 01463 238323
Email: info@caleymarina.com
www.caleymarina.com

VHF	Ch 74
ACCESS	H24

Caley Marina is a family run business based near Inverness. With the four flight Muirtown locks and the Kessock Bridge providing a dramatic backdrop, the marina runs alongside the Caledonian Canal which, opened in 1822, is regarded as one of the most spectacular waterways in Europe. Built as a short cut between the North Sea and the Atlantic Ocean, thus avoiding the potentially dangerous Pentland Firth on the north coast of Scotland, the canal is around 60 miles long and takes about three days to cruise from east to west. With the prevailing winds behind you, it takes slightly less time to cruise in the other direction.

FACILITIES AT A GLANCE

WICK MARINA

Wick Marina
Harbour Office, Wick, Caithness, KW1 5HA
Tel: 01955 602030
Email: office@wickharbour.co.uk

VHF	Ch 14, 16
ACCESS	H24

This is the most northerly marina on the British mainland and the last stop before the Orkney and Shetland Islands. Situated an easy five minutes walk from the town centre Wick Marina accommodates 80 fully serviced berths with all the support facilities expected in a modern marina.

This part of Scotland with its rugged coastline and rich history is easily accessible by air and a great starting point for cruising in the northern isles, Moray Firth, Caledonian Canal and Scandinavia, a comfortable 280-mile sail.

FACILITIES AT A GLANCE

Harbour Quay

River Pier

North Pier

RNLI Station

The Jetty

Outer Harbour

7

KIRKWALL MARINA

Kirkwall Marina
Harbour Street, Kirkwall, Orkney, KW15
Tel: 07810 465835 Fax: 01856 871313
Email: info@orkneymarinas.co.uk www.orkneymarinas.co.uk

VHF	Ch 14
ACCESS	H24

The Orkney Isles, comprising 70 islands in total, provides some of the finest cruising grounds in Northern Europe. The Main Island, incorporating the ancient port of Kirkwall, is the largest, although 16 others have lively communities and are rich in archaeological sites as well as spectacular scenery and wildlife.

Kirkwall Marina, an all year facility, is located within the harbour and just yards from the visitor attractions of this ancient port. Local shops, hotels and restaurants are all within walking distance.

FACILITIES AT A GLANCE

STROMNESS MARINA

Stromness Marina
Stromness, Orkney, KW16
Tel: 07483 366655 Fax: 01856 871313
Email: info@orkneymarinas.co.uk
www.orkneymarinas.co.uk

VHF	Ch 14
ACCESS	H24

Stromness lies on the south-western tip of the Orkney Isles' Mainland. Sitting beneath the rocky ridge known as Brinkie's Brae, it is considered one of Orkney's major seaports, with sailors first attracted to the fine anchorage provided by the bay of Hamnavoe.

Stromness offers comprehensive and repair services. Also on hand are an internet café, a fitness suite and swimming pool as well as car and bike hire.

FACILITIES AT A GLANCE

Key
a Terminal building, Harbour Master's office
b Cafe

SAIL TO ORKNEY

ORKNEY MARINAS

The Orkney islands are an exciting cruising destination with an abundance of wildlife, history and outstanding coastal scenery.

Westray

Mainland

Stromness   Kirkwall

Hoy

+44 (0)1856 871313 | info@orkneymarinas.co.uk | www.orkneymarinas.co.uk
Orkney Marinas Ltd, Dunkirk, Shore Street, Kirkwall.

NORTH WEST SCOTLAND – Cape Wrath to Crinan Canal

Key to Marina Plans symbols

	Bottled gas	P	Parking
	Chandler		Pub/Restaurant
	Disabled facilities		Pump out
	Electrical supply		Rigging service
	Electrical repairs		Sail repairs
	Engine repairs		Shipwright
	First Aid		Shop/Supermarket
	Fresh Water		Showers
D	Fuel - Diesel		Slipway
P	Fuel - Petrol	WC	Toilets
	Hardstanding/boatyard		Telephone
@	Internet Café		Trolleys
	Laundry facilities	V	Visitors berths
	Lift-out facilities		Wi-Fi

Area 8 - North West Scotland

MARINAS
Telephone Numbers
VHF Channel
Access Times

Stornoway Marina
01851 702688
Ch 12 H24

Ullapool

Portree

Mallaig Marina
07824 331031
Ch 09/16 H24

Mallaig

Corpach

Tobermory
07917 832497
Ch 68 H24

Salen

Dunstaffnage Marina
01631 566555 Ch M H24

Kerrera Marina
01631 565333
Ch 80 H24

Craobh Haven Marina
01852 500222
Ch M, 80 H24

Melfort Pier
01852 200333

Ardfern Yacht Centre
01852 500247
Ch 80 H24

8

STORNOWAY MARINA

Stornoway Port Authority
Amity House, Esplanade Quay,
Stornoway, Isle of Lewis, HS1 2XS
Tel: 01851 702688
Email: info@stornowayport.com

VHF	Ch 12
ACCESS	HW24

Stornoway Marina is sheltered and has easy access at all states of the tide and weather conditions. Vessels up to 24 metres in length and 3 metres draft can be accommodated.

The 80-berth marina provides a safe haven for island hoppers and days sailors. The marina is particularly popular as it is located right in the heart of the bustling town centre. Fresh water, electricity, wi-fi, toilet, shower and laundry facilities are available quayside for all visitors.

FACILITIES AT A GLANCE

MALLAIG MARINA

Mallaig Marina
East Bay, Mallaig, Inverness-shire, PH41 4QS
Tel: 07824 331031 Fax: 01687 462172
Email: info@mallaigharbourauthority.com

VHF	Ch 09, 16
ACCESS	H24

Mallaig Marina is truly the gateway to the Western Isles. The 50-berth marina, part funded by EU Sail West project, provides the ideal location for experiencing and exploring the magnificent sailing opportunities available on the west coast of Scotland. Onshore facilities including a small laundry are available in the Marina Centre.

The marina is a short walk from the village centre, which offers a range of options for the discerning diner, shopper or tourist. Fishing boats still operate from the busy harbour, and there is regular activity with various ferries to and fro Knoydart, the Small Isles and the Western Isles. The village also welcomes the Jacobite Steam Train twice daily in the high season.

FACILITIES AT A GLANCE

TOBERMORY

Tobermory Harbour Association
Taigh Solais, Ledaig, Tobermory, Isle of Mull, PA75 6NR
Mob: 07917 832497 Tel: 01688 302876
www.tobermoryharbour.co.uk
Email: admin@tobermoryharbour.co.uk

VHF	Ch 68
ACCESS	H24

Tobermory is an iconic Scottish west coast destination, a natural historic harbour, and a protected anchorage. Harbour pontoons are located on the west shore of Tobermory Bay with direct access to the town. To supplement the 58 pontoon berths there are also 38 swinging moorings for hire – look for the blue moorings with the white top.

Within easy walking distance, Tobermory offers an array of shops, bars, and restaurants offering local produce. Mull Aquarium is in the Harbour Building and is Europe's first 'Catch and Release' Aquarium. Situated adjacent to the main car park, the pontoon has access to public transport to and from mainland ferry links.

FACILITIES AT A GLANCE

Key a Tobermory Harbour Association office
b Recycling
c Cruise ship tenders and charter boats
d Large vessels
e Shallow draft vessels

DUNSTAFFNAGE MARINA

Dunstaffnage Marina Ltd
Dunbeg, by Oban, Argyll, PA37 1PX
Tel: 01631 566555 Fax: 01631 571044
Email: info@dunstaffnagemarina.com

VHF	Ch M
ACCESS	H24

Located just two to three miles north of Oban, Dunstaffnage Marina has been renovated to include an additional 36 fully serviced berths, a new breakwater providing shelter from NE'ly to E'ly winds and an increased amount of hard standing. Also on site is the Wide Mouthed Frog, offering a convivial bar, restaurant and accommodation with stunning views of the 13th century Dunstaffnage Castle.

The marina is perfectly placed to explore Scotland's west coast and Hebridean Islands. Only 10M NE up Loch Linnhe is Port Appin, while sailing 15M S, down the Firth of Lorne, brings you to Puldohran where you can walk to an ancient hostelry situated next to the C18 Bridge Over the Atlantic.

FACILITIES AT A GLANCE

KERRERA MARINA

Kerrera Marina
Isle of Kerrera, Oban, Argyll, PA34 4SX
Tel: 01631 565333
Email: office@kerreramarina.com www.kerreramarina.com

VHF Ch 80
ACCESS H24

A warm welcome awaits at Kerrera Marina. Access all tides, 70 pontoon berths, 30 moorings along with winter storage & full boat yard services with 50T hoist. Shore base facilities are extensive - gas, diesel, water, showers, laundry, wi-fi and a cosy lounge with TV & library. We offer a pre-booked ferry service into Oban, please see our website.

Kerrera is a magical place to explore, full of amazing wildlife, beautiful beaches & wonderful views. Our bar and restaurant overlooks the sheltered bay of Ardantrive serving delicious local produce. The island also has a tearoom, two farm shops and a castle steeped in history.

FACILITIES AT A GLANCE

Key
a Reception
b Showers/toilets
c Bar & grill
d Shed

MELFORT PIER AND HARBOUR

Melfort Pier and Harbour
Kilmelford, by Oban, Argyll
Tel: 01852 200333
Email: melharbour@aol.com www.mellowmelfort.com

VHF
ACCESS

Melfort Pier & Harbour is situated on the shores of Loch Melfort, one of the most peaceful lochs on the south west coast of Scotland. Overlooked by the Pass of Melfort and the Braes of Lorn, it lies approximately 18 miles north of Lochgilphead and 16 miles south of Oban. Its onsite facilities include showers, laundry, free Wi-Fi access and parking – pets welcome. Fuel, power and water are available at nearby Kilmelford Yacht Haven.

For those who want a few nights on dry land, Melfort Pier & Harbour offers lochside houses, each one equipped with a sauna, spa bath and balcony offering stunning views over the loch - available per night.

FACILITIES AT A GLANCE

CRAOBH MARINA

Craobh Marina
By Lochgilphead, Argyll, Scotland, PA31 8UA
Tel: 01852 500222 Fax: 01852 500252
Out of hours: 07702 517038
Email: info@craobhmarina.co.uk www.craobhmarina.co.uk

VHF Ch 80
ACCESS H24

Craobh Marina is idyllically situated in the heart of Scotland's most sought after cruising grounds. Not only does Craobh offer ready access to a wonderful choice of scenic cruising throughout the western isles, the marina is conveniently close to Glasgow and its international transport hub.

Craobh Marina has been developed from a near perfect natural harbour, offering secure and sheltered berthing for up to 250 vessels to 40m LOA and with a draft of 4m. With an unusually deep and wide entrance Craobh Marina provides shelter and a warm welcome for all types of craft.

FACILITIES AT A GLANCE

Key
a Office, chandlery, facilities
b Boat shed
c Waste, recycle
d Bar, restaurant, shop
e Holiday cottages

ARDFERN YACHT CENTRE

Ardfern Yacht Centre
Ardfern, by Lochgilphead, Argyll, PA31 8QN
Tel: 01852 500247 Fax: 01852 500624
www.ardfernyacht.co.uk Email: office@ardfernyacht.co.uk

VHF Ch 80
ACCESS H24

Developed around an old pier once frequented by steamers, Ardfern Yacht Centre lies at the head of Loch Craignish, one of Scotland's most sheltered and picturesque sea lochs. With several islands and protected anchorages nearby, Ardfern is an ideal place from which to cruise the west coast of Scotland and the Outer Hebrides.

The Yacht Centre comprises pontoon berths and swinging moorings as well as a workshop, boat storage and well-stocked chandlery, while a grocery store and eating places can be found in the village. Among the onshore activities available locally are horse riding, cycling, and walking.

FACILITIES AT A GLANCE

Key
a Workshop
b Showers, toilets and launderette
c Chandlery and office

8

Aberdeenshire Harbours

Aberdeenshire Council operates six pleasure harbours along the east coast of Scotland. From Stonehaven, at the gateway to Royal Deeside, Johnshaven and Gourdon, to the Marina at Banff Harbour, Portsoy and Rosehearty.

These well serviced and picturesque harbours with local facilities, visitor attractions and museums, are ideally placed to explore from Royal Deeside to the Moray Firth, including the Whisky and Castle Trails.

Experience a warm welcome at the many restaurants and hotels in the area providing excellent Scottish cruising.

Macduff is Aberdeenshire's main commercial harbour involved in fishing, general cargo, vessel repair and build.

Gourdon

Johnshaven

Portsoy

Rosehearty

Stonehaven

Macduff

Aberdeenshire
COUNCIL

Harbour Authority ■ Aberdeenshire Council
Infrastructure Services ■ St Leonards ■ Sandyhill Road ■ Banff AB45 1SD
Web: www.aberdeenshireharbours.co.uk
Email: harboursadmin@aberdeenshire.gov.uk

SOUTH WEST SCOTLAND – Crinan Canal to Mull of Galloway

Key to Marina Plans symbols

Symbol	Description	Symbol	Description
	Bottled gas	P	Parking
	Chandler		Pub/Restaurant
	Disabled facilities		Pump out
	Electrical supply		Rigging service
	Electrical repairs		Sail repairs
	Engine repairs		Shipwright
	First Aid		Shop/Supermarket
	Fresh Water		Showers
	Fuel - Diesel		Slipway
	Fuel - Petrol	WC	Toilets
	Hardstanding/boatyard		Telephone
@	Internet Café		Trolleys
	Laundry facilities	V	Visitors berths
	Lift-out facilities		Wi-Fi

Area 9 - South West Scotland

MARINAS
Telephone Numbers
VHF Channel
Access Times

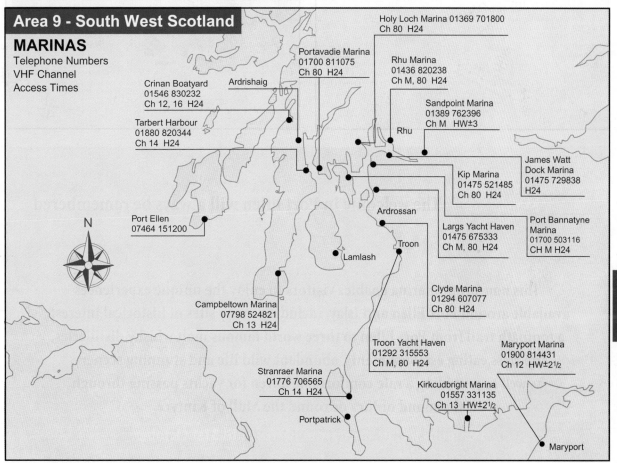

Holy Loch Marina 01369 701800
Ch 80 H24

Portavadie Marina
01700 811075
Ch 80 H24

Rhu Marina
01436 820238
Ch M, 80 H24

Crinan Boatyard
01546 830232
Ch 12, 16 H24

Ardrishaig

Sandpoint Marina
01389 762396
Ch M   HW±3

Tarbert Harbour
01880 820344
Ch 14 H24

Rhu

James Watt
Dock Marina
01475 729838
H24

Kip Marina
01475 521485
Ch 80 H24

Port Ellen
07464 151200

Ardrossan

Port Bannatyne
Marina
01700 503116
CH M H24

Largs Yacht Haven
01475 675333
Ch M, 80 H24

Troon

Lamlash

Clyde Marina
01294 607077
Ch 80 H24

Campbeltown Marina
07798 524821
Ch 13 H24

Troon Yacht Haven
01292 315553
Ch M, 80 H24

Maryport Marina
01900 814431
Ch 12 HW±2½

Stranraer Marina
01776 706565
Ch 14 H24

Kirkcudbright Marina
01557 331135
Ch 13 HW±2½

Portpatrick

Maryport

9

PORT ELLEN MARINA

Port Ellen Marina
Port Ellen, Islay, Argyll, PA42 7DB
Tel: 07464 151200 www.portellenmarina.co.uk
Email: portellenmarina@outlook.com

VHF	
ACCESS	H24

A safe and relaxed mooring superbly located in the quaint village of Port Ellen, making it an ideal stopping off point whether planning to sail north or south. Islay is world-renowned for its many malt whisky distilleries, nine at the last count and one to reopen shortly.

Meeting guests and short term storage is trouble free with the excellent air and ferry services to the mainland and Glasgow. Once on Islay you will be tempted to extend your stay so be warned, check www.portellenmarina.com for the many reasons to visit.

FACILITIES AT A GLANCE

Key
a   Office
b   Hotel

Local boats only

Dredged to 3m 2006
Stay inside green markers

CRINAN BOATYARD

Crinan Boatyard Ltd
Crinan, Lochgilphead, Argyll, PA31 8SW
Tel: 01546 830232 Fax: 01546 830281
Email: info@crinanboatyard.co.uk
www.crinanboatyard.co.uk

VHF	Ch 12, 16
ACCESS	H24

Situated at the westerly entrance of the scenic Crinan Canal, Crinan Boatyard offers swinging moorings nightly or longer term, a fuelling/loading berth, a well stocked Chandlery, heads, showers, laundry and an experienced work force for repair work all on site. A hotel and coffee shop, just a short walk away at the Canal basin, great walking and the historic Kilmartin Glen close by are some of the attractions on shore.

The nearby town of Lochgilphead 7 miles away offers shopping and good travel links to Glasgow (85 miles) and its International Airport.

FACILITIES AT A GLANCE

Eilean da Mhèin

Small craft moorings

R 15–17
G 5–11
R 14–11
Y 7–9
R 18–21
R 1–10
B 6–8
W 6–8
VR 22–24
R 25–27

Crinan Boatyard

WC

Hotel

Lock

Crinan Canal

Port Ellen
MARINA

The welcome in Port Ellen will always be remembered

This non-profit marina enables visitors to enjoy the unique experiences available around Port Ellen and Islay, including many sites of historical interest, a footpath trail from Port Ellen to three world famous malt whisky distilleries, top class eating establishments, abundant wild life and stunning scenery, as well as providing a safe comfortable haven for yachts passing through the sound of Jura or round the Mull of Kintyre.

Pontoons will be open from Easter until 31st October.

20 new visitor berths were added last year.

38 berths have inclusive water and power.

www.portellenmarina.co.uk   T: 07464 151200   E: portellenmarina@outlook.com

Registered charity SC032157

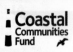
Coastal
Communities
Fund

TARBERT HARBOUR

Tarbert Harbour Authority
Harbour Office, Garval Road, Tarbert, Argyll, PA29 6TR
Tel: 01880 820344
Email: info@tarbertharbour.co.uk

VHF	Ch 14
ACCESS	H24

East Loch Tarbert is situated on the western shores of Loch Fyne. The naturally sheltered harbour is accessible through an easily navigated narrow entrance, and is a prefect stopping point for those heading north to the Crinan Canal.

The pontoons can accommodate up to 100 visiting vessels of various sizes, with fresh water, electricity and wi-fi available FOC. Toilet, shower and laundry facilities are accessible 24/7, and the unique recreation area and community marquee are available to use - perfect for families, gatherings and musters. The marina pontoons are situated at the heart of the heritage village of Tarbert, which boasts a busy festival calendar and offers a wide range of amenities.

FACILITIES AT A GLANCE

PORT BANNATYNE MARINA

Port Bannatyne Marina
Marine Road, Port Bannatyne, PA20 0LT
Tel: 01700 503116 Mobile: 07711 319992
Email: portbannatynemarina@btinternet.com

VHF	Ch M1
ACCESS	H24

Nestled in the bay at Port Bannatyne on the Isle of Bute, the marina is set in breathtakingly beautiful surroundings. The shore facilities include toilets and showers, lifting and winter storage and all boat repairs. Free wi-fi is available throughout the marina. Protected by a breakwater and accessible H24 the marina is dredged to –2.4m CD.

The village of Port Bannatyne offers a Post Office for essential groceries. There are frequent bus services to both Rothesay and Ettrick Bay where a walk along a beautiful beach with amazing views can be completed with either a meal or tea and cake at the beach side restaurant.

FACILITIES AT A GLANCE

PORTAVADIE MARINA

Portavadie Marina
Portavadie, Loch Fyne, Argyll, PA21 2DA
Tel: 01700 811075 Fax: 01700 811074
Email: info@portavadiemarina.com

VHF	Ch 80
ACCESS	H24

Portavadie Marina offers deep and sheltered berthing to residential and visiting boats in an area renowned for its superb cruising waters. Situated on the east side of Loch Fyne in close proximity to several islands and the famous Kyles of Bute, Portavadie is within easy sailing distance of the Crinan Canal, giving access to the Inner and Outer Hebrides. The marina has 230 berths 40 of which are reserved for visitors, plus comprehensive on shore facilities, including a choice of restaurants, bars and self catering accommodation. There is also a shop and small chandlery overlooking the marina, a dedicated fuel berth for petrol and diesel and bike hire.

This unspoiled area of Argyll which is less than two hours by road from Glasgow offers an ideal base for boat owners looking for a safe and secure haven.

FACILITIES AT A GLANCE

Key
a Reception, offices, conference room, open deck viewing platform
b Bar & restaurant
c WC, Showers & laundry
d Luxury self-catering apartments
e Leisure complex

Berthing
A-H pontoons
Odd numbers on the north side
Even numbers on the south side
Numbers start at the inner end

Visitor S pontoon
Mostly alongside with just S46 to S60 at the access bridge remaining

Visitor N pontoon
Runs from N1 at the north end to N19 at the access bridge

9

CAMPBELTOWN MARINA

Campbeltown Marina Ltd
Dubh Artach, Roading, Campbeltown, PA28 6LU
Tel: 07798 524821
Email: campbeltownmarina@btinternet.com

VHF	Ch 13
ACCESS	H24

Campbeltown Marina is a brand new facility opened in June 2015 and is situated in the town centre at the head of the deep, sheltered waters of Campbeltown Loch on the SE aspect of the Kintyre Peninsula. It is within easy reach of the Antrim Coast, Ayrshire and the Upper Clyde. Diesel is available at the Old Quay and gas is across the road. Petrol can be bought a 5-minute walk away and a well stocked chandlery is situated in the town centre.

Campbeltown is the perfect getaway destination with plenty to offer the whole family. Golf, cycling and walking routes, modern swimming pool and horse riding are some of the activities on offer. Situated directly in the town centre there is a wide choice of shops, cafes, bars, restaurants and supermarkets within easy walking distance.

FACILITIES AT A GLANCE

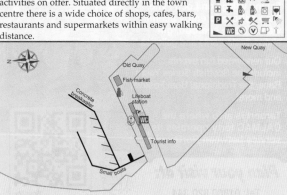

HOLY LOCH MARINA

Holy Loch Marina
Rankin's Brae, Sandbank, Dunoon, PA23 8FE
Tel: 01369 701800
Email: info@holylochmarina.co.uk www.holylochmarina.co.uk

VHF	Ch 80
ACCESS	H24

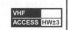

Holy Loch Marina, the marine gateway to Loch Lomond and the Trossachs National Park, lies on the south shore of the loch, roughly half a mile west of Lazaretto Point. Holy Loch is among the Clyde's most beautiful natural harbours and, besides being a peaceful location, offers an abundance of wildlife, places of local historical interest as well as excellent walking and cycling through the Argyll Forest Park. The marina can be entered in all weather conditions and is within easy sailing distance of Loch Long and Upper Firth.

FACILITIES AT A GLANCE

Key
a Office/Harbourmaster
b Boat storage
c Holy Loch Sailing Club
d Pier

Sandbank Village

RHU MARINA

Rhu Marina
Boatfolk Marinas Ltd, Pier Road, Rhu, G84 8LH
Tel: 01436 820238
Email: rhu@boatfolk.co.uk
www.boatfolk.co.uk/rhumarina

VHF	Ch M, 80
ACCESS	H24

Located on the north shore of the Clyde Estuary, Rhu Marina is accessible at all states of the tide and can accommodate yachts up to 24m in length. It also operates 40 swinging moorings in the bay adjacent to the marina, with a ferry service provided.

Within easy walking distance of the marina is Rhu village, a conservation village incorporating a few shops, a pub and the beautiful Glenarn Gardens as well as the Royal Northern & Clyde Yacht Club. A mile or two to the east lies the holiday town of Helensburgh, renowned for its attractive architecture and elegant parks and gardens, while Glasgow city is just 25 miles away and can be easily reached by train.

FACILITIES AT A GLANCE

SANDPOINT MARINA

Sandpoint Marina Ltd
Sandpoint, Woodyard Road, Dumbarton, G82 4BG
Tel: 01389 762396 Fax: 01389 732605
Email: sales@sandpoint-marina.co.uk
www.sandpoint-marina.co.uk

VHF	
ACCESS	HW±3

Lying on the north bank of the Clyde estuary on the opposite side of the River Leven from Dumbarton Castle, Sandpoint Marina provides easy access to some of the most stunning cruising grounds in the United Kingdom. It is an independently run marina, offering a professional yet personal service to every boat owner. Among the facilities to hand are an on site chandlery, storage areas, a 40 ton travel hoist and 20 individual workshop units.

Within a 20-minute drive of Glasgow city centre, the marina is situated close to the shores of Loch Lomond, the largest fresh water loch in Britain.

FACILITIES AT A GLANCE

Key
a Marina office
b Workshops
c Undercover storage shed

KIP MARINA

Kip Marina, The Yacht Harbour
Inverkip, Renfrewshire, Scotland, PA16 0AS
Tel: 01475 521485
www.kipmarina.co.uk Email: info@kipmarina.co.uk

VHF	Ch 80
ACCESS	H24

Inverkip is a small village which lies on the south shores of the River Kip as it enters the Firth of Clyde. Once established for fishing, smuggling and, in the 17th century, witch-hunts, it became a seaside resort in the 1860s as a result of the installation of the railway. Today it is a yachting centre, boasting a state-of-the-art marina with over 600 berths and full boatyard facilities. With the capacity to accommodate yachts of up to 23m LOA, Kip Marina offers direct road and rail access to Glasgow and its international airport, therefore making it an ideal location for either a winter lay up or crew changeover.

FACILITIES AT A GLANCE

Key
a   Boat sales, chandlery and reception
b   Workshop and contractors
c   Chartroom bar and restaurant

JAMES WATT DOCK MARINA

James Watt Dock Marina
East Hamilton Street
Greenock, Renfrewshire, PA15 2TD
Tel: 01475 729838
www.jwdmarina.co.uk Email: info@jwdmarina.co.uk

VHF	80
ACCESS	H24

James Watt Dock Marina offers around 170 berths alongside or on finger pontoons for craft ranging in size from 7m to 100+m within a historic dock setting. With excellent motorway and public transport connections and easy access to some of the best sailing waters at all states of tide, James Watt Dock Marina provides unbeatable opportunities for boaters

The marina is a short distance from Greenock's cinema, pool, ice rink, restaurants and shops, and with nearby transport connections, the marina will be a great location for both visitors and regular berthers.

FACILITIES AT A GLANCE

Key
a   Marina office

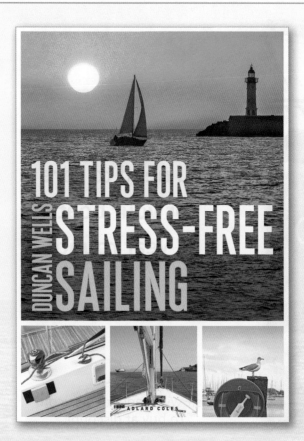

A step-by-step handbook with tried and tested solutions for handling the most common sailing situations

Visit www.adlardcoles.com
to buy at discount

LARGS YACHT HAVEN

Largs Yacht Haven Ltd
Irvine Road, Largs, Ayrshire, KA30 8EZ
Tel: 01475 675333
Email: largs@yachthavens.com www.yachthavens.com

VHF Ch M, 80
ACCESS H24

Largs Yacht Haven offers a superb location among lochs and islands, with numerous fishing villages and harbours nearby. Sheltered cruising can be enjoyed in the inner Clyde, while the west coast and Ireland are only a day's sail away. With a stunning backdrop of the Scottish mountains, Largs incorporates 700 fully serviced berths and provides a range of on site facilities including chandlers, sailmakers, engineers, shops, restaurants and club.

A 20-minute coastal walk brings you to the town of Largs, which has all the usual amenities as well as excellent road and rail connections to Glasgow.

FACILITIES AT A GLANCE

Key
a Reception
b Restaurant
c Largs Sailing Club
d Shops, offices, service companies
e Sail loft
f Boat repair shed
g Boat sales

CLYDE MARINA

Clyde Marina Ltd
The Harbour, Ardrossan, Ayrshire, KA22 8DB
Tel: 01294 607077 Fax: 01294 607076
www.clydemarina.com Email: info@clydemarina.com

VHF Ch 80
ACCESS H24

CLYDE MARINA

Situated on the Clyde Coast between Irvine and Largs, Clyde Marina is Scotland's third largest marina and boatyard. It is set in a landscaped environment boasting a 50T hoist and active boat sales. A deep draft marina berthing vessels up to 30m LOA, draft up to 5m. Peviously accommodated vessels include tall ships and Whitbread 60s plus a variety of sail and power craft. Fully serviced pontoons plus all the yard facilities you would expect from a leading marina including boatyard and boatshed for repairs or storage. Good road and rail connections and only 30 minutes from Glasgow and Prestwick airports.

FACILITIES AT A GLANCE

key
a Winter storage shed
b Secure winter hard standing area

Numbering starts from shoreside
For pontoons B-E from shoreside:
Even nos - starboard side of pontoon
Odd nos - port side of pontoon

TROON YACHT HAVEN

Troon Yacht Haven Ltd
The Harbour, Troon, Ayrshire, KA10 6DJ
Tel: 01292 315553
Email: troon@yachthavens.com
www.yachthavens.com

VHF Ch 80
ACCESS H24

Troon Yacht Haven, situated on the Southern Clyde Estuary, benefits from deep water at all states of the tide. Tucked away in the harbour of Troon, it is well sheltered and within easy access of the town centre.

There are plenty of cruising opportunities to be had from here, whether it be hopping across to the Isle of Arran, with its peaceful anchorages and mountain walks, sailing round the Mull or through the Crinan Canal to the Western Isles, or heading for the sheltered waters of the Clyde.

FACILITIES AT A GLANCE

Key
a Main building
   Toilets
   Showers
   Baths
   Laundry
b Marina office

STRANRAER MARINA

Stranraer Marina
West Pier, Market Street, Stranraer, DG9 7RE
Tel: 01776 706565 Mob: 07734 073421
Email: lesley.smith@dumgal.gov.uk

VHF Ch 14
ACCESS H24

Stranraer Marina is at the southern end of beautiful Loch Ryan with 24H access and modern facilities with a 30T boat crane, transporter and hardstanding available. The visitor berths are those immediately adjacent to the breakwater. Craft over 12m are advised to call ahead for availability.

Stranraer town centre is only a short walk from the marina. Berthing rates are available at www.dumgal.gov.uk/harbours. It should be noted that the marina is exposed in strong N winds. Two ferry terminals are located on the E side of the loch approximately 6M N of the marina and extra care should be taken in this area.

FACILITIES AT A GLANCE

KIRKCUDBRIGHT MARINA

Kirkcudbright Marina
HM Office, Harbour Square, Kirkcudbright, DG6 4HY
Tel: 01557 331135 Mob: 07709 479663
Email: robbie.garside@dumgal.gov.uk

VHF Ch 16, 73
ACCESS HW±2.5

A very well sheltered picturesque marina accessed HW+/-2.5 hrs via a 3.5 mile long, narrow channel that is well marked and lit, contact should be made with Range Safety vessel 'Gallovidian' prior to approach. Limited visitors berths so vessels should contact the harbour master in advance.

The marina is only 250m from the centre of Kirkcudbright, an historic 'artist's' town where visitors may enjoy a wide range of facilities and tourist attractions including castle, museum, tollbooth, art galleries and traditional shops. There is a superb programme of summer festivities.

FACILITIES AT A GLANCE

Kirkcudbright Bridge

Main Quay wall

Drying grid

MARYPORT MARINA

Maryport Harbour and Marina Ltd
Marine Road, Maryport, Cumbria, CA15 8AY
Tel: 01900 814431
www.maryportmarina.com
Email: enquiries@maryportmarina.com

VHF Ch 12,16
ACCESS HW±2.5

Maryport Marina is located in the historic Senhouse Dock, which was originally built for sailing clippers in the late 19th century. The old stone harbour walls provide good shelter to the 190 berths from the prevailing south westerlies.

Maryport town centre and its shops, pubs and other amenities is within easy walking distance from the marina. Maryport a perfect location from which to explore the west coast of Scotland as well as the Isle of Man and the Galloway Coast. For those who wish to venture inland, then the Lake District is only seven miles away.

FACILITIES AT A GLANCE

Key
a Marina Office
b Boat repair facility
c Coastguard building
d Fish handling building
e Cafe
f Aquarium, cafe
g Play area
h Amenity block

House (conspic)

Senhouse Dock

Elizabeth Dock

NW ENGLAND, ISLE OF MAN & N WALES – Mull of Galloway to Bardsey Is

Key to Marina Plans symbols

Bottled gas		P	Parking
Chandler			Pub/Restaurant
Disabled facilities			Pump out
Electrical supply			Rigging service
Electrical repairs			Sail repairs
Engine repairs			Shipwright
First Aid			Shop/Supermarket
Fresh Water			Showers
Fuel - Diesel			Slipway
Fuel - Petrol		WC	Toilets
Hardstanding/boatyard			Telephone
Internet Café			Trolleys
Laundry facilities		V	Visitors berths
Lift-out facilities			Wi-Fi

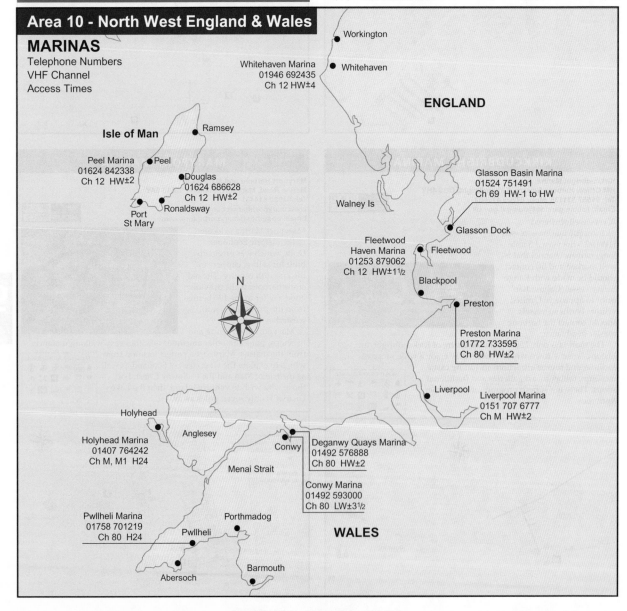

Area 10 - North West England & Wales

MARINAS
Telephone Numbers
VHF Channel
Access Times

Workington

Whitehaven Marina
01946 692435
Ch 12 HW±4

Whitehaven

ENGLAND

Isle of Man

Ramsey

Peel Marina
01624 842338
Ch 12 HW±2

Peel

Douglas
01624 686628
Ch 12 HW±2

Glasson Basin Marina
01524 751491
Ch 69 HW-1 to HW

Walney Is

Port
St Mary

Ronaldsway

Glasson Dock

Fleetwood
Haven Marina
01253 879062
Ch 12 HW±1½

Fleetwood

Blackpool

N

Preston

Preston Marina
01772 733595
Ch 80 HW±2

Liverpool

Liverpool Marina
0151 707 6777
Ch M HW±2

Holyhead

Holyhead Marina
01407 764242
Ch M, M1 H24

Anglesey

Conwy

Deganwy Quays Marina
01492 576888
Ch 80 HW±2

Menai Strait

Conwy Marina
01492 593000
Ch 80 LW±3½

Pwllheli Marina
01758 701219
Ch 80 H24

Porthmadog

Pwllheli

WALES

Abersoch

Barmouth

WHITEHAVEN MARINA

Whitehaven Marina Ltd
Harbour Office, Bulwark Quay, Whitehaven, Cumbria, CA28 7HS
Tel: 01946 692435
Email: enquiries@whitehavenmarina.co.uk
www.whitehavenmarina.co.uk

VHF	Ch 12
ACCESS	HW±4

Whitehaven Marina can be found at the south-western entrance to the Solway Firth, providing a strategic departure point for those yachts heading for the Isle of Man, Ireland or Southern Scotland. The harbour is one of the more accessible ports of refuge in NW England, affording a safe entry in most weathers. The approach channel across the outer harbour is dredged to about 1.0m above chart datum, allowing entry into the inner harbour via a sea lock at around HW±4. Over 100 new walk ashore berths were installed in 2013.

Conveniently situated for visiting the Lake District, Whitehaven is an attractive Georgian town, renowned in the C18 for its rum and slave imports.

FACILITIES AT A GLANCE

GLASSON WATERSIDE & MARINA

Glasson Waterside & Marina
School Lane, Glasson Dock, Lancaster, LA2 0AW
Tel: 01524 751491 Fax: 01524 752626
Email: glasson@aquavista.com
www.aquavista.com

VHF	Ch 69
ACCESS	HW-1 to HW

Glasson Basin Marina lies on the River Lune, west of Sunderland Point. Access is via the outer dock which opens 45 minutes before HW. Liverpool and thence via BWB lock into the inner basin. It is recommended to leave Lune No. 1 Buoy approx 1.5 hrs before HW. Contact the dock on Channel 69. The Marina can only be contacted by telephone. All the necessary requirements can be found either on site or within easy reach of Glasson Dock, including boat, rigging and sail repair services as well as a launderette, ablution facilities, shops and restaurants.

FACILITIES AT A GLANCE

Key
a   Marina office
b   Glasson Sailing Club
c   Harbour House

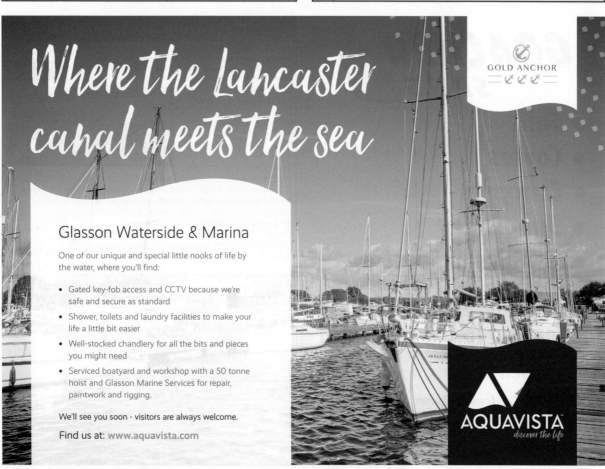

DOUGLAS MARINA

Douglas Marina
Sea Terminal Building, Douglas, IM1 2RF
Tel: 01624 686628
www.gov.im/harbours/
Email: harbours@gov.im

VHF	Ch 12, 16
ACCESS	HW±2

Douglas Marina is accessible HW±2 with 2.5m retained at LW. The depth of water inside the marina can vary so please advise draft. The maximum length accommodated on pontoons is 15m. Wall berths are also available. Douglas Marina Operations Centre requires clearance for entrance to the outer harbour due to commercial traffic. Please inform arrival on VHF Ch 12 10 minutes before port entry.

The marina has many facilities including electricity, fresh water, diesel, lift out, drying pad, gas, chandlery and showers/toilet facilities.

Douglas Marina is in the heart of the Isle of Man's capital so all local amenities and transport links such as the Steam Railway just a short walk.

FACILITIES AT A GLANCE

PEEL MARINA

Peel Marina
The Harbour Office, East Quay, Peel, IM5 1AR
Tel: 01624 842338 Fax: 01624 843610
www.gov.im/harbours/
Email: harbours@gov.im

VHF	Ch 12
ACCESS	HW±2

The Inner harbour has provision on pontoons for visiting vessels up 15m with rafting also available on the harbour walls. Access is available HW±2hrs with a maximum draft of 2.5m retained at low water but this does vary so please advise vessel dimensions on approach via VHF Ch 12.

Fresh water and electricity are available on all pontoon and some wall berths. Diesel fuel is available at the quayside with petrol sourced from a local forecourt in Peel.

Peel is a lovely active fishing port with many local amenities and a beautiful castle overlooking the harbour.

FACILITIES AT A GLANCE

FLEETWOOD HAVEN MARINA

Fleetwood Haven Marina
c/o ABP, Port & Marina Office, Fleetwood, FY7 8BP
Tel: 01253 879062 Fax: 01253 879063
Email: fleetwoodhaven@abports.co.uk

VHF	Ch 12
ACCESS	HW±1.5

Fleetwood Haven Marina provides a good location from which to cruise Morecambe Bay and the Irish Sea. To the north west is the Isle of Man, the north is the Solway Firth and the Clyde Estuary, while to the south west is Conwy, the Menai Straits and Holyhead.

Tucked away in a protected dock which dates to 1835, the marina has 182 full service berths and offers extensive facilities including a 75-tonne boat hoist, laundry and a first class shower/bathroom block.

Call Fleetwood Dock Radio on VHF Channel 12 (Tel 01253 872351) for permission to enter the dock channel.

FACILITIES AT A GLANCE

PRESTON MARINA

Preston Marine Services Ltd
The Boathouse, Navigation Way, Preston, PR2 2YP
Tel: 01772 733595
Email: info@prestonmarina.co.uk www.prestonmarina.co.uk

VHF Ch 80
ACCESS HW±2

Preston Marina forms part of the comprehensive Riversway Docklands development, meeting all the demands of modern day boat owners. With the docks' history dating back over 100 years, today the marina comprises 40 acres of fully serviced pontoon berths sheltered behind the lock gates.

Lying 15 miles up the River Ribble, which itself is an interesting cruising ground with an abundance of wildlife, Preston is well placed for sailing to parts of Scotland, Ireland or Wales. The Docklands development includes a wide choice of restaurants, shops and cinemas as well as being in easy reach of all the cultural and leisure facilities provided by a large town.

FACILITIES AT A GLANCE

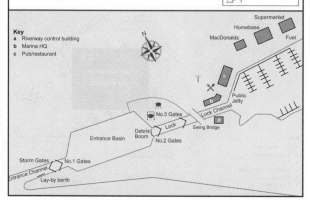

Key
a Riverway control building
b Marina HQ
c Pub/restaurant

LIVERPOOL MARINA

Liverpool Marina
Coburg Wharf, Sefton Street, Liverpool, L3 4BP
Tel: 0151 707 6777 Fax: 0151 707 6770
Email: mail@liverpoolmarina.co.uk

VHF Ch M
ACCESS HW±2

Liverpool Marina is ideally situated for yachtsmen wishing to cruise the Irish Sea. Access is through a computerised lock that opens two and a half hours either side of high water between 0600 and 2200 daily. Once in the marina, you can enjoy the benefits of the facilities on offer, including a first class club bar and restaurant.

Liverpool is a thriving cosmopolitan city, with attractions ranging from numerous bars and restaurants to museums, art galleries and the Beatles Story.

FACILITIES AT A GLANCE

Key
a Clubhouse bar, toilets and showers
b Fuel berth
c Hardstanding yard

CONWY MARINA

Conwy Marina
Conwy, LL32 8EP
Tel: 01492 593000
Email: conwy@boatfolk.co.uk
www.boatfolk.co.uk/conwymarina

VHF Ch 80
ACCESS LW±3.5

Situated in an area of outstanding natural beauty, with the Mountains of Snowdonia National Park providing a stunning backdrop, Conwy is the first purpose-built marina to be developed on the north coast of Wales. Enjoying a unique site next to the 13th century Conwy Castle, the third of Edward I's great castles, it provides a convenient base from which to explore the cruising grounds of the North Wales coast. The unspoilt coves of Anglesey and the beautiful Menai Straits prove a popular destination, while further afield are the Llyn Peninsula and the Islands of Bardsey and Tudwells. The marina incorporates about 500 fully serviced berths which are accessible through a barrier gate at half tide.

FACILITIES AT A GLANCE

Key
a Main services
   Marina office
b Network Yacht Brokers
   Seawake
   Yachtshop
   The Mulberry Stores
   Rowlands Marine Electronics
c Toilets/showers
   Laundry store

DEGANWY MARINA

Deganwy Marina
Deganwy, Conwy, LL31 9DJ
Tel: 01492 576888 Fax: 01492 580066
Email: enquiries@deganwymarina.co.uk
www.deganwymarina.co.uk

VHF Ch 80
ACCESS HW±3

Deganwy Marina is located in the centre of the north Wales coastline on the estuary of the Conwy River and sits between the river and the small town of Deganwy with the beautiful backdrop of the Vardre hills. The views from the marina across the Conwy River are truly outstanding with the medieval walled town and Castle of Conwy outlined against the foothills of the Snowdonia National Park.

Deganwy Marina has 165 fully serviced berths, which are accessed via a tidal gate between half tide and high water.

FACILITIES AT A GLANCE

HOLYHEAD MARINA

Holyhead Marina Ltd
Newry Beach, Holyhead, Gwynedd, LL65 1YA
Tel: 01407 764242 Fax: 01407 769152
Email: info@holyheadmarina.co.uk

VHF Ch M
ACCESS H24

One of the few natural deep water harbours on the Welsh coast, Anglesey is conveniently placed as a first port of call if heading to North Wales from the North, South or West. Its marina at Holyhead, accessible at all states of the tide, is sheltered by Holyhead Mountain as well as an enormous harbour breakwater and extensive floating breakwaters, therefore offering good protection from all directions.

Anglesey boasts numerous picturesque anchorages and beaches in addition to striking views over Snowdonia, while only a tide or two away are the Isle of Man and Eire.

FACILITIES AT A GLANCE

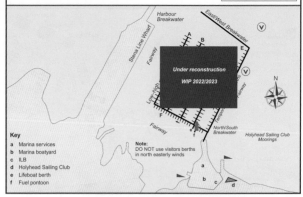

Key
a   Marina services
b   Marina boatyard
c   ILB
d   Holyhead Sailing Club
e   Lifeboat berth
f   Fuel pontoon

Note:
DO NOT use visitors berths in north easterly winds

PWLLHELI MARINA

Pwllheli Marina
Glan Don, Pwllheli, North Wales, LL53 5YT
Tel: 01758 701219
Email: hafanpwllheli@gwynedd.llwy.cymru

VHF Ch 80
ACCESS

Pwllheli is an old Welsh market town providing the gateway to the Llyn Peninsula, which stretches out as far as Bardsey Island to form an 'Area of Outstanding Natural Beauty'. Enjoying the spectacular backdrop of the Snowdonia Mountains, Pwllheli's numerous attractions include an open-air market every Wednesday, 'Neuadd Dwyfor', offering a mix of live theatre and latest films, and beautiful beaches.

Pwllheli Marina is situated on the south side of the Llyn Peninsula. One of Wales' finest marinas and sailing centres, it has over 400 pontoon berths and excellent onshore facilities.

FACILITIES AT A GLANCE

Key
a   Marina offices   b   Domestic refuse point
    Toilets   c   Short stay boat park
    Showers   d   Pwllheli sailing club
    Baby change   e   Chandlery
    Launderette   f   Events pontoons

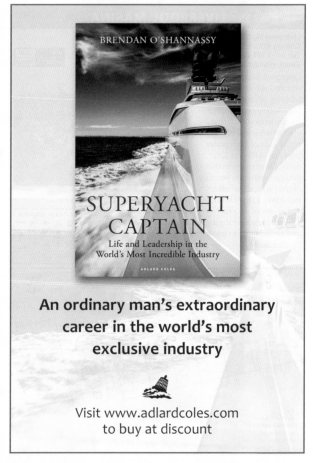

SOUTH WALES & BRISTOL CHANNEL – Bardsey Island to Land's End

Reeds PDF ebooks

In response to popular demand, all the Reeds Almanacs are now available as searchable, highlightable PDF ebooks. (All ebooks incorporate the Marina Guide.)

Visit www.reedsnauticalalmanac.co.uk for further information

Key to Marina Plans symbols

Bottled gas		P	Parking
Chandler			Pub/Restaurant
Disabled facilities			Pump out
Electrical supply			Rigging service
Electrical repairs			Sail repairs
Engine repairs			Shipwright
First Aid			Shop/Supermarket
Fresh Water			Showers
Fuel - Diesel			Slipway
Fuel - Petrol		WC	Toilets
Hardstanding/boatyard			Telephone
@ Internet Café			Trolleys
Laundry facilities		V	Visitors berths
Lift-out facilities			Wi-Fi

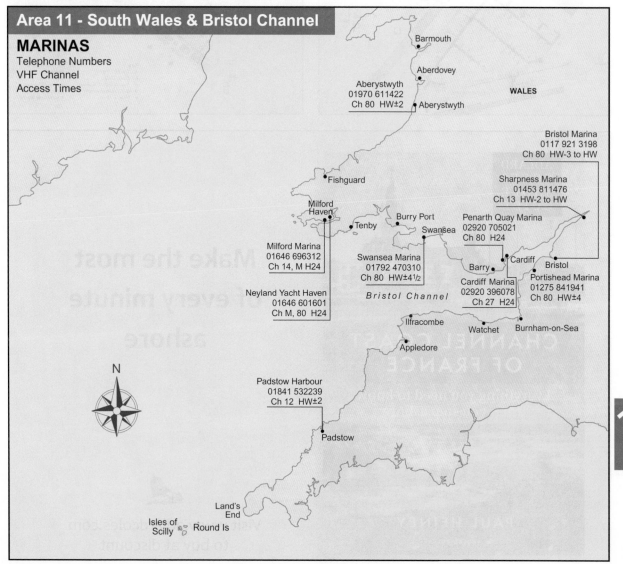

Area 11 - South Wales & Bristol Channel

MARINAS
Telephone Numbers
VHF Channel
Access Times

Barmouth

Aberdovey

Aberystwyth
01970 611422
Ch 80 HW±2
Aberystwyth

WALES

Bristol Marina
0117 921 3198
Ch 80 HW-3 to HW

Sharpness Marina
01453 811476
Ch 13 HW-2 to HW

Fishguard

Milford Haven

Burry Port

Penarth Quay Marina
02920 705021
Ch 80 H24

Tenby

Swansea

Milford Marina
01646 696312
Ch 14, M H24

Cardiff

Bristol

Barry

Swansea Marina
01792 470310
Ch 80 HW±4½

Cardiff Marina
02920 396078
Ch 27 H24

Portishead Marina
01275 841941
Ch 80 HW±4

Neyland Yacht Haven
01646 601601
Ch M, 80 H24

Bristol Channel

Ilfracombe

Watchet

Burnham-on-Sea

Appledore

Padstow Harbour
01841 532239
Ch 12 HW±2

N

Padstow

Land's End

Isles of Scilly

Round Is

11

ABERYSTWYTH MARINA

Aberystwyth Marina
Trefechan, Aberystwyth, Ceredigion, SY23 1AS
Tel: 01970 611422 Fax: 01970 624122
Email: aber@themarinegroup.co.uk

VHF Ch 80
ACCESS HW±2

Aberystwyth Marina offers 165 first class berths providing safe, secure and sheltered moorings for motor boats and yachts.

The onsite chandlery has a selection of clothing, safety equipment, ropes, maintenance, navigation and electrical equipment. The brokerage has a range of motor boats and yachts for sale. In addition, the marina offers a range of boatyard and engine servicing. Other facilities include a slipway and 10t hoist.

Aberystwyth has a range of cafes, seaside fish and chip shops, restaurants, pubs and bars, many a short walk from the marina. The seafront, Promenade and pier is a great location for a walk and to look out over the Irish Sea.

FACILITIES AT A GLANCE

Key
a Offices
b Offices
c Marina office
d Apartments
e Aberystwyth BC

MILFORD MARINA

Milford Marina
Milford Docks, Milford Haven, Pembrokeshire, SA73 3AF
Tel: 01646 696312 Fax: 01646 696314
Email: enquiries@milfordmarina.com www.milfordmarina.com

VHF Ch 14
ACCESS H24

Set within one of the deepest natural harbours in the world, Milford Marina is situated in a non-tidal basin within the UK's only coastal National Park, the ideal base for discovering the fabulous coastline in Pembrokeshire, Wales and Ireland. Continued investment has meant that the marina provides safe, secure and sheltered boat berths with a full range of shoreside facilities in the heart of SW Wales.

Accessed via an entrance lock (with waiting pontoons both inside and outside the lock), the marina is perfect for exploring the picturesque upper reaches of the River Cleddau or cruising out beyond St Ann's Head to the unspoilt islands of Skomer, Skokholm and Grassholm.

FACILITIES AT A GLANCE

Key
a The Fish Plaice
b Galley Café
c Quadra Marine Services
d COCO's Restaurant
e Phoenix Bowl
f All Pets Vet Care
g Museum
h Marina Control
Martha's Vineyard
Dyfed Electronics
i Windjammer Marine

NEYLAND YACHT HAVEN

Neyland Yacht Haven Ltd
Brunel Quay, Neyland, Pembrokeshire, SA73 1PY
Tel: 01646 601601
Email: neyland@yachthavens.com www.yachthavens.com

| VHF | Ch M, 80 |
| ACCESS | H24 |

Approximately 10 miles from the entrance to Milford Haven lies Neyland Yacht Haven. Tucked away in a well protected inlet just before the Cleddau Bridge, this marina has 420 berths and can accommodate yachts up to 25m LOA with draughts of up to 2.5m. The marina is divided into two basins, with the lower one enjoying full tidal access, while entry to the upper one is restricted by a tidal sill. Visitor and annual berthing enquiries welcome.

Offering a comprehensive range of services, Neyland Yacht Haven is within a five minute walk of the town centre where the various shops and takeaways cater for most everyday needs; bicycle hire is also available. The Yacht Haven is a member of the TransEurope Group.

FACILITIES AT A GLANCE

Key

a	Marine services building		Disabled persons toilets		yacht repair yard, yard, chandlery
	Harbour Master's office	b	Storage compound - refuse disposal	g	Tidal sill with depth gauge
	Laundry	c	Upper Basin - showers and toilets	h	Yacht club and slipway
	Bottled gas and café	d	Refuse, recycling, battery disposal	i	Waste oil and used
	Restaurant and bar	e	Holding berth		battery collection point
	Showers and toilets	f	Dale Sailing Co Ltd	j	Glamping pods
	Weather information collection point				**NB Berth numbering flows from low outer**

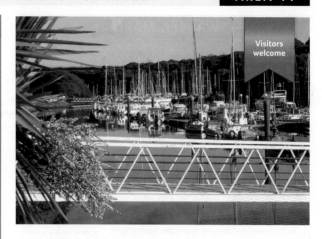

Visitors welcome

Neyland Yacht Haven
Full tidal access

- Pembrokeshire's Picturesque Marina
- Full tidal access within a well-protected creek
- TransEurope Member – visitor discounts
- Popular Café & Bar Restaurant on-site
- Chandlery, on-water diesel & petrol by Dale Sailing
- FREE Wi-Fi for berth holders & visitors
- Haven Pods, floating waterfront cabins to hire
- Family-friendly Bike Hire

Call **01646 601601** or **VHF Ch 37 & 80**
or visit **yachthavens.com**

Neyland Yacht Haven

11

SWANSEA MARINA

Swansea Marina
Lockside, Maritime Quarter, Swansea, SA1 1WG
Tel: 01792 470310 Fax: 01792 463948
www.swansea.gov.uk/swanseamarina
Email: swanmar@swansea.gov.uk

VHF	Ch 80
ACCESS	HW±4.5

At the hub of the city's redeveloped and award winning Maritime Quarter, Swansea Marina can be accessed HW±4½ hrs via a lock. Surrounded by a plethora of shops, restaurants and marine businesses to cater for most yachtsmen's needs, the marina is in close proximity to the picturesque Gower coast, where there is no shortage of quiet sandy beaches off which to anchor. It also provides the perfect starting point for cruising to Ilfracombe, Lundy Island, the North Cornish coast or West Wales.

Within easy walking distance of the marina is the city centre, boasting a covered shopping centre and market. For those who prefer walking or cycling, take the long promenade to the Mumbles fishing village from where there are plenty of coastal walks.

FACILITIES AT A GLANCE

Key
a Leisure Centre
b Maritime Museum
c Pumphouse Restaurant
d Yacht Club
e Repair shed
f Mariott Hotel

PENARTH MARINA

Penarth Marina
Penarth, Vale of Glamorgan, CF64 1TQ
Tel: 02920 705021
Email: penarth@boatfolk.co.uk
www.boatfolk.co.uk/penarthmarina

VHF	Ch 80
ACCESS	H24

Penarth Marina has been established in the historic basins of Penarth Docks for over 20 years and is the premier boating facility in the region. The marina is Cardiff Bay's only 5 Gold Anchor marina and provides an ideal base for those using the Bay and the Bristol Channel.

With 24hr access there is always water available for boating. Penarth and Cardiff boast an extensive range of leisure facilities, shops and restaurants making this marina an ideal base or destination. The marina has a blue flag and is a member of the TransEurope Group.

FACILITIES AT A GLANCE

CARDIFF BAY

Key
a Marina office
b Inner basin services building
c Boat shed
d Refuse compound/recycling
e Boat sales/Café
f Restaurant

CARDIFF MARINA

Cardiff Marina
Watkiss Way, Cardiff, CF11 0SY
Tel: 02920 396078   Fax: 02920 345116
Email: info@themarinegroup.co.uk
www.themarinegroup.co.uk

VHF	Ch M
ACCESS	H24

A sheltered haven on the River Ely, Cardiff Marina offers 350 fully serviced berths within Cardiff Bay. Adjacent to Cardiff Marina, the waterside setting of Bayscape, a new mixed-use development of 115 apartments, is also home to the brand-new marina management suite, laundry and washrooms. The south facing terrace of the lounge bar, is a great location for berth holders to relax and unwind. Marina facilities also include a 50t Sealift, platform crane for mast work and brokerage. In addition, Cardiff Marine Village is home to Cardiff Marine Services, Wales' leading boatyard and refit and repair centre. The 3-acre site also has ample space for hard standing storage.

FACILITIES AT A GLANCE

Key
a Marina Office
b Showers, toilets
c Workshop

BRISTOL MARINA

Bristol Marina Ltd
Hanover Place, Bristol, BS1 6UH
Tel: 0117 921 3198
Email: info@bristolmarina.co.uk

VHF	Ch 80
ACCESS	HW-3 to HW

Situated in the heart of the city, Bristol is a fully serviced marina providing over 100 pontoon berths for vessels up to 20m LOA. Among the facilities are a new fuelling berth and pump out station as well as an on site chandler and sailmaker. It is situated on the south side of the Floating Harbour, about eight miles from the mouth of the River Avon. Accessible from seaward via the Cumberland Basin, passing through both Entrance Lock and Junction Lock, it can be reached approximately three hours before HW.

Shops, restaurants, theatres and cinemas are all within easy reach of the marina, while local attractions include the SS *Great Britain*, designed by Isambard Kingdom Brunel, and the famous Clifton Suspension Bridge, which has an excellent visitors' centre depicting its fascinating story.

FACILITIES AT A GLANCE

Key
a Albion Boatyard
b Marina office

PORTISHEAD MARINA

Portishead Marina
Newfoundland Way, Portishead, North Somerset, BS20 7DF
Tel: 01275 841941
Email: portishead@boatfolk.co.uk
www.boatfolk.co.uk/portisheadmarina

VHF	Ch 80
ACCESS	HW±3.5

Portishead Marina is a popular destination for cruising in the Bristol Channel. Providing an excellent link between the inland waterways at Bristol and Sharpness and offering access to the open water and marinas down channel. The entrance to the marina is via a lock, with a minimum access of HW+/-3.5hrs. Contact the marina on Ch 80 ahead of time for next available lock. The marina provides 320 fully serviced berths and can accommodate vessels up to 40m LOA, draft up to 5.5m. The marina has a 35 tonnes boat hoist and the boatyard offers all the facilities you would expect from a boatfolk site.

FACILITIES AT A GLANCE

Key
a Marina control building (reception, facilities & laundry)
b Advance Marine Services & Chandlery
c A&W Building & Coastguard
d Boatyard facilities, fishing tackle supplies & café
e Ray Williams Marine Engineer
f Hall & Woodhouse pub (facilities & laundry)
g Co-op supermarket

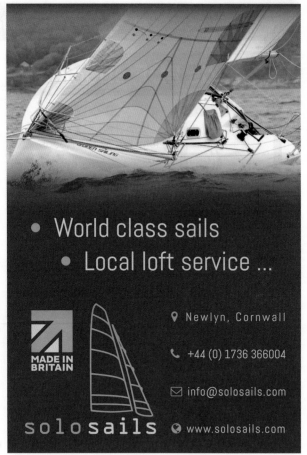
PADSTOW HARBOUR

Padstow Harbour Commissioners
The Harbour Office, Padstow, Cornwall, PL28 8AQ
Tel: 01841 532239
Email: harbourmaster@padstow-harbour.co.uk
www.padstow-harbour.co.uk

VHF	Ch 12, 16
ACCESS	HW±2

Padstow is a small commercial port with a rich history situated 1.5 miles from the sea within the estuary of the River Camel. The inner harbour is serviced by a tidal gate – part of the 1988–1990 flood defence scheme, which is open approximately two hours either side of high water. A minimum of 3m of water is maintained in the inner harbour at all times. Onshore facilities are excellent, please enquire at the Harbour Office.

This is a thriving fishing port, so perhaps it wasn't surprising that celebrity chefs like Rick Stein and Paul Ainsworth would set up shop in the town. This is a great resting point for everything Cornish from surf and coastal walks to fish and chips and cream teas.

FACILITIES AT A GLANCE

Key
a Residents' pontoons
b Harbour office
* Electricity and water points
1-20 around harbour denote ladder numbers

11

SOUTH IRELAND – Malahide, clockwise to Liscannor Bay

Key to Marina Plans symbols

Symbol	Description	Symbol	Description
	Bottled gas	P	Parking
	Chandler		Pub/Restaurant
	Disabled facilities		Pump out
	Electrical supply		Rigging service
	Electrical repairs		Sail repairs
	Engine repairs		Shipwright
	First Aid		Shop/Supermarket
	Fresh Water		Showers
	Fuel - Diesel		Slipway
	Fuel - Petrol	WC	Toilets
	Hardstanding/boatyard		Telephone
@	Internet Café		Trolleys
	Laundry facilities	V	Visitors berths
	Lift-out facilities		Wi-Fi

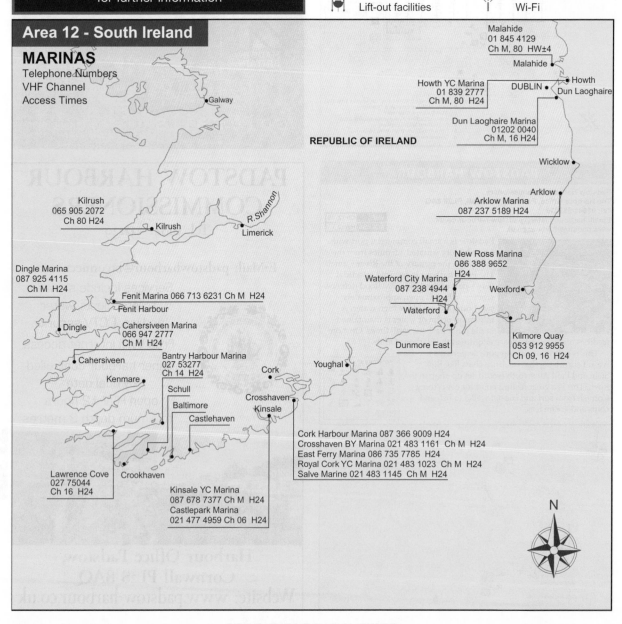

Area 12 - South Ireland

MARINAS
Telephone Numbers
VHF Channel
Access Times

REPUBLIC OF IRELAND

Malahide
01 845 4129
Ch M, 80 HW±4

Howth YC Marina
01 839 2777
Ch M, 80 H24

Dun Laoghaire Marina
01202 0040
Ch M, 16 H24

Arklow Marina
087 237 5189 H24

New Ross Marina
086 388 9652
H24

Waterford City Marina
087 238 4944
H24

Kilmore Quay
053 912 9955
Ch 09, 16 H24

Kilrush
065 905 2072
Ch 80 H24

Dingle Marina
087 925 4115
Ch M H24

Fenit Marina 066 713 6231 Ch M H24

Cahersiveen Marina
066 947 2777
Ch M H24

Bantry Harbour Marina
027 53277
Ch 14 H24

Cork Harbour Marina 087 366 9009 H24
Crosshaven BY Marina 021 483 1161 Ch M H24
East Ferry Marina 086 735 7785 H24
Royal Cork YC Marina 021 483 1023 Ch M H24
Salve Marine 021 483 1145 Ch M H24

Lawrence Cove
027 75044
Ch 16 H24

Kinsale YC Marina
087 678 7377 Ch M H24
Castlepark Marina
021 477 4959 Ch 06 H24

Galway · Limerick · Dublin · Howth · Dun Laoghaire · Wicklow · Arklow · Wexford · Waterford · Dunmore East · Youghal · Cork · Crosshaven · Kinsale · Baltimore · Schull · Castlehaven · Crookhaven · Kenmare · Cahersiveen · Dingle · Fenit Harbour · Kilrush · Malahide

N

MALAHIDE MARINA

Malahide Marina
Malahide, Co. Dublin
Tel: +353 1 845 4129 Fax: +353 1 845 4255
Email: info@malahidemarina.net
www.malahidemarina.net

VHF	Ch M, 80
ACCESS	HW±4

Malahide Marina, situated just 10 minutes from Dublin Airport and 20 minutes north of Dublin's city centre, is a fully serviced marina accommodating up to 350 yachts. Capable of taking vessels of up to 75m in length, its first class facilities include a boatyard with hard standing for approximately 170 boats and a 30-ton mobile hoist. Its on site restaurant provides a large seating area in convivial surroundings. The village of Malahide has plenty to offer the visiting yachtsmen, with a wide variety of eating places, nearby golf courses and tennis courts as well as a historic castle and botanical gardens.

FACILITIES AT A GLANCE

Key
a Boat handling & storage area
b Refuelling bay
c Marina centre
d Boatyard
e Marina access bridge
f Restaurant
g Wash area

HOWTH MARINA

Howth Marina
Howth Marina, Harbour Road, Howth, Co. Dublin
Tel: +353 1 8392777 Fax: +353 1 8392430
Email: marina@hyc.ie
www.hyc.ie

VHF	Ch M, 80
ACCESS	H24

Based on the north coast of the rugged peninsula that forms the northern side of Dublin Bay, Howth Marina is ideally situated for north or south-bound traffic in the Irish Sea. Well sheltered in all winds, it can be entered at any state of the tide. Overlooking the marina is Howth Yacht Club, which has in recent years been expanded and is now said to be the largest yacht club in Ireland. With good road and rail links, Howth is in easy reach of Dublin's airport and ferry terminal, making it an obvious choice for crew changeovers.

FACILITIES AT A GLANCE

Key
a Harbour office
b RNLI boathouse
c Clubhouse
d Drying pad
e Waiting pontoons (A&B)

Berth numbering starts at hammerheads

DUN LAOGHAIRE MARINA

Dun Laoghaire Marina
Harbour Road, Dun Laoghaire, Co Dublin, Ireland
Tel: +353 1 202 0040
Email: info@dlmarina.com www.dlmarina.com

VHF	Ch M, 16
ACCESS	H24

Dun Laoghaire Marina – Gateway to Dublin and the first marina in the Republic of Ireland to be awarded five Gold anchors by THYA and also achieved the ICOMIA 'Clean Marina' accreditation – is the largest marina in Ireland. 24 hour access in all weather conditions. The town centre is located within 400m. Serviced berthing for 820 boats from 6m to 23m with visitors mainly on the hammerheads.

Larger vessels up to 46m and 160 tonnes can be berthed alongside breakwater pontoons. Minimum draft is 4.0m LWS. Three phase power is available. With Dublin rail station 12km and airport 35km, this is an ideal base for Irish culture and entertainment, as well as crew changes etc. Easy access to Dublin Bay, home to the biennial Dun Laoghaire Regatta.

FACILITIES AT A GLANCE

Key
a Royal Irish Yacht Club
b Marina office
c WC
d Royal St George Yacht Club
Berth numbering - odds to port, evens to starboard, increase inwards

ARKLOW MARINA

Arklow Marina
North Quay, Arklow, Co. Wicklow, Ireland
Mobiles: +353 87 2375189 or + 353 87 2588078
Email: personnel@asl.ie
www.arklowmarina.com

VHF	
ACCESS	H24

Arklow is a popular fishing port and seaside town situated at the mouth of the River Avoca, 16 miles south of Wicklow and 11 miles north east of Gorey. The town is ideally placed for visiting the many beauty spots of County Wicklow including Glenmalure, Glendalough and Clara Lara, Avoca (Ballykissangel).

Arklow Marina is on the north bank of the river (dredged 2014) just upstream of the commercial quays, with 42 berths in an inner harbour and 30 berths on pontoons outside the marina entrance. Vessels over 14m LOA should moor on the river pontoons.

FACILITIES AT A GLANCE

NEW ROSS MARINA

New Ross Marina
The Tholsel, Quay Street, New Ross, Co Wexford, Y34 CF64
Tel: +353 86 3889652
www.newrossmarina.com
Email: newrossmarina@wexfordcoco.ie

VHF	
ACCESS	H24

Situated on the River Barrow, New Ross Marina is an ideal base for those sailing the south and east of Ireland. A 60-berth marina located 18M from Hook Head, New Ross is a short hop from Kilmore Quay, Dunmore East and Waterford City Marinas.

The River Barrow is the second longest river in Ireland and an important link to the Inland Waterways Network throughout the island, connecting New Ross to Dublin, Limerick, Carrick on Shannon, Enniskillen and the NW. The replica famine ship Dunbrody is a stroll up the quays, and the Kennedy Homestead just a few miles down the road.

FACILITIES AT A GLANCE

KILMORE QUAY

Kilmore Quay
Wexford, Ireland
Tel: +353 53 9129955 www.kilmorequaymarina.com
Email: assistant.marineofficer@wexfordcoco.ie

VHF	Ch 09, 16
ACCESS	H24

Located in the SE corner of Ireland, Kilmore Quay is a small rural fishing village situated approximately 14 miles from the town of Wexford and 12 miles from Rosslare ferry port.

Its 55-berthed marina, offering shelter from the elements as well as various on shore facilities, including diesel available 24/7, has become a regular port of call for many cruising yachtsmen. With several nearby areas of either historical or natural significance accessible using local bike hire, Kilmore is renowned for its 'green' approach to the environment.

FACILITIES AT A GLANCE

Key
a   Harbour master's office - onshore facilities
b   Lifeboat station
c   Information board
d   Stella Maris - community centre

WATERFORD CITY MARINA

Waterford City Marina
Waterford, Ireland
Tel: +353 87 2384944
Email: jcodd@waterfordcouncil.ie

VHF	
ACCESS	H24

Famous for its connections with Waterford Crystal, manufactured in the city centre, Waterford is the capital of the SE region of Ireland. As a major city, it benefits from good rail links with Dublin, and Limerick, a regional airport with daily flights to Britain and an extensive bus service to surrounding towns and villages. The marina is found on the banks of the River Suir, in the heart of this historic Viking city dating back to the ninth century. Yachtsmen can make the most of Waterford's wide range of shops, restaurants and bars without having to walk too far from their boats. With 100 fully serviced berths and first rate security, Waterford City Marina now provides shower, toilet and laundry facilities in its new reception building.

FACILITIES AT A GLANCE

CROSSHAVEN BOATYARD MARINA

Crosshaven Boatyard Marina
Crosshaven, Co Cork, Ireland
Tel: +353 214 831161 Fax: +353 214 831603
Email: info@crosshavenboatyard.com

VHF	Ch M
ACCESS	H24

One of three marinas at Crosshaven, Crosshaven Boatyard was founded in 1950 and originally made its name from the construction of some of the most world-renowned yachts, including *Gypsy Moth* and Denis Doyle's *Moonduster*. Nowadays, however, the yard has diversified to provide a wide range of services to both the marine leisure and professional industries. Situated on a safe and sheltered river only 12 miles from Cork City Centre, the marina boasts 100 fully-serviced berths along with the capacity to accommodate yachts up to 35m LOA with a 4m draught. In addition, it is ideally situated for cruising the stunning south west coast of Ireland.

FACILITIES AT A GLANCE

SALVE MARINE

Salve Marine
Crosshaven, Co Cork, Ireland
Tel: +353 21 483 1145 Fax: +353 21 483 1747
Email: salvemarineltd@gmail.com

VHF **Ch M**
ACCESS **H24**

Crosshaven is a picturesque seaside resort providing a gateway to Ireland's south and south west coasts. Offering a variety of activities to suit all types, its rocky coves and quiet sandy beaches stretch from Graball to Church Bay and from Fennell's Bay to nearby Myrtleville. Besides a selection of craft shops selling locally produced arts and crafts, there are plenty of pubs, restaurants and takeaways to suit even the most discerning of tastes. Lying within a few hundred metres of the village centre is Salve Marine, accommodating yachts up to 43m LOA with draughts of up to 4m. Its comprehensive services range from engineering and welding facilities to hull and rigging repairs.

FACILITIES AT A GLANCE

CORK HARBOUR MARINA

Cork Harbour Marina
Monkstown, Co Cork, Ireland
Tel: +353 87 366 9009
Email: info@corkharbourmarina.ie www.corkharbourmarina.ie

VHF
ACCESS **H24**

Located in the picturesque town of Monkstown, Cork Harbour Marina is in the heart of Cork Harbour. The marina can cater for all boat types with a draft of up to 7m and the marina is accessible at all phases of the tide.

Within strolling distance from the marina is the 'Bosun' restaurant and 'Napoli', an Italian delicatessen. There is also a sailing club, tennis club and golf club located nearby. Monkstown is just a short riverside walk from Passage West, with all the amenities one might require.

There is a frequent bus service from the marina gates to Cork City. Cork Harbour Marina is 15km from Cork International Airport.

FACILITIES AT A GLANCE

ROYAL CORK YACHT CLUB

Royal Cork Yacht Club Marina
Crosshaven, Co Cork, Ireland
Tel: +353 21 483 1023 Fax: +353 21 483 2657
Email: mark@royalcork.com www.royalcork.com

⚓⚓⚓⚓

VHF **Ch M**
ACCESS **H24**

Founded in 1720, the Royal Cork Yacht Club is the oldest and one of the most prominent yacht clubs in the world. Organising, among many other events, the prestigious biennial Volvo Cork Week, it boasts a number of World, European and national sailors among its membership.

The Yacht Club's marina is situated at Crosshaven, on the hillside at the mouth of the Owenabue River, just inside the entrance to Cork Harbour. The harbour is popular with yachtsmen as it is accessible and well sheltered in all weather conditions. It also benefits from the Gulf Stream producing a temperate climate practically all year round.

FACILITIES AT A GLANCE

Blue Flag
An Taisce

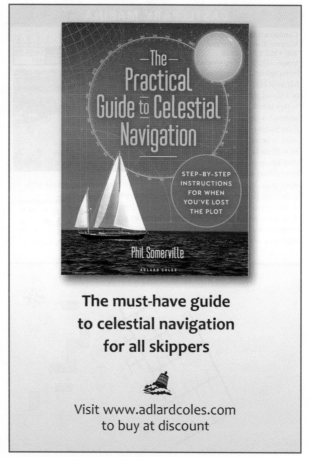

KINSALE YACHT CLUB MARINA

Kinsale Yacht Club Marina
Kinsale, Co Cork, Ireland
Tel: +353 876 787377
Email: kyc@iol.ie

VHF	Ch M
ACCESS	H24

Kinsale is a natural, virtually land-locked harbour on the estuary of the Bandon River, approximately 12 miles south west of Cork harbour entrance. Home to a thriving fishing fleet as well as frequented by commercial shipping, it boasts two fully serviced marinas, with the Kinsale Yacht Club

& Marina being the closest to the town. Visitors to this marina automatically become temporary members of the club and are therefore entitled to make full use of the facilities, which include a fully licensed bar and restaurant serving evening meals on Wednesdays, Thursdays and Saturdays. Fuel, water and repair services are also available.

FACILITIES AT A GLANCE

BANTRY HARBOUR MARINA

Bantry Harbour Marina
Trefechan, Aberystwyth, Ceredigion, SY23 1AS
Tel: +353 2753277 Fax: +353 2751202
Email: mpatmurphy@bantrybayport.com

VHF	Ch 14
ACCESS	H24

Bantry Harbour Marina is situated on the eastern most corner of Bantry Bay. Lying off Bantry town in Co. Cork on the southwest coast of Ireland the marina offers straightforward access on any state of the tide, The northern route round Whiddy Island is the preferred route with a deep-water channel marked by large lit navigational buoys.

The facilities at the Marina include toilets, EHU and rubbish/recycling disposal, you will also find a Petrol/Diesel garage with shop essentials 2 minutes away or it is only a 10min walk to the larger SuperValu supermarket, the main Bantry town is just a 5-minute walk away.

FACILITIES AT A GLANCE

CASTLEPARK MARINA

Castlepark Marina Centre
Kinsale, Co Cork, Ireland
Tel: +353 21 4774959
Email: info@castleparkmarina.com

VHF	Ch 16, 14
ACCESS	H24

Situated on the south side of Kinsale Harbour, Castlepark is a small marina with deep water pontoon berths that are accessible at all states of the tide. Surrounded by rolling hills, it boasts its own beach as well as being in close proximity to the parklands of James Fort and a traditional

Irish pub. The attractive town of Kinsale, with its narrow streets and slate-clad houses, lies just 1.5 miles away by road or five minutes away by ferry. Known as Ireland's 'fine food centre', it incorporates a number of gourmet food shops and high quality restaurants as well as a wine museum.

FACILITIES AT A GLANCE

LAWRENCE COVE MARINA

Lawrence Cove Marina
Lawrence Cove, Bere Island, Co Cork, Ireland
Tel: +353 27 75044 mob: +353 879 125930
Email: rachelsherig@gmail.com
www.lawrencecovemarina.ie

VHF	Ch 16
ACCESS	H24

Lawrence Cove enjoys a peaceful location on an island at the entrance to Bantry Bay. Privately owned and run, it offers sheltered and secluded waters as well as excellent facilities and fully serviced pontoon berths. A few hundred yards from the marina you will find a shop,

pub and restaurant, while the mainland, with its various attractions, can be easily reached by ferry. Lawrence Cove lies at the heart of the wonderful cruising grounds of Ireland's south west coast and, just two hours from Cork airport, is an ideal place to leave your boat for long or short periods.

FACILITIES AT A GLANCE

CAHERSIVEEN MARINA

Cahersiveen Marina
The Pier, Cahersiveen, Co. Kerry, Ireland
Tel: +353 66 9472777
Email: acardsiveen@gmail.com
www.cahersiveenmarina.ie

VHF	Ch M, 80
ACCESS	H24

Situated two miles up Valentia River from Valentia Harbour, Cahersiveen Marina is well protected in all wind directions and is convenient for sailing to Valentia Island and Dingle Bay as well as for visiting some of the spectacular uninhabited islands in the surrounding area. Boasting a host of sheltered sandy beaches, the region is renowned for salt and fresh water fishing as well as being good for scuba diving.

Within easy walking distance of the marina lies the historic town of Cahersiveen, incorporating an array of convivial pubs and restaurants.

FACILITIES AT A GLANCE

DINGLE MARINA

Dingle Marina
c/o Dingle Fishery Harbour Centre, Strand Street, Dingle, Co Kerry, Ireland
Tel: +353 (0)87 925 4115 Fax: +353 (0)69 5152546
Email:dingleharbour@agriculture.gov.ie
www.dinglemarina.ie

VHF	Ch 14
ACCESS	H24

Dingle is Ireland's most westerly marina, lying at the heart of the sheltered Dingle Harbour, and is easily reached both day and night via a well buoyed approach channel. The surrounding area is an interesting and unfrequented cruising ground, with several islands, bays and beaches for the yachtsman to explore.

The marina lies in the heart of the old market town, renowned for its hospitality and traditional Irish pub music. Besides enjoying the excellent seafood restaurants and 52 pubs, other recreational pastimes include horse riding, golf, climbing and diving.

FACILITIES AT A GLANCE

Key
a Marina centre building - cafe, dive centre, sailing and rowing centre, chandlery and showers
b Sea Life Centre
c Commercial berths - FVs & ferries
d Marina office

FENIT HARBOUR MARINA

Fenit Harbour & Marina
Fenit, Tralee, Co. Kerry, Republic of Ireland
Tel: +353 66 7136231 Fax: +353 66 7136473
Email: fenit.harbour@kerrycoco.ie www.kerrycoco.ie

VHF	Ch M
ACCESS	H24

Fenit Harbour Marina is tucked away in Tralee Bay, not far south of the Shannon Estuary. Besides offering a superb cruising ground, being within a day's sail of Dingle and Kilrush, the marina also provides a convenient base from which to visit inland attractions such as the picturesque tourist towns of Tralee and Killarney. This 120-berth marina accommodates boats up to 15m LOA and benefits from deep water at all states of the tide.

The small village of Fenit incorporates a grocery shop as well a several pubs and restaurants, while among the local activities are horse riding, swimming from one of the nearby sandy beaches and golfing.

FACILITIES AT A GLANCE

Key
a Warehouse
b Marina services, harbour office, lifeboat station

KILRUSH MARINA

Kilrush Marina Ltd
Kilrush, Co. Clare, Ireland
Tel: +353 65 9052072 Mobile: +353 86 2313870
Email: info@kilrushmarina.ie

VHF	Ch 80
ACCESS	H24

Kilrush Marina and boatyard is well placed for exploring the unspoilt west coast of Ireland, including Galway Bay, Dingle, W Cork and Kerry. It also provides a gateway to over 150 miles of cruising on Lough Derg, the R Shannon and the Irish canal system. Accessed via lock gates, the marina lies at one end of the main street in Kilrush, the marina centre provides all the facilities for the visiting sailor. Kilrush is a vibrant market town with a long maritime history. A 15-minute ferry ride from the marina takes you to Scattery Is, once a 6th century monastic settlement but now only inhabited by wildlife. The Shannon Estuary is reputed for being the country's first marine Special Area of Conservation (SAC) and is home to Ireland's only known resident group of bottlenose dolphins.

FACILITIES AT A GLANCE

craftinsure.com

Boat Insurance made easy

Get a quote in 20 seconds

On cover in 2 minutes

Low on-line premiums

 Get the App - craftinsure.com/app

> craftinsure.com

☎ 03452 607888

Authorised and regulated by the Financial Conduct Authority

NORTH IRELAND – Liscannor Bay, clockwise to Lambay Island

Reeds PDF ebooks

REEDS 2023 NAUTICAL ALMANAC
ATLANTIC EUROPE FROM THE TIP OF DENMARK TO GIBRALTAR (INCLUDES MARINAS AND AZORES)

In response to popular demand, all the Reeds Almanacs are now available as searchable, highlightable PDF ebooks. (All ebooks incorporate the Marina Guide.)

Visit www.reedsnauticalalmanac.co.uk for further information

Key to Marina Plans symbols

⌀	Bottled gas	P	Parking
⚓	Chandler	✕	Pub/Restaurant
♿	Disabled facilities	♒	Pump out
⚡	Electrical supply	△	Rigging service
⚡	Electrical repairs	⚲	Sail repairs
⚒	Engine repairs	✕	Shipwright
✚	First Aid	🛒	Shop/Supermarket
⚲	Fresh Water		Showers
D	Fuel - Diesel	◣	Slipway
P	Fuel - Petrol	WC	Toilets
⚏	Hardstanding/boatyard	☏	Telephone
@	Internet Café	🛒	Trolleys
⬚	Laundry facilities	Ⓥ	Visitors berths
⬛	Lift-out facilities	Ⓨ	Wi-Fi

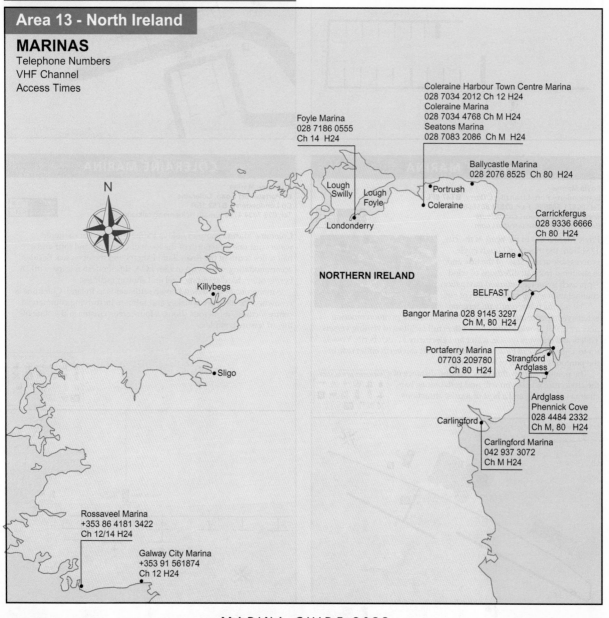

Area 13 - North Ireland

MARINAS
Telephone Numbers
VHF Channel
Access Times

N

Coleraine Harbour Town Centre Marina
028 7034 2012 Ch 12 H24
Coleraine Marina
028 7034 4768 Ch M H24
Seatons Marina
028 7083 2086 Ch M H24

Ballycastle Marina
028 2076 8525 Ch 80 H24

Foyle Marina
028 7186 0555
Ch 14 H24

Lough Swilly
Lough Foyle
Londonderry
Portrush
Coleraine

Carrickfergus
028 9336 6666
Ch 80 H24

Larne

NORTHERN IRELAND

Killybegs

BELFAST

Bangor Marina 028 9145 3297
Ch M, 80 H24

Portaferry Marina
07703 209780
Ch 80 H24

Strangford
Ardglass

Sligo

Ardglass
Phennick Cove
028 4484 2332
Ch M, 80 H24

Carlingford

Carlingford Marina
042 937 3072
Ch M H24

Rossaveel Marina
+353 86 4181 3422
Ch 12/14 H24

Galway City Marina
+353 91 561874
Ch 12 H24

GALWAY CITY MARINA

Galway City Marina
Galway Harbour Co, Harbour Office, Galway, Ireland
Tel: +353 91 561874 Fax: +353 91 563738
Email: info@theportofgalway.com

VHF	Ch 12
ACCESS	HW-2 to HW

The Galway harbour Company operates a small marina in the confines of Galway Harbour with an additional 60m of pontoon-walkway. Freshwater and electrical power is available at the pontoons. Power cars can be purchased from the harbour office during the day. A number of visitors pontoons are available for hire during the summer and for winter layup. Sailors intending to call to Galway Harbour should first make contact with the Harbour office to determine if a berth is available — advisable as demand is high in this quiet and beautiful part of Ireland.

FACILITIES AT A GLANCE

ROSSAVEEL MARINA

Rossaveel Marina
Ros An Mhil, Galway, Ireland
Tel: +353 86 41813422
Email: padraic.otoole@agriculture.gov.ie

VHF	Ch 12/14
ACCESS	H24

Nestled on the north coast of Galway Bay, the Rossaveel marinas (North and South) are a relatively new development in a busy working port and fishing harbour. The North Marina has a minimum depth of 2.6m for 166, although planning is underway for a further 60. The South Marina has 2m water for 44 vessels. All berths are serviced with water and electricity and fuel can be bought locally. Two slips are available for both tidal work and trailer launching.

Rossaveel has all the usual conveniences of a small town and from here ferries can be taken to the Aran Islands.

FACILITIES AT A GLANCE

FOYLE MARINA

Foyle Marina
Londonderry Port, Lisahally, L'Derry, BT47 6FL
Tel: 02871 860555 Fax: 02871 861656
www.londonderryport.com/leisure
Email: info@londonderryport.com

VHF	Ch 14
ACCESS	H24

Foyle Marina lies in the heart of the city, 17M from the mouth of Lough Foyle, is accessible at any state of the tide and is sheltered from all directions of wind. Approach is via well-marked navigation channel with a maintained depth of 8m.

The marina has recently undergone extensive improvements with over 680m of secure pontoon mooring now available. Foyle Marina now offers full facilities to visiting vessels. Toilets and showers on site, water and electricity at each berth. Vessels up to 130m LOA can be accommodated. Craft can berth either side of the pontoons in depths of 5–7m at LW.

The pontoons are within easy walking distance of the city centre where you will find restaurants, bars, cinemas, shopping and a host of tourist attractions.

FACILITIES AT A GLANCE

Key a Council offices
     b Appartments
     c Doctor's surgery

River Foyle

COLERAINE MARINA

Coleraine Marina
64 Portstewart Road, Coleraine,
Co Londonderry, BT52 1RR
Tel: 028 7034 4768 Email: rickiemac@talktalk.net

VHF	Ch M
ACCESS	H24

Coleraine Marina complex enjoys a superb location in sheltered waters just one mile north of the town of Coleraine and four and a half miles south of the River Bann Estuary and the open sea. Besides accommodating vessels up to 18m LOA, this modern marina with 78 berths offers hard standing, fuel and shower facilities.

Among one of the oldest known settlements in Ireland, Coleraine is renowned for its linen, whiskey and salmon. Its thriving commercial centre includes numerous shops, a four-screen cinema and a state-of-the-art leisure complex.

FACILITIES AT A GLANCE

SEATONS MARINA

Seatons Marina
Drumslade Rd, Coleraine, Londonderry, BT52 1SE
Tel: 028 7083 2086 Mobile 07718 883099
Email: jill@seatonsmarina.co.uk www.seatonsmarina.co.uk

VHF
ACCESS H24

Seatons Marina is a privately owned business on the north coast of Ireland, which was established by Eric Seaton in 1962. It lies on the east bank of the River Bann, approximately two miles downstream from Coleraine and three miles from the sea. Long term pontoon berths are

available for yachts up to 11.5 with a maximum draft of 2.4m; fore and aft moorings are available for larger vessels. Lift out and mast stepping facilities are provided by a 12 tonne trailer hoist.

FACILITIES AT A GLANCE

Seaton's Marina

COLERAINE HARBOUR MARINA

Coleraine Harbour Town Centre Marina
Coleraine Harbour Office, 4 Riversdale Road, Coleraine, BT52 1XA
Tel: 028 7034 2012 Mobile: 07742 242788
Email: info@coleraineharbour.com
www.coleraineharbour.com

VHF Ch 12
ACCESS H24

The Marina lies upstream about five miles from the sea. Ideally situated in a sheltered location in the centre of the town, just a few minutes stroll from a selection of shops, cafes, restaurants and bars. It is the ideal location for a short or long stay.

In addition to the pontoon berths there is a 40 tonne Roodberg slipway launch/ recovery trailer. Hard standing and covered storage are available.

FACILITIES AT A GLANCE

Landing stages   River Bann   Coleraine Harbour Town Centre pontoons   Millenium Footbridge

Coleraine Harbour Town Centre west bank pontoons   Coleraine Bridge

BALLYCASTLE MARINA

Ballycastle Marina
Bayview Road, Ballycastle, Northern Ireland
Tel: 028 2076 8525/07803 505084 Fax: 028 2076 6215
Email: info@moyle-council.org

VHF Ch 80
ACCESS H24

Ballycastle is a traditional seaside town situated on Northern Ireland's North Antrim coast. The 74-berthed, sheltered marina provides a perfect base from which to explore the well known local attractions such as the Giant's Causeway world heritage site, the spectacular

Nine Glens of Antrim, and Rathlin, the only inhabited island in Northern Ireland. The most northern coastal marina in Ireland, Ballycastle is accessible at all states of the tide, although yachts are required to contact the marina on VHF Ch 80 before entering the harbour. Along the seafront are a selection of restaurants, bars and shops, while the town centre is only about a five minute walk away.

FACILITIES AT A GLANCE

2.5m   2m   Visitors berths   3.0m   2.0m   A B C D

P

Marina Office   WC   Public Telephone

CARRICKFERGUS MARINA

Carrickferus Marina
3 Quayside, Carrickfergus, Co. Antrim, BT38 8BJ
Tel: 028 9336 6666 Fax: 028 9335 0505
Email: marina.reception@midandeastantrim.gov.uk
www.midandeastantrim.gov.uk

VHF Ch 80
ACCESS H24

Carrickfergus Marina is situated on the north shore of Belfast Lough overlooked by the town's medieval 12th century Norman Castle. Known as the gateway to the Causeway Coastal Route, Carrickfergus is also well connected to main arterial

routes headed to Belfast (7 miles) and further afield.

Our 300-berth, fully serviced marina has earned the prestigious 5 Gold Anchor Award and European Blue Flag status. No detail is overlooked in our exclusive berth holder facilities. From immaculately presented showers and personal laundry service, together with bespoke marine services, these are just some of the facilities available during a stay.

FACILITIES AT A GLANCE

Key
a   Apartments
b   Hotel/bar/restaurant
c   Marina office
d   Cinema/café/restaurant
e   Retail superstore

d   e

Apartments   Apartments   Apartments   a   c   b

Apartments

B D   C
F   E
H   G
J
L   Low-high   K
N   M

Sailing Club

Marine Services

BANGOR MARINA

Bangor Marina
Bangor, Co. Down, BT20 5ED
Tel: 028 9145 3297 Fax: 028 9145 3450
Email: bangor@boatfolk.co.uk
www.boatfolk.co.uk/bangormarina

VHF Ch 11, 80
ACCESS H24

Situated on the south shore of Belfast Lough, Bangor is located close to the Irish Sea cruising routes. The marina is right at the town's centre, within walking distance of shops, restaurants, hotels and bars. The Tourist information centre is across the road from marina reception and there are numerous visitors' attractions in the Borough. The Royal Ulster Yacht Club and the Ballyholme Yacht Club are both nearby and welcome visitors.

FACILITIES AT A GLANCE

Key
a Boat hoist - BJ Marine
b Boat yard - BJ Marine
c Bregenz House
d Chandlery/brokerage BJ Marine
e Dinghy berths
f Access bridge
g Lifeboat slipway
h Domestic waste facilities
i Waste oil tank
j Disabled berthing
NB Berth numbers low outer to high inner, odd numbers on right, even left

CARLINGFORD MARINA

Carlingford Marina
Co. Louth, Ireland
Tel: +353 (0)42 937 3072 Fax: +353 (0)42 937 3075
Email: info@carlingfordmarina.ie
www.carlingfordmarina.ie

VHF Ch M
ACCESS H24

Carlingford Lough is an eight-mile sheltered haven between the Cooley Mountains to the south and the Mourne Mountains to the north. The marina is situated on the southern shore, about four miles from Haulbowline Lighthouse, and can be easily reached via a deep water shipping channel. Among the most attractive destinations in the Irish Sea, Carlingford is only 60 miles from the Isle of Man and within a day's sail from Strangford Lough and Ardglass. Full facilities in the marina include a first class bar and restaurant offering superb views across the water.

FACILITIES AT A GLANCE

Key
a Bar and restaurant
b Toilets, showers and laundry
c Refuse
d Office
e Chandlery
f Marina office
g Waiting pontoon

ARDGLASS MARINA

Ardglass Marina
19 Quay Street, Ardglass, BT30 7SA
Tel: 028 4484 2332
Email: infoardglassmarina@gmail.com
www.ardglassmarina.co.uk

VHF Ch M, 80
ACCESS H24

Situated just south of Strangford, Ardglass has the capacity to accommodate up to 22 yachts as well as space for small craft. Despite being relatively small in size, the marina boasts an extensive array of facilities, either on site or close at hand. Recent access improvements have been made for wheelchair users in the shower/WC and reception. Grocery stores, a post office, chemist and off-licence, are all within a five-minute walk from the marina. Among the local onshore activities are golf, mountain climbing in Newcastle, which is 18 miles south, as well as scenic walks at Ardglass and Delamont Park.

FACILITIES AT A GLANCE

Key
a Administration building
b Boat storage

Additional Facilities
Reception car park - 60 vehicles
Waste oil tanks
Local charts for Strangford Lough
Heavy duty battery charging
High pressure water washing
Internet and email access
Barbeque facilities
Car hire
Weather fax

PORTAFERRY MARINA

Portaferry Marina
1 Mill View, Portaferry, BT22 1LQ
Mobile: 07703 209780 Fax: 028 4272 9784
Email: info@portaferrymarina.co.uk

VHF Ch 80
ACCESS H24

Portaferry Marina lies on the east shore of the Narrows, the gateway to Strangford Lough on the north east coast of Ireland. A marine nature reserve of outstanding natural beauty, the Lough offers plenty of recreational activities. The marina, which caters for draughts of up to 2.5m, is fairly small, accommodating around 30 yachts. The office is situated about 200m from the marina itself, where you will find ablution facilities along with a launderette.

Portaferry incorporates several pubs and restaurants as well as a few convenience stores, while one of its prime attractions is the Exploris Aquarium. Places of historic interest in the vicinity include Castleward, an 18th century mansion in Strangford, and Mount Stewart House & Garden in Newtownards.

FACILITIES AT A GLANCE

CHANNEL ISLANDS – Guernsey & Jersey

Key to Marina Plans symbols

Bottled gas		Parking	
Chandler		Pub/Restaurant	
Disabled facilities		Pump out	
Electrical supply		Rigging service	
Electrical repairs		Sail repairs	
Engine repairs		Shipwright	
First Aid		Shop/Supermarket	
Fresh Water		Showers	
Fuel - Diesel		Slipway	
Fuel - Petrol		Toilets	
Hardstanding/boatyard		Telephone	
Internet Café		Trolleys	
Laundry facilities		Visitors berths	
Lift-out facilities		Wi-Fi	

Area 14 - Channel Islands

MARINAS
Telephone Numbers
VHF Channel
Access Times

ALDERNEY

Beaucette Marina
01481 245000
Ch 80 HW±3

GUERNSEY

HERM

SARK

St Peter Port
Victoria Marina
01481 720229
Ch 12, Ch 80 HW±2½

Maître Ile

N

JERSEY

St Helier Marina
01534 447708
Ch 14 HW±3

BEAUCETTE MARINA

Beaucette Marina
Vale, Guernsey, GY3 5BQ
Tel: 01481 245000 Fax: 01481 247071
Mobile: 07781 102302
Email: info@beaucettemarina.com

VHF	Ch 80
ACCESS	HW±3

Situated on the north east tip of Guernsey, Beaucette enjoys a peaceful, rural setting in contrast to the more vibrant atmosphere of Victoria Marina. Now owned by a private individual and offering a high standard of service, the site was originally formed from an old quarry.

There is a general store close by, while the bustling town of St Peter Port is only 20 minutes away by bus.

FACILITIES AT A GLANCE

Key
a Harbour office
b Restaurant
c Showers/toilets
d Laundry & telephone
e Manager's cabin
f Boatyard

ST PETER PORT

Guernsey Harbours
PO Box 631, St Julian's Emplacement, St Peter Port
Tel: 01481 720229
Email: guernsey.harbour@gov.gg

VHF	Ch 12, 80
ACCESS	HW±2.5

The harbour of St Peter Port comprises the Queen Elizabeth II Marina to the N and Victoria and Albert Marinas to the S, with visiting yachtsmen usually accommodated in Victoria Marina.

St Peter Port is the capital of Guernsey. Its regency architecture and picturesque cobbled streets filled with restaurants and boutiques help to make it one of the most attractive harbours in Europe. Among the places of interest are Hauteville House, home of the writer Victor Hugo, and Castle Cornet. There are regular bus services to all parts of the island for visitors to explore a rich heritage.

FACILITIES AT A GLANCE

Key
a Customs shed
b Tourist Information
c Royal Channel Islands Yacht Club
d Toilets, showers, launderette, shops, pub and restaurant
e Guernsey Yacht Club
f Ferry terminal

ST PETER PORT VICTORIA MARINA

Guernsey Harbours
PO Box 631, St Julian's Emplacement, St Peter Port
Tel: 01481 720229 Fax: 01481 714177
Email: guernsey.harbour@gov.gg

VHF	Ch 80
ACCESS	HW±2.5

Victoria Marina in St Peter Port accommodates some 300 visiting yachts. In the height of the season it gets extremely busy, but when full visitors can berth on 5 other pontoons in the Pool or pre-arrange a berth in the QE II or Albert marinas. There are no visitor moorings in the Pool. Depending on draught, the marina is accessible approximately two and a half hours either side of HW, with yachts crossing over a sill drying to 4.2m. The marina dory will direct you to a berth on arrival or else will instruct you to moor on one of the waiting pontoons just outside.

Guernsey is well placed for exploring the rest of the Channel Islands and nearby French ports.

FACILITIES AT A GLANCE

Key
a Toilets, showers, launderette and shops
b Royal Channel Islands Yacht Club
c Refuse skip
d Marina control, port office
e Dinghy/tender landing pontoon
f Pub/restaurant
g Tourist information

SEA START ™
MEMBERSHIP
CELEBRATING **30** YEARS

24/7 MARINE BREAKDOWN SERVICE

DON'T CAST OFF WITHOUT US

- **90% of boats are repaired on scene**
- **Dedicated marine engineers**
- **Home berth start**
- **Unlimited callouts**

JOIN TODAY 0800 885500

24 7

MARINE BREAKDOWN

'Le Shed'

JOIN TODAY: 0800 885500
membership@seastart.co.uk • www.seastart.co.uk

ST HELIER HARBOUR

St Helier Harbour
Maritime House, La Route du Port Elizabeth
St Helier, Jersey, JE1 1HB
Tel: 01534 447708
www.portofjersey.je Email: marinas@ports.je

VHF Ch 14
ACCESS HW±3

Set in the Norman Breton Gulf, Jersey is the most southerly of the Channel Islands, offering over 200 visitor berths on a flexible daily, weekly or monthly basis. With its close proximity to the adjacent French coast and with sheltered bays and anchorages there are plenty of opportunities to explore new cruising areas, making Jersey an ideal base. Jersey airport is only 15 minutes away from St Helier Marina by bus or car.

Visiting craft are directed into St Helier Marina which is located in the town with access is HW±3. Alternatively, there is a holding pontoon just outside of the marina entrance providing full services and walk ashore access. Visiting vessels of up to 20m may be directed into Elizabeth Marina by prior arrangement.

FACILITIES AT A GLANCE

Key
a Marina office
b Water/toilets/public phone
c Tourism
d Harbour office and Customs
e Maritime house
f Waiting pontoon
g Passenger Terminal
h Trailer park
i Port control
j Marina shop
k Cafe
l Self-service fuel

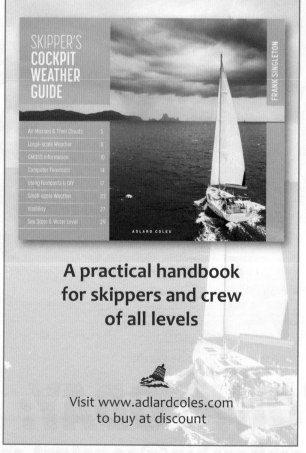

Adhesives 100	Electronic Devices & Equipment 109	Safety Equipment 118
Associations............................ 100	Engines & Accessories 110	Sailmakers & Repairs 119
Berths & Moorings.......................... 100	Foul Weather Gear.............................. 111	Solar Power 120
Boatbuilders & Repairs..................... 100	General Marine Equipment & Spares. 111	Sprayhoods & Dodgers...................... 120
Boatyard Services & Supplies 101	Harbour Masters 111	Surveyors & Naval Architects 120
Boat Deliveries & Storage 103	Harbours 113	Tape Technology................................ 121
Books & Charts/Publishers 104	Insurance & Finance........................... 113	Transport/Yacht Deliveries 121
Bow Thrusters 104	Liferaft & Inflatables.......................... 113	Tuition/Sailing Schools...................... 121
Breakdown 104	Marinas.. 113	Waterside Accommodation &
Chandlers................................ 104	Marine Engineers.............................. 115	Restaurants.................................... 123
Chart Agents 108	Masts/Spars & Rigging 117	Weather Info 123
Clothing 108	Navigational Equipment - General..... 117	Wood Fittings.................................... 123
Code of Practice Examiners.............. 108	Paint & Osmosis 118	Yacht Brokers.................................... 123
Computers & Software..................... 108	Propellers & Sterngear/Repairs.......... 118	Yacht Charters & Holidays 124
Deck Equipment........................ 108	Radio Courses/Schools 118	Yacht Clubs....................................... 124
Diesel Marine & Fuel Additives 108	Reefing Systems 118	Yacht Designers................................. 128
Divers..................................... 108	Repair Materials & Accessories........... 118	Yacht Management............................ 128
Electrical & Electronic Engineers....... 109	Rope & Wire 118	Yacht Valeting................................... 128

SECTION 2
MARINE SUPPLIES AND SERVICES GUIDE

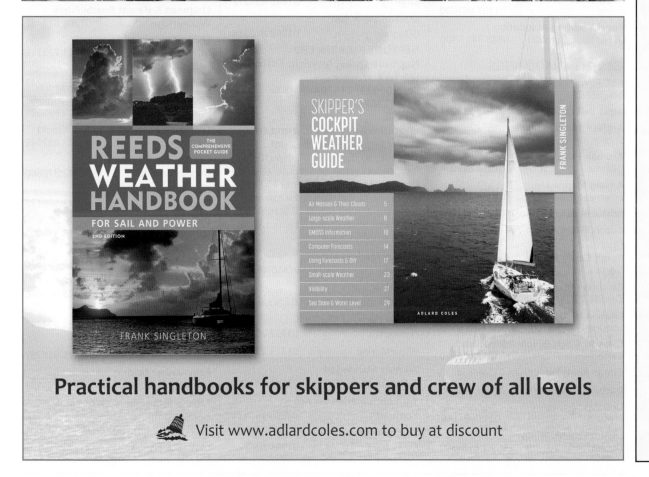

Practical handbooks for skippers and crew of all levels

Visit www.adlardcoles.com to buy at discount

ADHESIVES

Casco Adhesives
Darwen   07710 546899

CC Marine Services Ltd
West Mersea   07751 734510

Industrial Self Adhesives Ltd
Nottingham   0115 9681895

Sika Ltd Garden City   01707 394444

Technix Rubber & Plastics Ltd
Southampton   01489 789944

Tiflex Liskeard   01579 320808

Trade Grade Products Ltd
Poole   01202 820177

UK Epoxy Resins
Burscough   01704 892364

Wessex Resins & Adhesives Ltd
Romsey   01794 521111

3M United Kingdom plc
Bracknell   01344 858315

ASSOCIATIONS/ AGENCIES

Cruising Association
London   020 7537 2828

**Fishermans Mutual Association
(Eyemouth) Ltd**
Eyemouth   01890 750373

Maritime and Coastguard Agency
Southampton   0870 6006505

Royal Institute of Navigation
London   020 7591 3130

Royal National Lifeboat Institution
Poole   01202 663000

**Royal Yachting Association
(RYA)** Southampton   0845 345 0400

BERTHS & MOORINGS

ABC Powermarine
Beaumaris   01248 811413

Aqua Bell Ltd Norwich   01603 713013

Ardfern Yacht Centre
Lochgilphead   01852 500247/500636

Ardmair Boat Centre
Ullapool   01854 612054

Arisaig Marine Ltd
Inverness-shire   01687 450224

Bristol Boat Ltd Bristol   01225 872032

British Waterways
Argyll   01546 603210

Burgh Castle Marine
Norfolk   01493 780331

Cambrian Marine Services Ltd
Cardiff   029 2034 3459

Chelsea Harbour Ltd
London   020 7225 9108

Clapson & Son (Shipbuilders) Ltd
Barton-on-Humber   01652 635620

Crinan Boatyard, Crinan 01546 830232

Dartside Quay Brixham 01803 845445

Douglas Marine
Preston   01772 812462

Dublin City Moorings
Dublin   +353 1 8183300

Emsworth Yacht Harbour
Emsworth   01243 377727

Exeter Ship Canal   01392 274306

HAFAN PWLLHELI
Glan Don, Pwllheli, Gwynedd LL53 5YT
Tel: (01758) 701219
Fax: (01758) 701443 VHF Ch80
Hafan Pwllheli has over 400 pontoon berths and offers access at virtually all states of the tide. Ashore, its modern purpose-built facilities include luxury toilets, showers, launderette, a secure boat park for winter storage, 40-ton travel hoist, mobile crane and plenty of space for car parking. Open 24-hours a day, 7 days a week.

Highway Marine
Sandwich   01304 613925

Iron Wharf Boatyard
Faversham   01795 536296

Jalsea Marine Services Ltd
Northwich   01606 77870

Jersey Harbours
St Helier   01534 447788

Jones (Boatbuilders), David
Chester   01244 390363

Lawrenny Yacht Station
Kilgetty   01646 651212

MacFarlane & Son
Glasgow   01360 870214

NEPTUNE MARINA LTD
Neptune Quay, Ipswich, Suffolk IP4 1AX
Tel: (01473) 215204
Fax: (01473) 215206
e-mail:
enquiries@neptune-marina.com
www.neptune-marina.com
The quay to the heart of Ipswich! Call Ipswich lock gates on Channel 68 and Neptune Marina on Channel 80. Bring your crew to the wonderful Ipswich waterfront, with plenty of watering holes and town centre activities. You won't want to leave!

Orkney Marinas Ltd
Kirkwall   07810 465835

V Marine
Shoreham-by-Sea   01273 461491

Sutton Harbour Marina
Plymouth   01752 204186

WicorMarine Fareham   01329 237112

Winters Marine Ltd
Salcombe   01548 843580

Yarmouth Marine Service
Yarmouth   01983 760521

Youngboats
Faversham   01795 536176

BOAT BUILDERS & REPAIRS

ABC Hayling Island   023 9246 1968

ABC Powermarine
Beaumaris   01248 811413

Advance Yacht Systems
Southampton   023 8033 7722

Aqua-Star Ltd
St Sampsons   01481 244550

ArdoFran Marine
Oban   01631 566123

Baumbach Bros Boatbuilders
Hayle   01736 753228

Beacon Boatyard
Rochester   01634 841320

Bedwell & Co
Walton on the Naze   01255 675873

Blackwell, Craig
Co Meath   +353 87 677 9605

Boyd Boat Building
Falmouth   07885 436722

Boatcraft
Ardrossan   01294 603047

B+ St Peter Port   01481 726071

Brennan, John
Dun Laoghaire   +353 1 280 5308

Burghead Boat Centre
Findhorn   01309 690099

Carrick Marine Projects
Co Antrim   02893 355884

Chapman & Hewitt Boatbuilders
Wadebridge   01208 813487

Chicks Marine Ltd
Guernsey   01481 723716

Clarence Boatyard
East Cowes   01983 294243

Cooks Maritime Craftsmen - Poliglow
Lymington   01590 675521

Creekside Boatyard (Old Mill Creek)
Dartmouth   01803 832649

CTC Marine & Leisure
Middlesbrough   01642 372600

Davies Marine Services
Ramsgate   01843 586172

Dickie International
Bangor   01248 363400

Dickie International
Pwllheli   01758 701828

East Llanion Marine Ltd
Pembroke Dock   01646 686866

Emblem Enterprises
East Cowes   01983 294243

Fairlie Quay
Fairlie   01475 568267

Fairweather Marine
Fareham   01329 283500

Farrow & Chambers Yacht Builders
Humberston
             www.farrowandchambers.co.uk

Fast Tack Plymouth   01752 255171

Fergulsea Engineering
Ayr 01292 262978

Ferrypoint Boat Co
Youghal +353 24 94232

Floetree Ltd (Loch Lomond Marina)
Balloch 01389 752069

Freshwater Boatyard
Truro 01326 270443

Frogmore Boatyard
Kingsbridge 01548 531257

Furniss Boat Building
Falmouth 01326 311766

Gallichan Marine Ltd
Jersey 01534 746387

Garvel Clyde
Greenock 01475 725372

Goodchild Marine Services
Great Yarmouth 01493 782301

Gosport Boatyard
Gosport 023 9252 6534

Gweek Quay Boatyard
Helston 01326 221657

Halls
Walton on the Naze 01255 675596

Harris Pye Marine
Barry 01446 720066

Haven Boatyard
Lymington 01590 677073

Hayling Yacht Company
Hayling Island 023 9246 3592

Hoare Ltd, Bob
Poole 01202 736704

Holyhead Boatyard
Holyhead 01407 760111

Jackson Marine
Lowestoft 01502 539772

Jackson Yacht Services
Jersey 01534 743819

JEP Marine
Canterbury 01227 710102

JWS Marine Services
Southsea 023 9275 5155

Kimelford Yacht Haven
Oban 01852 200248

Kingfisher Marine
Weymouth 01305 766595

Kingfisher Ultraclean UK Ltd
Tarporley 0800 085 7039

King's Boatyard
Pin Mill 01473 780258

Kinsale Boatyard
Kinsale +353 21477 4774

Kippford Slipway Ltd
Dalbeattie 01556 620249

Lawrenny Yacht Station
Lawrenny 01646 651212

Lencraft Boats Ltd
Dungarvan +353 58 682220

Mackay Boatbuilders
Arbroath 01241 872879

Marine Blast
Holy Loch 01369 705394

Marine Services
Norwich 01692 582239

Mashford Brothers
Torpoint 01752 822232

Mayor & Co Ltd, J
Preston 01772 812250

Mears, HJ Axmouth 01297 23344

Mill, Dan, Galway +353 86 337 9304

Miller Marine
Tyne & Wear 01207 542149

Morrison, A
Killyleagh 028 44828215

Moss (Boatbuilders), David
Thornton-Cleveleys 01253 893830

Multi Marine Composites Ltd
Torpoint 01752 823513

Newing, Roy E
Canterbury 01227 860345

Noble and Sons, Alexander
Girvan 01465 712223

Northney Marine Services
Hayling Island 023 9246 9246

Northshore Sport & Leisure
King's Lynn 01485 210236

O'Sullivans Marine Ltd
Tralee +353 66 7124957

Pachol, Terry
Brighton 01273 682724

Partington Marine Ltd, William
Pwllheli 01758 612808

Pasco's Boatyard
Truro 01326 270269

Penrhos Marine
Aberdovey 01654 767478

Penzance Marine Services
Penzance 01736 361081

PJ Bespoke Boat Fitters Ltd
Crewe 01270 812244

Preston Marine Services Ltd
Preston 01772 733595

Red Bay Boats Ltd
Cushendall 028 2177 1331

Reliance Marine
Wirral 0151 625 5219

Reever, Adrian
Maldon 07548 744090

Retreat Boatyard Ltd
Exeter 01392 874720/875934

Richardson Boatbuilders, Ian
Stromness 01856 850321

Richardson Yacht Services Ltd
Newport 01983 821095

Roberts Marine Ltd, S
Liverpool 0151 707 8300

Rothman Pantall & Co
Fareham 01329 280221

Rustler Yachts
Falmouth 01326 310210

Salterns Boatyard
Poole 01202 707391

Sea & Shore Ship Chandler
Dundee 01382 450666

Seamark-Nunn & Co
Felixstowe 01394 275327

Seapower
Woolverstone 01473 780090

Slipway Cooperative Ltd
Bristol 0117 907 9938

Small, Donal
Galway +353 83 1831057

Smith, GB, & Sons
Rock 01208 862815

Spicer Boatbuilder, Nick
Weymouth Marina 01305 767118

Squadron Marine Ltd
Poole 01202 674531

Storrar Marine Store
Newcastle upon Tyne 0191 266 1037

TT Marine Ashwell 01462 742449

Waterfront Marine
Bangor 01248 352513

Way, A&R, Boat Building
Tarbert, Loch Fyne 01546 606657

WestCoast Marine
Troon 01292 318121

Western Marine
Dublin +353 1 280 0321

Wigmore Wright Marine Services
Penarth 029 2070 9983

Williams, Peter
Fowey 01726 870987

WQI Ltd
Bournemouth 01202 771292

Yarmouth Marine Service
01983 760521

Youngboats
Faversham 01795 536176

BOATYARD SERVICES & SUPPLIES

ABC Marine
Hayling Island 023 9246 1968

Abersoch Boatyard Services Ltd
Abersoch 01758 713900

Amble Boat Co Ltd
Amble 01665 710267

Amsbrisbeg Ltd
Port Bannatyne 01700 831215

Ardmair Boat Centre
Ullapool 01854 612054

Ardmaleish Boat Building Co Rothesay
01700 502007

www.ardoran.co.uk
W coast Scotland. All marine facilities.

Ardrishaig Boatyard
Lochgilphead   01546 603280

Arklow Slipway
Arklow   +353 402 33233

Baltic Wharf Boatyard
Totnes   01803 867922

Baltimore Boatyard
Baltimore   +353 28 20444

Bates, Declan
Kilmore Quay   +353 87 252 9936

Bedwell and Co
Walton-on-the-Naze   01255 675873

Berthon Boat Co
Lymington   01590 673312

Birdham Shipyard
Chichester   01243 512310

BJ Marine Ltd Bangor   028 91271434

Blagdon, A
Plymouth   01752 561830

Boatcraft Ardrossan   01294 603047

Boatworks + Ltd
St Peter Port   01481 726071

Brennan, John
Dun Laoghaire   +353 1 280 5308

Brighton Marina Boatyard
Brighton   01273 819919

Bristol Marina (Yard)
Bristol   0117 921 3198

Buckie Shipyard Ltd
Buckie   01542 831245

Bucklers Hard Boat Builders Ltd
Brockenhurst   01590 616214

C & J Marine Services
Newcastle Upon Tyne   0191 295 0072

Caley Marina Inverness   01463 236539

Cambrian Boat Centre
Swansea   01792 655925

Cambrian Marine Services Ltd
Cardiff   029 2034 3459

Cantell and Son Ltd
Newhaven   01273 514118

Canvey Yacht Builders Ltd
Canvey Island   01268 696094

Carroll's Ballyhack Boatyard
New Ross   +353 51 389164

Castlepoint Boatyard
Crosshaven   +353 21 4832154

Chabot, Gary
Newhaven   07702 006767

Chapman & Hewitt Boatbuilders
Wadebridge   01208 813487

Chippendale Craft Rye   01797 227707

Clapson & Son (Shipbuilders) Ltd
Barton on Humber   01652 635620

Clarence Boatyard
East Cowes   01983 294243

Coastal Marine Boatbuilders
Eyemouth   01890 750328

Coastcraft Ltd
Cockenzie   01875 812150

Coates Marine Ltd
Whitby   01947 604486

Connor, Richard
Coleraine   07712 115751

Coombes, AA
Bembridge   01983 872296

Corpach Boatbuilding Company
Fort William   01397 772861

Craobh Marina
By Lochgilphead   01852 500222

Creekside Boatyard (Old Mill Creek)
Dartmouth   01803 832649

Crinan Boatyard
By Lochgilphead   01546 830232

Crosshaven Boatyard Co Ltd
Crosshaven   +353 21 831161

Dale Sailing Co Ltd
Neyland   01646 603110

Darthaven Marina
Kingswear   01803 752242

Dartside Quay
Brixham   01803 845445

Dauntless Boatyard Ltd
Canvey Island   01268 793782

Davis's Boatyard Poole   01202 674349

Dinas Boat Yard Ltd
Y Felinheli   01248 671642

Dorset Lake Shipyard Ltd
Poole   01202 674531

Dorset Yachts Co Ltd
Poole   01202 674531

Douglas Boatyard
Preston   01772 812462

Dover Yacht Co Dover   01304 201073

Dun Laoghaire Marina
Dun Laoghaire   +353 1 2020040

Elephant Boatyard
Southampton   023 8040 3268

Elton Boatbuilding Ltd
Kirkcudbright   01557 330177

Felixstowe Ferry Boatyard
Felixstowe   01394 282173

Ferguson Engineering
Wexford   +353 6568 66822133

Ferry Marine South
Queensferry   0131 331 1233

Findhorn Boatyard
Findhorn   01309 690099

Firmhelm Ltd Pwllheli   01758 612251

Fowey Boatyard
Fowey   01726 832194

Fox's Marina Ipswich   01473 689111

Frank Halls & Son
Walton on the Naze   01255 675596

Freeport Marine
Jersey   01534 888100

Furniss Boat Building
Falmouth   01326 311766

Garval Clyde
Greenock   01475 725372

Goodchild Marine Services
Great Yarmouth   01493 782301

Gosport Boatyard
Gosport   023 9252 6534

Gweek Quay Boatyard
Helston   01326 221657

Haines Boatyard
Chichester   01243 512228

Harbour Marine
Plymouth   01752 204691

Harbour Marine Services Ltd
Southwold   01502 724721

Harris Pye Marine Barry 01446 720066

Hartlepool Marine Engineering
Hartlepool   01429 867883

Hayles, Harold
Yarmouth, IoW   01983 760373

Henderson, J Shiskine   01770 860259

Heron Marine
Whitstable   01227 361255

Hewitt, George
Binham   01328 830078

Holyhead Marina & Trinity Marine Ltd
Holyhead   01407 764242

Instow Marine Services
Bideford   01271 861081

Ipswich Haven Marina
Ipswich   01473 236644

Iron Wharf Boatyard
Faversham   01795 536296

Island Boat Services
Port of St Mary   01624 832073

Isle of Skye Yachts
Ardvasar   01471 844216

Jalsea Marine Services Ltd Weaver
Shipyard, Northwich   01606 77870

JBS Group
Peterhead   01779 475395

J B Timber Ltd
North Ferriby   01482 631765

Jersey Harbours Dept
St Helier   01534 885588

Kilnsale Boatyard
Kinsale   +353 21 4774774

Kingfisher Ultraclean UK Ltd
Tarporley   01928 787878

Kilrush Marina Boatyard
Kilrush   +35 87 7990091

Kinsale Boatyard   +353 21477 4774

KPB Beaucette   07781 152581

Lake Yard Poole   01202 674531

Lallow, C Isle of Wight   01983 292112

Latham's Boatyard
Poole   01202 748029

Laxey Towing
Douglas, Isle of Man   07624 493592

Leonard Marine, Peter
Newhaven   01273 515987

Lincombe Marine
Salcombe   01548 843580

Lomax Boatbuilders
Cliffony   +353 71 66124

Lymington Yt Haven   01590 677071

MacDougalls Marine Services
Isle of Mull   01681 700294

Macduff Shipyard Ltd
Macduff   01261 832234

Madog Boatyard
Porthmadog   01766 514205/513435

Mainbrayce Marine
Alderney   01481 822772

Malakoff and Moore
Lerwick   01595 695544

Mallaig Boat Building and Engineering
Mallaig   01687 462304

Maramarine
Helensburgh   01436 810971

Marindus Engineering
Kilmore Quay   +353 53 29794

Mariners Farm Boatyard
Gillingham   01634 233179

Marvig Boatyard
Marvig, Lewis   07771 763662

McGruar and Co Ltd
Helensburgh   01436 831313

Mevagh Boatyard
Mulroy Bay   +353 74 915 4470

Mill, Dan, Galway   +353 86 337 9304

Mitchell's Boatyard
Poole   01202 747857

Mooney Boats
Killybegs   +353 73 31152/31388

Moore & Son, J
St Austell   01726 842964

Morrison, A Killyleagh   028 44828215

Moss (Boatbuilders), David
Thornton-Cleveleys   01253 893830

Mustang Marine
Milford Haven   01646 696320

New Horizons Rhu   01436 821555

Noble and Sons, Alexander
Girvan   01465 712223

North Pier (Oban)
Oban   01631 562892

North Wales Boat Centre
Conwy   01492 580740

Northam Marine
Brightlingsea   01206 302003

Northshore Yacht Yard
Chichester   01243 512611

Oban Yachts and Marine Services
By Oban   01631 565333

Pearn and Co, Norman
Looe   01503 262244

Penrhos Marine
Aberdovey   01654 767478

Penzance Dry Dock and Engineering Co Ltd Penzance   01736 363838

Philip & Son Dartmouth   01803 833351

Phillips, HJ Rye   01797 223234

Pierce-Purcell
Galway   +353 87 279 3821

Ponsharden Boatyard
Penryn   01326 372215

Powersail and Island Chandlers Ltd
East Cowes Marina   01983 299800

Priors Boatyard
Burnham-on-Crouch   01621 782160

R K Marine Ltd
Swanwick   01489 583572

Rat Island Sailboat Company (Yard) St Mary's   01720 423399

Rennison, Russell
Gosport   07734 688819

Retreat Boatyard Ltd
Exeter   01392 874720/875934

Rice and Cole Ltd
Burnham-on-Crouch   01621 782063

Richardson Boatbuilders, Ian Stromness
01856 850321

Richardsons Boatbuilders
Binfield   01983 821095

Riverside Yard
Shoreham Beach   01273 592456

River Yar Boatyard
Yarmouth, IoW   01983 761000

Robertsons Boatyard
Woodbridge   01394 382305

Rossbrin Boatyard
Schull   +353 28 37352

Rossiter Yachts Ltd
Christchurch   01202 483250

Rossreagh Boatyard
Rathmullan   +353 74 9150182

Rudders Boatyard & Moorings
Milford Haven   01646 600288

Ryan & Roberts Marine Services
Askeaton   +353 61 392198

Rye Harbour Marina Rye
                             01797 227667

Rynn Engineering, Pat
Galway   +353 91 562568

Salterns Boatyard Poole 01202 707391

Sandbanks Yacht Company
Poole   01202 611262

Scarborough Marine Engineering Ltd
Scarborough   01723 375199

Severn Valley Cruisers Ltd (Boatyard)
Stourport-on-Severn   01299 871165

Shepards Wharf Boatyard Ltd
Cowes   01983 297821

Shipshape
King's Lynn   01553 764058

Shotley Marina Ltd
Ipswich   01473 788982

Shotley Marine Services Ltd
Ipswich   01473 788913

Silvers Marina Ltd
Helensburgh   01436 831222

Skinners Boat Yard
Baltimore   +353 28 20114

Smith, GB, & Sons
Rock   01208 862815

Smith & Gibbs
Eastbourne   07802 582009

Sparkes Boatyard
Hayling Island   023 92463572

Spencer Sailing Services, Jim
Brightlingsea   01206 302911

Standard House Boatyard
Wells-next-the-Sea   01328 710593

Storrar Marine Store
Newcastle upon Tyne   0191 266 1037

Strand Shipyard Rye   01797 222070

Surry Boatyard
Shoreham-by-Sea   01273 461491

The Shipyard
Littlehampton   01903 713327

Titchmarsh Marina
Walton-on-the-Naze   01255 672185

Tollesbury Marina
Tollesbury   01621 869202

T J Rigging Conwy   07780 972411

Toms and Son Ltd, C
Fowey   01726 870232

Tony's Marine Service
Coleraine   028 7035 6422

Torquay Marina
Torquay   01803 200210

Trinity Marine & Holyhead Marina
Holyhead   01407 763855

Trouts Boatyard (River Exe)
Topsham   01392 873044

Upson and Co, RF
Aldeburgh   01728 453047

Versatility Workboats
Rye   01797 224422

Weir Quay Boatyard
Bere Alston   01822 840474

West Solent Boatbuilders
Lymington   01590 642080

WicorMarine Fareham   01329 237112

Woodrolfe Boatyard
Maldon   01621 869202

Yarmouth Marine Services
Yarmouth, IoW   01983 760521

BOAT DELIVERIES & STORAGE

ABC Marine
Hayling Island   023 9246 1968

Abersoch Boatyard Services Ltd
Pwllheli   01758 713900

Ambrisbeg Ltd
Port Bannatyne   01700 502719

Arisaig Marine
Inverness-shire   01687 450224

Bedwell and Co Walton-on-the-Naze	01255 675873
Berthon Boat Company Lymington	01590 673312
Boat Shifters	07733 344018/01326 210548
C & J Marine Services Newcastle upon Tyne	0191 295 0072
Caley Marine Inverness	01463 233437
Carrick Marine Projects Co Antrim	02893 355884
Challenger Marine Penryn	01326 377222
Coates Marine Ltd Whitby	01947 604486
Convoi Exceptionnel Ltd Hamble	023 8045 3045
Creekside Boatyard (Old Mill Creek) Dartmouth	01803 832649
Crinan Boatyard Ltd Crinan	01546 830232
Dale Sailing Co Ltd Neyland	01646 603110
Dart Marina Ltd Dartmouth	01803 833351
Dartside Quay Brixham	01803 845445
Dauntless Boatyard Ltd Canvey Island	01268 793782
Debbage Yachting Ipswich	01473 601169
Douglas Marine Preston	01772 812462
East & Co, Robin Kingsbridge	01548 531257
East Coast Offshore Yachting	01480 861381
Emsworth Yacht Harbour Emsworth	01243 377727
Exeter Ship Canal	01392 274306
Exmouth Marina	01395 269314
Firmhelm Ltd Pwllheli	01758 612244
Forrest Marine Ltd Exeter	08452 308335
Fowey Boatyard Fowey	01726 832194
Freshwater Boatyard Truro	01326 270443
Hafan Pwllheli Pwllheli	01758 701219
Houghton Boat Transport Tewkesbury	07831 486710
Gweek Quay Boatyard Helston	01326 221657
Iron Wharf Boatyard Faversham	01795 536296
Jalsea Marine Services Ltd Northwich	01606 77870
KG McColl Oban	01852 200248
Latham's Boatyard Poole	01202 748029
Lincombe Boat Yard Salcombe	01548 843580

Marine Blast Holy Loch	01369 705394
Marine Resource Centre Ltd Oban	01631 720291
Marine & General Engineers Guernsey	01481 245808
Milford Marina Milford Haven	01646 696312/3
Moonfleet Sailing Poole	01202 682269
Murphy Marine Services Cahersiveen	+353 66 9476365
Southerly Chichester	01243 512611
Pasco's Boatyard Truro	01326 270269
Pearn and Co, Norman Looe	01503 262244
Performance Yachting Plymouth	01752 565023
Peters & May Ltd Southampton	023 8048 0480
Ponsharden Boatyard Penryn	01326 372215
Portsmouth Marine Engineering Fareham	01329 232854
Priors Boatyard Burnham-on-Crouch	01621 782160
Reeder School of Seamanship, Mike Lymington	01590 674560
Rossiter Yachts Christchurch	01202 483250
Sealand Boat Deliveries Ltd Liverpool	01254 705225
Shearwater Sailing Southampton	01962 775213
Shepards Wharf Boatyard Cowes Harbour Commission Cowes	01983 297821
Silvers Marina Ltd Helensburgh	01436 831222
Southcoasting Navigators Devon	01626 335626
Waterfront Marine Bangor	01248 352513
West Country Boat Transport	01566 785651
WicorMarine Fareham	01329 237112
Winters Marine Ltd Salcombe	01548 843580
Wolff, David	07659 550131
Yacht Solutions Ltd Portsmouth	023 9275 5155
Yarmouth Marine Service Yarmouth, IoW	01983 760521
Youngboats Faversham	01795 536176

BOOKS, CHARTS & PUBLISHERS

Adlard Coles Nautical London	020 7631 5600
Brown Son & Ferguson Ltd Glasgow	0141 429 1234
Cooke & Son Ltd, B Hull	01482 223454
Dubois Phillips & McCallum Ltd Liverpool	0151 236 2776
Imray, Laurie, Norie & Wilson Huntingdon	01480 462114
Kelvin Hughes Southampton	023 8063 4911
Lilley & Gillie Ltd, John	0191 257 2217
Marine Chart Services Wellingborough	01933 441629
Price & Co Ltd, WF Bristol	0117 929 2229
QPC Fareham	01329 287880
Stanford Charts Bristol	0117 929 9966
Stanford Charts London	020 7836 1321
Stanford Charts Manchester	0845 880 3730 / 0870 890 3730
Wiley Nautical Chichester	01243 779777

BOW THRUSTERS

ARS Anglian Diesels Ltd Wakefield	01924 332492
Buckler's Hard Boat Builders Ltd Beaulieu	01590 616214
JS Mouldings International Bursledon	023 8063 4400

BREAKDOWN

BJ Marine Ltd Bangor, Ireland	028 9127 1434
Seastart National	0800 885500

CHANDLERS

ABC Powermarine Beaumaris	01248 811413
Admiral Marine Supplies Bootle	01469 575909
Allgadgets.co.uk Exmouth	01395 227727
Alpine Room & Yacht Equipment Chelmsford	01245 223563
Aquatogs Cowes	01983 295071
Arbroath Fishermen's Association Arbroath	01241 873132
Ardfern Yacht Centre Ltd Argyll	01852 500247
Ardoran Marine Oban	01631 566123
Arthurs Chandlery Gosport	023 9252 6522

Arun Canvas and Rigging Ltd
Littlehampton 01903 732561

Aruncraft Chandlers
Littlehampton 01903 713327

ASAP Supplies – Equipment & Spares Worldwide
Beccles 0845 1300870

Auto Marine Southsea 02392 825601

Bayside Marine
Brixham 01803 856771

Bedwell and Co
Walton on the Naze 01255 675873

BJ Marine Ltd Bangor 028 9127 1434

Bluecastle Chandlers
Portland 01305 822298

Blue Water Marine Ltd
Pwllheli 01758 614600

Boatacs
Westcliffe on Sea 01702 475057

Boathouse, The
Penryn 01326 374177

Booley Galway +353 91 562869

Boston Marina 01205 364420

Bosun's Locker, The
Falmouth 01326 312212

Bosun's Locker, The
Ramsgate 01843 597158

Bosuns Locker, The
South Queensferry 0131 331 3875/4496

B+ St Peter Port 01481 726071

Bridger Marine, John
Exeter 01392 250970

Bristol Boat Ltd Bristol 01225 872032

Brixham Yacht Supplies Ltd
Brixham 01803 882290

Brunel Chandlery Ltd
Neyland 01646 601667

Buccaneer Ltd
Macduff 01261 835199

Bucklers Hard Boat Builders
Beaulieu 01590 616214

Burghead Boat Centre
Findhorn 01309 690099

Bussell & Co, WL
Weymouth 01305 785633

Buzzard Marine
Yarmouth 01983 760707

C & M Marine
Bridlington 01262 672212

Cabin Yacht Stores
Rochester 01634 718020

Caley Marina Inverness 01463 236539

Cambrian Boat Centre
Swansea 01792 655925

Cantell & Son Ltd
Newhaven 01273 514118

Captain Watts Plymouth 01752 927067

Carne (Sales) Ltd, David
Penryn 01326 374177

Carrickcraft
Malahide +353 1 845 5438

Caters Carrick Ltd
Carrickfergus 028 93351919

CH Marine (Cork) +353 21 4315700

CH Marine Skibbereen +353 28 23190

Charity & Taylor Ltd
Lowestoft 01502 581529

Chertsey Marine Ltd
Penton Hook Marina 01932 565195

Chicks Marine Ltd
Guernsey 01481 740771

Christchurch Boat Shop
Christchurch 01202 482751

Clancy Hardware
Kilrush +35 65 905 1085

Clapson & Son (Shipbuilders) Ltd South
Ferriby Marina 01652 635620

Clarke, Albert, Marine
Newtownards 028 9187 2325

Clyde Chandlers
Ardrossan 01294 607077

CMC Campbeltown 01586 551441

Coastal Marine Boatbuilders Ltd
(Dunbar) Eyemouth 01890 750328

Coates Marine Ltd
Whitby 01947 604486

Collins Marine
St Helier 01534 732415

Compass Marine
Lancing 01903 761773

Cosalt International Ltd
Aberdeen 01224 588327

Cosalt International Ltd
Southampton 023 8063 2824

Cotter, Kieran
Baltimore +353 28 20106

Cox Yacht Charter Ltd, Nick
Lymington 01590 673489

C Q Chandlers Ltd Poole 01202 682095

Crinan Boats Ltd
Lochgilphead 01546 830232

CTC Marine & Leisure
Middlesbrough 01642 372600

Dale Sailing Co Ltd
Milford Haven 01646 603110

Danson Marine
Sidcup 0208 304 5678

Dartmouth Chandlery
Dartmouth 01803 839292

Dartside Quay
Brixham 01803 845445

Dauntless Boatyard Ltd
Canvey Island 01268 793782

Davis's Yacht Chandler
Littlehampton 01903 722778

Denney & Son, EL
Redcar 01642 483507

Deva Marine Conwy 01492 572777

Dickie & Sons Ltd, AM
Bangor 01248 363400

Dickie & Sons Ltd, AM
Pwllheli 01758 701828

Dinghy Supplies Ltd/Sutton Marine Ltd
Sutton +353 1 832 2312

Diverse Yacht Services
Hamble 023 80453399

Dixon Chandlery, Peter
Exmouth 01395 273248

Doling & Son, GW
Barrow In Furness 01229 823708

Dovey Marine
Aberdovey 01654 767581

Down Marine Co Ltd
Belfast 028 9048 0247

Douglas Marine Preston 01772 812462

Dubois Phillips & McCallum Ltd
Liverpool 0151 236 2776

Duncan Ltd, JS Wick 01955 602689

Duncan Yacht Chandlers
Ely 01353 663095

East Anglian Sea School
Ipswich 01473 659992

Eccles Marine Co
Middlesbrough 01642 372600

Ely Boat Chandlers
Hayling Island 023 9246 1968

Emsworth Chandlery
Emsworth 01243 375500

Force 4 Chandlery
Stroud 0845 1300710

Exe Leisure Exeter 01392 879055

Express Marine Services
Chichester 01243 773788

Fairways Chandlery
Burnham-on-Crouch 01621 782659

Fairweather Marine
Fareham 01329 283500

Fal Chandlers
Falmouth Marina 01326 212411

Ferrypoint Boat Co
Youghal +353 24 94232

Findhorn Marina & Boatyard
Findhorn 01309 690099

Firmhelm Ltd P
wllheli 01758 612244

Fisherman's Mutual Asssociation (Eyemouth) Ltd
Eyemouth 01890 750373

Floetree Ltd (Loch Lomond Marina)
Balloch 01389 752069

Force 4 (Deacons)
Bursledon 023 8040 2182

Force 4 Chichester 01243 773788

Force 4 Chandlery
Mail order 0845 1300710

Force 4 Chandlery
Plymouth 01752 252489

Force 4 (Hamble Point)
Southampton 023 80455 058

Force 4 (Mercury)
Southampton 023 8045 4849

Force 4 (Port Hamble)
Southampton   023 8045 4858

Force 4 (Shamrock)
Southampton   023 8063 2725

Force 4 (Swanwick)
Swanwick   01489 881825

Freeport Marine
Jersey   01534 888100

French Marine Motors Ltd
Brightlingsea   01206 302133

Furneaux Riddall & Co Ltd
Portsmouth   023 9266 8621

Gael Force Glasgow   0141 941 1211

Gael Force Stornoway   01851 705540

Gallichan Marine Ltd
Jersey   01534 746387

Galway Maritime
Galway   +353 91 566568

GB Attfield & Company
Dursley   01453 547185

Gibbons Ship Chandlers Ltd
Sunderland   0191 567 2101

Goodwick Marine
Fishguard   01348 873955

Gorleston Marine Ltd
Great Yarmouth   01493 661883

GP Barnes Ltd
Shoreham   01273 591705/596680

Great Outdoors
Clarenbridge, Galway +353 87 2793821

Green Marine, Jimmy
Fore St Beer   01297 20744

Grimsby Rigging Services Ltd
Grimsby   01472 362758

Gunn Navigation Services, Thomas
Aberdeen   01224 595045

Hale Marine, Ron
Portsmouth   023 92732985

Harbour Marine Services Ltd (HMS)
Southwold   01502 724721

Hardware & Marine Supplies
Wexford   +353 53 29791

Hartlepool Marine Supplies
Hartlepool   01429 862932

Harwoods Yarmouth   01983 760258

Hawkins Marine Shipstores, John
Rochester   01634 840812

Hayles, Harold
Yarmouth   01983 760373

Herm Seaway Marine Ltd
St Peter Port   01481 726829

Highway Marine
Sandwich   01304 613925

Hoare Ltd, Bob, Poole   01202 736704

Hodges, T Coleraine   028 7035 6422

Iron Stores Marine
St Helier   01534 877755

Isles of Scilly Steamship Co
St Mary's   01720 422710

Jackson Yacht Services
Jersey   01534 743819

Jamison and Green Ltd
Belfast   028 9032 2444

Jeckells and Son Ltd
Lowestoft   01502 565007

JF Marine Chandlery Rhu 01436 820584

JNW Services Aberdeen 01224 594050

JNW Services Peterhead 01779 477346

JSB Ltd
Tarbert, Loch Fyne   01880 820180

Johnston Brothers
Mallaig   01687 462215

Johnstons Marine Stores
Lamlash   01770 600333

Kearon Ltd, George
Arklow   +353 402 32319

Kelvin Hughes Ltd
Southampton   023 80634911

Kildale Marine Hull   01482 227464

Kingfisher Marine
Weymouth   01305 766595

Kings Lock Chandlery
Middlewich   01606 737564

Kip Chandlery Inverkip
Greenock   01475 521485

Kirkcudbright Scallop Gear Ltd
Kirkcudbright   01557 330399

Kyle Chandlers Troon   01292 311880

Landon Marine, Reg
Truro   01872 272668

Largs Chandlers Largs   01475 686026

Lencraft Boats Ltd
Dungarvan   +353 58 68220

Lincoln Marina Lincoln   01522 526896

Looe Chandlery
West Looe   01503 264355

Lynch Ltd, PA Morpeth   01670 512291

Mackay Boatbuilders (Arbroath) Ltd
Aberdeen   01241 872879

Mackay Marine Services
Aberdeen   01224 575772

Mailspeed Marine
Crawley   01273837823

Mailspeed Marine
Essex Marina   01342 710618

Mailspeed Marine
Warrington   01342 710618

Mainbrayce Chandlers
Braye, Alderney   01481 822772

Manx Marine Ltd
Douglas   01624 674842

Marine & Leisure Europe Ltd
Plymouth   01752 268826

Marine MegaStore
Hamble   023 8045 4400

Marine MegaStore
Morpeth   01670 516151

Marine Parts Direct
Swords, Co Dublin   +353 1 807 5144

Marine Scene Bridgend   01656 671822

Marine Scene
Cardiff   029 2070 5780

Marine Services
Jersey   01534 626930

Marine Store Wyatts
West Mersea   01206 384745

Marine Store
Maldon   01621 854280

Marine Store
Titchmarsh Marina   01255 679028

Marine Store
Walton on the Naze   01255 679028

Marine Superstore Port Solent Chandlery
Portsmouth   023 9221 9843

MarineCo Torpoint   01752 816005

Maryport Harbour and Marina
Maryport   01900 814431

Matthews Ltd, D
Cork   +353 214 277633

McClean
Greenock   01475 728234

McCready Sailboats Ltd
Holywood   028 9042 1821

Moore, Kevin Cowes   01983 289699

Moore & Son, J
Mevagissey   01726 842964

Morgan & Sons Marine, LH
Brightlingsea   01206 302003

Mount Batten Boathouse
Plymouth   01752 482666

Murphy Marine Services
Cahersiveen   +353 66 9476365

Murphy, Nicholas
Dunmore East   +353 51 383259

MUT Wick   07753 350143

Mylor Chandlery & Rigging
Falmouth   01326 375482

Nautical World Bangor   028 91460330

New World Yacht Care
Helensburgh   01436 820586

Newhaven Chandlery
Newhaven   01273 612612

Nifpo Ardglass   028 4484 2144

Norfolk Marine
Great Yarmouth   01692 670272

Norfolk Marine Chandlery Shop
Norwich   01603 783150

Ocean Leisure Ltd
London   020 7930 5050

One Stop Chandlery
Maldon   01621 853558

O'Sullivans Marine Ltd
Tralee   +353 66 7129635

Partington Marine Ltd, William
Pwllheli   01758 612808

Pascall Atkey & Sons Ltd
Isle of Wight   01983 292381

Pennine Marine Ltd
Skipton   01756 792335

Penrhos Marine
Aberdovey   01654 767478

Penzance Marine Services
Penzance   01736 361081

Perry Marine, Rob
Axminster   01297 631314

Pepe Boatyard
Hayling Island   023 9246 1968

Performance Yachting & Chandlery
Plymouth   01752 565023

Pinnell & Bax
Northampton   01604 592808

Piplers of Poole Poole   01202 673056

Pirate's Cave, The
Rochester   01634 295233

Powersail Island Chandlers Ltd
East Cowes Marina   01983 299800

Preston Marine Services Ltd
Preston   01772 733595

Price & Co Ltd, WF
Bristol   0117 929 2229

PSM Ltd Alderney   07781 106635

Purcell Marine
Clarenbridge   +353 87 279 3821

Purple Sails & Marine
Walsall   08456 435510

Quay West Marine
Poole   01202 732445

Quayside Marine
Salcombe   01548 844300

R&A Fabrication
Kirkcudbright   01557 330399

Racecourse Yacht Basin (Windsor) Ltd
Windsor   01753 851501

Rat Rigs Water Sports
Cardiff   029 2062 1309

Reliance Marine Wirral   0151 625 5219

Rigmarine Padstow   01841 532657

Riversway Marine
Preston   0844 879 4901

RHP Marine Cowes   01983 290421

RNS Marine Northam   01237 474167

Sail Loft Bideford   01271 860001

Sailaway
St Anthony   01326 231357

Salcombe Boatstore
Salcombe   01548 843708

Salterns Chandlery
Poole   01202 701556

Shipmate Salcombe   01548 844555

Sandrock Marine Rye   01797 222679

Schull Watersports Centre
Schull   +353 28 28554

Sea & Shore Ship Chandler
Dundee   01382 450666

Sea Cruisers of Rye Rye 01797 222070

Sea Span Edinburgh   0131 552 2224

Sea Teach Ltd Emsworth 01243 375774

Seafare Tobermory   01688 302277

Seahog Boats Preston   01772 633016

Seamark-Nunn & Co
Felixstowe   01394 451000

Seaquest Marine Ltd
St Peter Port   01481 721773

Seaware Ltd Penryn   01326 377948

Seaway Marine Macduff 01261 832877

Sharp & Enright Dover   01304 206295

Shearwater Engineering Services Ltd
Dunoon   01369 706666

Shipshape Marine
King's Lynn   01553 764058

Ship Shape Ramsgate   01843 597000

Shorewater Sports
Chichester   01243 672315

Simpson Marine Ltd
Newhaven   01273 612612

Simpson Marine Ltd, WA
Dundee   01382 566670

Sketrick Marine Centre
Killinchy   028 9754 1400

Smith AM (Marine) Ltd
London   020 8529 6988

Solent Marine Chandlery Ltd
Gosport   023 9258 4622

South Coast Marine
Christchurch   01202 482695

South Pier Shipyard
St Helier   01534 711000

Southampton Yacht Services Ltd
Southampton   023 803 35266

Sparkes Chandlery
Hayling Island   02392 463572

S Roberts Marine Ltd
Liverpool   0151 707 8300

SSL Marine Eastbourne   01323 47900

Standard House Chandlery
Wells-next-the-Sea   01328 710593

Stornoway Fishermen's Co-op
Stornoway   01851 702563

Sunset Marine & Watersports
Sligo   +353 71 9162792

Sussex Marine
St Leonards on Sea   01424 425882

Sussex Yachts Ltd
Shoreham   01273 605482

Sussex Marine Centre
Shoreham   01273 454737

Sutton Marine (Dublin)
Sutton   +353 1 832 2312

SW Nets Newlyn   01736 360254

Tarbert Ltd, JSB Tarbert 01880 820180

TCS Chandlery
Essex Marina   01702 258094

TCS Chandlery Grays   01375 374702

TCS Chandlery Southend 01702 444423

Thulecraft Ltd Lerwick   01595 693192

Tony's Marine Services
Coleraine   07866 690436

Torbay Boating Centre
Paignton   01803 558760

Torquay Chandlers
Torquay   01803 211854

Trafalgar Yacht Services
Fareham   01329 822445

Trident UK N Shields   0191 490 1736

Union Chandlery Cork+353 21 4554334

Uphill Boat Services
Weston-Super-Mare   01934 418617

Upper Deck Marine and Outriggers
Fowey   01726 832287

V Ships (Isle of Man)
Douglas   01624 688886

V F Marine Rhu   01436 820584

Viking Marine Ltd
Dun Laoghaire   +353 1 280 6654

Walker Boat Sales
Deganwy   01492 555706

Waterfront Marine
Bangor   01248 352513

Wayne Maddox Marine
Margate   01843 297157

Western Marine
Dalkey   +353 1280 0321

Wetworks, The
Burnham-on-Crouch   01621 786413

Whitstable Marine
Whitstable   01227 274168

Williams Ltd, TJ
Cardiff   029 20 487676

Windjammer Marine
Milford Marina   01646 699070

Yacht & Boat Chandlery
Faversham   01795 531777

Yacht Chandlers Conwy   01492 572777

Yacht Equipment
Chelmsford   01245 223563

Yachtmail Ltd
Lymington   01590 672784

Yachtshop Conwy   01492 338505

Yachtshop Holyhead   01407 760031

You Boat Chandlery
Gosport   02392 522226

CHART AGENTS

Brown Son & Ferguson Ltd
Glasgow   0141 429 1234

Chattan Security Ltd
Edinburgh   0131 554 7527

Cooke & Son Ltd, B Hull 01482 223454

Dubois Phillips & McCallum Ltd
Liverpool   0151 236 2776

Imray Laurie Norie and Wilson Ltd
Huntingdon   01480 462114

Kelvin Hughes
Southampton   023 8063 4911

Lilley & Gillie Ltd, John
North Shields   0191 257 2217

Marine Chart Services
Wellingborough   01933 441629

Sea Chest Nautical Bookshop
Plymouth   01752 222012

Seath Instruments (1992) Ltd
Lowestoft   01502 573811

Small Craft Deliveries
Woodbridge   01394 382655

Smith (Marine) Ltd, AM
London   020 8529 6988

South Bank Marine Charts Ltd Grimsby
01472 361137

Stanford Charts Bristol 0117 929 9966

Stanford Charts
London   020 7836 1321

Todd Chart Agency Ltd
County Down   028 9146 6640

UK Hydrographics Office
Taunton   01823 337900

Warsash Nautical Bookshop
Warsash   01489 572384

CLOTHING

Absolute
Gorleston on Sea   01493 442259

Aquatogs Cowes   01983 245892

Crew Clothing
London   020 8875 2300

Crewsaver
Gosport   01329 820000

Douglas Gill
Nottingham   0115 9460844

Fat Face   fatface.com

Gul International Ltd
Bodmin   01208 262400

Guy Cotten UK Ltd
Liskeard   01579 347115

Harwoods
Yarmouth   01983 760258

Helly Hansen
Nottingham   0115 979 5997

Henri Lloyd
Manchester   0161 799 1212

Joules   0845 6066871

Mad Cowes Clothing Co
Cowes   0845 456 5158

Matthews Ltd, D
Cork   +353 214 277633

Mountain & Marine
Poynton   01625 859863

Musto Ltd Laindon   01268 491555

Purple Sails & Marine
Walsall   0845 6435510

Quba Sails
Lymington   01590 689362

Quba Sails Salcombe 01548 844599

Yacht Parts Plymouth 01752 252489

CODE OF PRACTICE EXAMINERS

Booth Marine Surveys, Graham
Birchington-on-Sea   01843 843793

Cannell & Associates, David M
Wivenhoe   01206 823337

COMPUTERS & SOFTWARE

Dolphin Maritime Software
White Cross   01524 841946

Forum Software Ltd
Nr Haverfordwest   01646 636363

Kelvin Hughes Ltd
Southampton   023 8063 4911

Memory-Map
Aldermaston   0844 8110950

PC Maritime Plymouth 01752 254205

DECK EQUIPMENT

Aries Van Gear Spares
Penryn   01326 377467

Ronstan Gosport   023 9252 5377

Harken UK Lymington 01590 689122

IMP Royston   01763 241300

Kearon Ltd George   +353 402 32319

Pro-Boat Ltd
Burnham-on-Crouch   01621 785455

Ryland, Kenneth
Stanton   01386 584270

Timage & Co Ltd
Braintree   01376 343087

DIESEL MARINE/ FUEL ADDITIVES

Corralls Poole   01202 674551

Cotters Marine & General Supplies
Baltimore   +353 28 20106

Expresslube
Henfield   01444 254115

Gorey Marine Fuel Supplies
Gorey   07797 742384

Hammond Motorboats
Dover   01304 206809

Iron Wharf Boatyard
Faversham   01795 536296

Lallow, Clare Cowes 01983 760707

Marine Support & Towage
Cowes   01983 200716/07860 297633

McNair, D
Campbeltown   01586 552020

Quayside Fuel
Weymouth   07747 182181

Rossiter Yachts
Christchurch   01202 483250

Sleeman & Hawken
Shaldon   01626 778266

DIVERS

Abco Divers Belfast 028 90610492

Andark Diving
Burseldon   01489 581755

Argonaut Marine
Aberdeen   01224 706526

Baltimore Diving and Watersports Centre West Cork +353 28 20300

C & C Marine Services
Largs   01475 687180

Cardiff Commercial Boat Operators Ltd
Cardiff   029 2037 7872

Clyde Diving Centre
Inverkip   01475 521281

Divetech UK King's Lynn 01485 572323

Diving & Marine Engineering
Barry   01446 721553

Donnelly, R
South Shields   07973 119455

DV Diving   028 9146 4671

Falmouth Divers Ltd
Penryn   01326 374736

Fathoms Ltd Wick   01955 605956

Felixarc Marine Ltd
Lowestoft   01502 509215

Grampian Diving Services
New Deer   01771 644206

Higgins, Noel   +353 872027650

Hudson, Dave
Trearddur Bay   01407 860628

Hunt, Kevin Tralee   +353 6671 25979

Kaymac Diving Services
Swansea   08431 165523

Keller, Hilary Buncrana +353 77 62146

Kilkee Diving Centre
Kilkee   +353 6590 56707

Leask Marine Kirkwall 01856 874725

Looe Divers Hannafore 01503 262727

MacDonald, D Nairn   01667 455661

Medway Diving Contractors Ltd
Gillingham   01634 851902

MMC Diving Services
Lake, Isle of Wight   07966 579965

Mojo Maritime
Penzance   01736 762771

Murray, Alex
Stornoway   01851 704978

New Dawn Dive Centre
Lymington   01590 675656

Northern Divers (Engineering) Ltd
Hull   01482 227276

Offshore Marine Services Ltd
Bembridge   01983 873125

Parkinson (Sinbad Marine Services), J
Killybegs   +353 73 31417

Port of London Authority
Gravesend   01474 560311

Purcell, D – Crouch Sailing School
Burnham 01621 784140/0585 33

Salvesen UK Ltd
Liverpool 0151 933 6038

Sea-Lift Diving Dover 01304 829956

Southern Cylinder Services
Fareham 01329 221125

Sub Aqua Services
North Ormesby 01642 230209

Teign Diving Centre
Teignmouth 01626 773965

Tuskar Rock Marine
Rosslare +353 53 33376

Underwater Services
Dyffryn Arbwy 01341 247702

Wilson Alan c/o Portrush Yacht Club
Portrush 028 2076 2225

Woolford, William
Bridlington 01262 671710

ELECTRICAL AND ELECTRONIC ENGINEERS

AAS Marine
Aberystwyth 01970 631090

Allworth Riverside Services, Adrian
Chelsea Harbour Marina
07831 574774

ASL Auto Services
Boston 01205 761560

Auto Marine Electrics
Holy Loch 01369 701555

Baker, Keith Brentford 07792 937790

Belson Design Ltd, Nick
Southampton 077 6835 1330

Biggs, John Weymouth Marina,
Weymouth 01305 778445

BJ Marine Ltd Bangor 028 9127 1434

BM Electrical
Kirkcudbright 07584 657192

Boat Electrics Troon 01292 315355

Buccaneer Ltd Macduff 01261 835199

Calibra Marine
Dartmouth 01803 833094

Campbell & McHardy Lossiemouth
Marina, Lossiemouth 01343 812137

CES Sandown Sparkes Marina,
Hayling Island 023 9246 6005

Colin Coady Marine
Malahide +353 87 265 6496

Contact Electrical
Arbroath 01241 874528

DDZ Marine Ardossan 01294 607077

Dean & Young
Bantry +353 275 0864

Dobson, Chris
Whitehaven 07986 086641

EC Leisure Craft
Essex Marina 01702 568482

Energy Solutions
Rochester 01634 290772

Enterprise Marine Electronic & Technical Services Ltd
Aberdeen 01224 593281

Eurotek Marine
Eastbourne 01323 479144

Evans, Lyndon
Brentford 07795 218704

Floetree Ltd (Loch Lomond Marina)
Balloch 01389 752069

Hall, Simon
Fleetwood 07850 738303

Hamble Marine
Hamble 02380 001088

HNP Engineers (Lerwick) Ltd
Lerwick 01595 692493

Jackson Yacht Services
Jersey 01534 743819

Jedynak, A Salcombe 01548 843321

Kippford Slipway Ltd
Dalbeattie 01556 620249

Lynch Ltd, PA Morpeth 01670 512291

Lynch, John Tralee +353 87 992 3102

Mackay Boatbuilders (Arbroath) Ltd
Aberdeen 01241 872879

Marine, AW Gosport 023 9250 1207

Marine Electrical Repair Service
London 020 7228 1336

Maxfield Electrical
Doncaster 07976 825349

MB Marine Troon 01292 311944

McMillan, Peter
Kilrush +35 86 8388617

MES Falmouth Marina,
Falmouth 01326 378497

Mount Batten Boathouse
Plymouth 01752 482666

New World Yacht Care
Rhu 01436 820586

Neyland Marine Services Ltd
Milford Haven 01646 600358

Powell, Martin Shamrock Quay,
Southampton 023 8033 2123

PR Systems
Plymouth 01752 936145

Radio & Electronic Services Beaucette Marina,
Guernsey 01481 728837

RHP Marine Cowes 01983 290421

Rothwell, Chris
Torquay Marina 01803 850960

Ruddy Marine
Galway +353 87 742 7439

Rutherford, Jeff Largs 01475 568026

SM International
Plymouth 01752 662129

Sussex Fishing Services
Rye 01797 223895

Tony's Marine Services
Coleraine 07866 690436

Ultra Marine Systems
Mayflower International Marina,
Plymouth 07989 941020

Upham, Roger
Chichester 01243 514511

Volspec Ipswich 01473 780144

Weyland Marine Services
Milford Haven 01646 600358

ELECTRONIC DEVICES AND EQUIPMENT

Anchorwatch UK
Edinburgh 0131 447 5057

Aquascan International Ltd
Newport 01633 841117

Atlantis Marine Power Ltd
Plymouth 01752 208810

Autosound Marine
Bradford 01274 688990

B&G Romsey 01794 518448

Brookes & Gatehouse
Romsey 01794 518448

Boat Electrics & Electronics Ltd
Troon 01292 315355

Cactus Navigation & Communication
London 020 7833 3435

CDL Aberdeen 01224 706655

Charity & Taylor Ltd
Lowestoft 01502 581529

Diverse Yacht Services
Hamble 023 8045 3399

Dyfed Electronics Ltd
Milford Haven 01646 694572

Echopilot Marine Electronics Ltd
Ringwood 01425 476211

Enterprise Marine
Aberdeen 01224 593281

Euronav Ltd
Portsmouth 023 9298 8806

Exposure Lights
Pulborough 01798 83930

Furuno UK
Fraserburgh 01346 518300
Havant 023 9244 1000

Garmin (Europe) Ltd
Romsey 0870 850 1242

Golden Arrow Marine Ltd
Southampton 023 8071 0371

Greenham Regis Marine Electronics
Lymington 01590 671144

Greenham Regis Marine Electronics
Poole 01202 676363

Greenham Regis Marine Electronics
Southampton — 023 8063 6555

ICS Electronics Arundel — 01903 731101

JG Technologies Ltd
Weymouth — 0845 458 9616

KM Electronics
Lowestoft — 01502 569079

Kongsberg Simrad Ltd
Aberdeen — 01224 226500

Kongsberg Simrad Ltd
Wick — 01955 603606

Landau UK Ltd
Hamble — 02380 454040

Enterprise Marine
Aberdeen — 01224 593281

Marathon Leisure
Hayling Island — 023 9263 7711

Marine Instruments
Falmouth — 01326 375483

MB Marine Troon — 01292 311944

Microcustom Ltd
Ipswich — 01473 215777

Nasa Marine Instruments
Stevenage — 01438 354033

Navionics UK Plymouth — 01752 204735

Ocean Leisure Ltd
London — 020 7930 5050

Plymouth Marine Electronics
Plymouth — 01752 227711

Radio & Electronic Services Ltd
St Peter Port — 01481 728837

Raymarine Ltd
Portsmouth — 02392 714700

Redfish Car Company
Stockton-on-Tees — 01642 633638

Robertson, MK Oban — 01631 563836

Satcom Distribution Ltd
Salisbury — 01722 410800

Seaquest Marine Ltd
Guernsey — 01481 721773

Seatronics Aberdeen — 01224 853100

Selex Communications
Aberdeen — 01224 890316

Selex Communications
Bristol — 0117 931 3550

Selex Communications
Brixham — 01803 882716

Selex Communications
Fraserburgh — 01346 518187

Selex Communications
Glasgow — 0141 882 6909

Selex Communications
Hull — 01482 326144

Selex Communications
Kilkeel — 028 4176 9009

Selex Communications
Liverpool — 01268 823400

Selex Communications
Lowestoft — 01502 572365

Selex Communications
Newcastle upon Tyne — 0191 265 0374

Selex Communications
Newlyn — 01736 361320

Selex Communications
Penryn — 01326 378031

Selex Communications
Plymouth — 01752 222878

Selex Communications
Rosyth — 01383 419606

Selex Communications
Southampton — 023 8051 1868

Silva Ltd Livingston — 01506 419555

SM International
Plymouth — 01752 662129

Sperry Marine Ltd
Peterhead — 01779 473475

Stenmar Ltd Aberdeen — 01224 827288

Transas Nautic
Portsmouth — 023 9267 4016

Veripos Precise Navigation
Aberdeen — 01224 965800

Wema (UK) Honiton — 01404 881810

Wilson & Co Ltd, DB
Glasgow — 0141 647 0161

Woodsons of Aberdeen Ltd
Aberdeen — 01224 722884

ENGINES AND ACCESSORIES

Airylea Motors
Aberdeen — 01224 872891

Amble Boat Co Ltd
Amble — 01665 710267

Anchor Marine Products
Benfleet — 01268 566666

Aquafac Ltd Luton — 01582 568700

Barrus Ltd, EP Bicester — 01869 363636

British Polar Engines Ltd
Glasgow — 0141 445 2455

Bukh Diesel UK Ltd
Poole — 01202 668840

CJ Marine Mechanical
Troon — 01292 313400

Cleghorn Waring Ltd
Letchworth — 01462 480380

Cook's Diesel Service Ltd
Faversham — 01795 538553

Southern Shipwright (SSL)
Brighton — 01273 601779

Southern Shipwright (SSL)
Eastbourne — 01323 479000

Fender-Fix
Maidstone — 01622 751518

Fettes & Rankine Engineering
Aberdeen — 01224 573343

Fleetwood & Sons Ltd, Henry
Lossiemouth — 01343 813015

Gorleston Marine Ltd
Great Yarmouth — 01493 661883

Halyard Salisbury — 01722 710922

Interseals (Guernsey) Ltd
Guernsey — 01481 246364

Kelpie Boats
Pembroke Dock — 01646 683661

Keypart Watford — 01923 330570

Lancing Marine
Brighton — 01273 410025

Lencraft Boats Ltd
Dungarvan — +353 58 68220

Lewmar Ltd Havant — 023 9247 1841

Liverpool Power Boats
Bootle — 0151 944 1163

Lynch Ltd, PA
Morpeth — 01670 512291

MacDonald & Co Ltd, JN
Glasgow — 0141 810 3400

Mariners Weigh
Shaldon — 01626 873698

MMS Ardrossan — 01294 604831

Mooring Mate Ltd
Bournemouth — 01202 421199

Murphy Marine Services
Cahersiveen — +353 66 9476365

Newens Marine, Chas
Putney — 020 8788 4587

Ocean Safety
Southampton — 023 8072 0800

RK Marine Ltd
Hamble — 01489 583585
Swanwick — 01489 583572

Sillette Sonic Ltd
Sutton — 020 8337 7543

Sowester Simpson-Lawrence Ltd
Poole — 01202 667700

Timage & Co Ltd
Braintree — 01376 343087

Thorne Boat Services
Thorne — 01405 814197

Vetus Den Ouden Ltd
Totton — 023 8045 4507

Western Marine
Dublin — +353 1 280 0321

Whitstable Marine
Whitstable — 01227 262525

Yates Marine, Martin
Galgate — 01524 751750

Ynys Marine
Cardigan — 01239 613179

FOUL-WEATHER GEAR

Aquatogs Cowes — 01983 295071

Crew Clothing London — 020 8875 2300

Century Finchampstead	0118 9731616
Crewsaver Gosport	01329 820000
Douglas Gill Nottingham	0115 946 0844
FBI Leeds	0113 270 7000
Gul International Ltd Bodmin	01208 262400
Helly Hansen Nottingham	0115 979 5997
Henri Lloyd Manchester	0161 799 1212
Musto Ltd Laindon	01268 491555
Pro Rainer Windsor	07752 903882

GENERAL MARINE EQUIPMENT & SPARES

Ampair Ringwood	01425 480780
Aries Vane Gear Spares Penryn	01326 377467
Arthurs Chandlery, R Gosport	023 9252 6522
Atlantis Marine Power Ltd Plymouth	01752 208810
Barden UK Ltd Fareham	01489 570770
Calibra Marine International Ltd Southampton	08702 400358
CH Marine (Cork)	+353 21 4315700
Chris Hornsey (Chandlery) Ltd Southsea	023 9273 4728
Compass Marine (Dartmouth) Dartmouth	01803 835915
Cox Yacht Charter Ltd, Nick Lymington	01590 673489
CTC Marine & Leisure Middlesbrough	01642 372600
Exposure Lights Pulborough	01798 83930
Frederiksen Boat Fittings (UK) Ltd Gosport	023 9252 5377
Furneaux Riddall & Co Ltd Portsmouth	023 9266 8621
Hardware & Marine Supplies Co Wexford	+353 (53) 29791
Index Marine Bournemouth	01202 470149
Kearon Ltd, George Arklow	+353 402 32319
Marathon Leisure Hayling Island	023 9263 7711
Pro-Boat Ltd Burnham-on-Crouch	01621 785455
Pump International Ltd Cornwall	01209 831937
Quay West Marine Poole	01202 732445
Rogers, Angie Bristol	0117 973 8276
Ryland, Kenneth Stanton	01386 584270

Tiflex Liskeard	01579 320808
Vetus Boating Equipment Southampton	02380 454507
Whitstable Marine Whitstable	01227 262525
Yacht Parts Plymouth	01752 252489

HARBOUR MASTERS

Aberaeron	01545 571645
Aberdeen	01224 597000
Aberdovey	01654 767626
Aberystwyth	01970 611433
Alderney & Burhou	01481 822620
Amble	01665 710306
Anstruther (remote)	03451 555555 Extn 461541
Appledore	01237 474569
Arbroath	01241 872166
Ardglass	028 4484 1291
Ardrossan Control Tower	01294 463972
Arinagour Piermaster	01879 230347
Arklow	+353 402 32466
Baltimore	+353 28 22145
Banff	01261 815544
Bantry Bay	+353 27 53277
Barmouth	01341 280671
Barry	01446 732665
Beaucette	01481 245000
Beaulieu River	01590 616200
Belfast Lough	028 90 553012
Belfast River Manager	028 90 328507
Bembridge	01983 872828
Berwick-upon-Tweed	07931 730165
Bideford	01237 346131
Blyth (Port Ops)	01670 357025
Boston	01205 362328
Bridlington	01262 670148/9
Bridport	01308 423222
Brighton	01273 819919
Bristol	0117 926 4797
Brixham	01803 853321
Buckie	01542 831700
Bude	01288 353111
Burghead	01542 831700
Burnham-on-Crouch	01621 783602
Burnham-on-Sea	0300 303 7799
Burtonport	+353 075 42155
Caernarfon	01286 672118

Caernarfon	07786 730865
Caledonian Canal Off. (Inverness)	01463 725500
Camber Berthing Offices – Portsmouth	023 92297395
Campbeltown	01586 552552 07825 732862
Canna	01687 310733
Cardiff	029 20400500
Carnlough Harbour	07703 606763
Castletown Bay	01624 823549
Charlestown	01726 67526
Chichester Harbour	01243 512301
Clovelly	01273 431549 07975 501380
Conwy	01492 596253
Cork	+353 21 4273125
Corpach Canal Sea Lock	01397 772249
Courtmacsherry	+353 8673 94299 +353 23 46311/46600
Coverack	01326 380679
Cowes	01983 293952
Crail	01333 450820
Craobh Haven	01852 502222
Crinan Canal Office	01546 603210
Cromarty Firth	01381 600479
Cromarty Harbour	01381 600493
Crookhaven	+353 28 35319
Cullen	01542 831700
Dingle	+353 66 9151629
Douglas	01624 686628
Dover	01304 240400 Ext 4520
Dublin	+353 1 874871
Dun Laoghaire	+353 1 280 1130/8074
Dunbar	07958 754858
Dundee	01382 224121
East Loch Tarbert	01859 502444
Eastbourne	01323 470099
Eigg Harbour	01687 482428
Elie	01333 330051
Estuary Control - Dumbarton	01389 726211
Exe	01392 274306
Exeter	01392 265791
Exmouth	01392 223265 07864 958658
Eyemouth	01890 750223 07885 742505

Felixstowe	07803 476621	Lough Foyle	028 7186 0555	Portsmouth Harbour Control	
Findochty	01542 831700	Lowestoft	01502 572286		023 92723694
Fisherrow	0131 665 5900	Lyme Regis	01297 442137	Portsmouth Harbour	023 92723124
Fishguard (Lower Harbour)		Lymington	01590 672014	Preston	01772 726711
	01348 874726	Lyness	01856 791387	Pwllheli	01758 701219
Fishguard	01348 404425	Macduff	01261 832236	Queenborough	01795 662051
Fleetwood	01253 872323	Maryport	01900 814431	Queens Gareloch/Rhu	01436 674321
Flotta	01856 701411	Menai Strait	01248 712312	Ramsey	01624 812245
Folkestone	01303 715354	Methil	01333 462725	Ramsgate	01843 572100
Fowey	01726 832471/2.	Mevagissey	01726 843305	River Bann & Coleraine	028 7034 2012
Fraserburgh	01346 515858	Milford Haven	01646 696100	River Blackwater	01621 856487
Galway Bay	+353 91 561874	Minehead (Mon-Fri)	01643 702566	River Colne (Brightlingsea)	01206 302200
Garlieston	01988 600274	Montrose	01674 672302	River Dart	01803 832337
Glasson Dock	07910 315606	Mousehole	01736 731511	River Deben	01473 736257
Gorey Port Control	01534 447788	Mullion Cove	01326 240222	River Exe Dockmaster	01392 274306
Gourdon	01569 762741	Nairn Harbour Office	01667 452453	River Humber	01482 327171
Great Yarmouth	01493 335501	Newhaven Harbour Admin		River Medway	01795 596593
Grimsby Dockmaster	01472 359181		01273 612872/612926	River Orwell	01473 231010
Groomsport Bay	028 91 278040	Newlyn	01736 731897	River Roach	01621 783602
Hamble River	01489 576387	Newquay	07737 387217	River Stour	01255 243000
Hayle	07500 993867	Newport Harbour Office		River Tyne/N Shields	0191 257 2080
Helford River	01326 732544		01983 823885	River Yealm	01752 872533
Helmsdale	01431 821692	North Berwick	00776 467373	Rivers Alde & Ore	07528 092635
Holy Island	01289 389217	Oban	01631 562892	Rosslare Europort	+353 53 915 7921
Holyhead	01407 763071	Padstow	01841 532239	Rothesay	01700 503842
Hopeman	01542 831700	Peel	01624 842338		07799 724225
Howth	+353 1 832 2252	Penrhyn Bangor	01248 352525	Ryde	01983 613903
Ilfracombe	01271 862108	Penzance	01736 366113	Salcombe	01548 843791
Inverness	01463 715715	Peterhead	01779 483630	Sark	01481 832323
Ipswich	01473 211771	Pierowall	01857 677216	Scalloway	01595 880574
Irvine	01294 487286	Pittenweem	01333 312591	Schull	+353 27 28136
Johnshaven	01561 362262	Plockton	01599 534589	Scarborough	01723 373530
Kettletoft Bay	01857 600227	Polperro	01503 272634	Scrabster	01847 892779
Killybegs	+353 73 31032		07966 528045	Seaham	07786 565205
Kilmore Quay	+353 53 912 9955	Poole	01202 440233	Sharpness, Gloucester Harbour Trustees	01453 811913
Kinlochbervie	01971 521235	Port Ellen Harbour Association		Shoreham	01273 598100
	07901 514350		01496 302458	Silloth	016973 31358
Kinsale	+353 21 4772503	Port Isaac	01208 880321	Sligo	+353 91 53819
Kirkcudbright	01557 331135		07855 429422	Southampton	023 8033 9733
Kirkwall	01856 872292	Port St Mary	01624 833205	Southend-on-Sea	01702 611889
Langstone Harbour	023 9246 3419	Porth Dinllaen	01758 720276	Southwold	01502 724712
Larne	02828 872100	Porthleven	01326 574207	St Helier	01534 447788
Lerwick	01595 692991	Porthmadog	01766 512927	St Ives	07793 515460
Littlehampton	01903 721215	Portknockie	01542 831700	St Margaret's Hope	01856 831454
Liverpool	0151 949 6134/5	Portland	01305 824044	St Mary's	01720 422768
Loch Gairloch	01445 712140	Portpatrick	01776 810355	St Michael's Mount	07870 400282
Loch Inver	01571 844267	Portree	01478 612926	St Monans (part-time)	07930 869538
	07958 734610	Portrush	028 70822307		
Looe	01503 262839	Portsmouth Harbour Commercial Docks	023 92297395		
	07918 728955				
Lossiemouth (Marina)	07969 213513				
	07969 213521				

St Peter Port	01481 720229
Stonehaven	01569 762741
Stornoway	01851 702688
Strangford Lough	028 44 881637
Stranraer	07734 073421
Stromness	07810 465825
Stronsay	01857 616317
Sullom Voe	01806 242551
Sunderland	0191 567 2626
Swale	01795 561234
Swansea	01792 653787
Tayport Hbr Trust	01382 553799
Tees & Hartlepool Port Authority	01429 277205
Teignmouth	01626 773165
Tenby	01834 842717
Thames Estuary	01474 562200
Tobermory Moorings Officer	07917 832497
Torquay	01803 292429
Troon	01292 281687
Truro	01872 272130
Ullapool	01854 612091
Waldringfield	01394 736291
Walton-on-the-Naze	01255 851899
Watchet	01643 703704
Waterford	+353 51 899801
Wells-next-the-Sea	01328 711646
West Bay (Bridport)	01308 423222
	07870 240636
Wexford	+353 53 912 2039
Weymouth	01305 206423
Whitby	01947 602354
Whitehaven	01946 692435
Whitehills	01261 861291
Whitstable	01227 274086
Wick	01955 602030
Wicklow	+353 404 67455
Workington	01900 602301
Yarmouth	01983 760321
Youghal	+353 24 92626
	+353 86 780 0878

HARBOURS

Bristol Harbour	0117 903 1484
Clyde Marina, Ardrossan	01294 607077
Jersey Hbrs St Helier	01534 885588
Maryport Harbour and Marina	
Maryport	01900 818447/4431

Peterhead Bay Authority
Peterhead 01779 474020

Sark Moorings – Channel Islands
01481 832260

INSURANCE/FINANCE

Admiral Marine Ltd
Salisbury 01722 416106

Bishop Skinner Boat Insurance
London 0800 7838057

Bluefin
London 0800 074 5200

Castlemain Ltd
St Peter Port 01481 721319

Craven Hodgson Associates
Leeds 0113 243 8443

Giles Insurance Brokers
Irvine 01294 315481

GJW Direct Liverpool 0151 473 8000

Haven Knox-Johnston
West Malling 01732 223600

Lombard
Southampton 023 8024 2171

Mercia Marine
Malvern 01684 564457

Nautical Insurance Services Ltd
Leigh-on-Sea 01702 470811

Navigators & General
Brighton 01273 863400

Pantaenius UK Ltd
Plymouth 01752 223656

Porthcawl Insurance Consultants
Porthcawl 01656 784866

Saga Boat Insurance
Folkestone 01303 771135

St Margarets Insurances
London 020 8778 6161

Towergate Insurance
Shrewsbury 0344 892 1987

LIFERAFTS & INFLATABLES

Adec Marine Ltd
Croydon 020 8686 9717

Avon Inflatables
Llanelli 01554 882000

Cosalt International Ltd
Aberdeen 01224 826662

Glaslyn Marine Supplies Ltd
Porthmadog 01766 513545

Hale Marine, Ron
Portsmouth 023 9273 2985

Guernsey Yacht Club
St Peter Port 01481 722838

IBS Boats South Woodham Ferrers
01245 323211/425551

KTS Seasafety
Kilkeel 028 918 28405

Nationwide Marine Hire
Warrington 01925 245788

Norwest Marine Ltd
Liverpool 0151 207 2860

Ocean Safety
Southampton 023 8072 0800

Polymarine Ltd
Conwy 01492 583322

Premium Liferaft Services
Burnham-on-Crouch 0800 243673

Ribeye Dartmouth 01803 832060

South Eastern Marine Services Ltd
Basildon 01268 534427

Suffolk Marine Safety
Ipswich 01473 833010

Whitstable Marine
Whitstable 01227 262525

MARINAS

Aberystwyth Marina	01970 611422
Amble Marina	01665 712168
Arbroath Harbour	01241 872166
Ardfern Yacht Centre Ltd	01852 500247
Ardglass Marina	028 44842332
Arklow Marina	+353 87 258 8078
Ballycastle Marina	028 2076 8525
Banff Harbour Marina	01261 832236
Bangor Marina	028 91 453297
Bantry Harbour Marina	+353 275 3277
Beaucette Marina	01481 245000
Bembridge Harbour Authority	01983 872828
Berthon Lymington Marina	01590 647405
Birdham Pool Marina	01243 512310
Blackwater Marina	01621 740264
Boston Gateway Marina	07480 525230
Bradwell Marina	01621 776235
Bray Marina	01628 623654
Brentford Dock Marina	020 8232 8941
Bridgemarsh Marine	01621 740414
Brighton Marina	01273 819919
Bristol Marina	0117 921 3198
Brixham Marina	01803 882929
Bucklers Hard Marina	01590 616200
Burnham Yacht Harbour Marina Ltd	01621 782150
Cahersiveen Marina	+353 66 947 2777
Caley Marina	01463 236539
Campbeltown Marina	07798 524821
Cardiff Marina	02920 396078
Carlingford Marina	+353 42 9373072
Carrickfergus Marina	028 9336 6666
Castlepark Marina	+353 21 477 4959
Chatham Maritime Marina	01634 899200

Marina	Phone
Chelsea Harbour Marina	07770 542783
Chichester Marina	01243 512731
Clyde Marina Ltd	01294 607077
Cobbs Quay Marina	01202 674299
Coleraine Harbour Town Centre Marina	028 7034 2012
Coleraine Marina	028 703 44768
Conwy Marina	01492 593000
Cork Harbour Marina	+353 87 3669009
Cowes Harbour Shepards Marina	01983 297821
Cowes Yacht Haven	01983 299975
Craobh Marina	01852 500222
Crinan Boatyard	01546 830232
Crosshaven Boatyard Marina	+353 21 483 1161
Dart Marina Yacht Harbour	01803 837161
Darthaven Marina	01803 752242
Dartside Quay	01803 845445
Deacons Marina & Boatyard	02380 402253
Deganwy Marina	01492 576888
Dingle Marina	+353 87 925 4115
Douglas Marina	01624 686628
Dover Marina	01304 241663
Dun Laoghaire Marina	+353 1 202 0040
Dunstaffnage Marina Ltd	01631 566555
East Cowes Marina	01983 293983
Emsworth Yacht Harbour	01243 377727
Essex Marina	01702 258531
Falmouth Haven Marina	01326 310991
Falmouth Marina	01326 316620
Fambridge Yacht Haven	01621 740370
Fambridge Yacht Station	01621 742911
Fenit Harbour & Marina	+353 66 7136231
Fleetwood Haven Marina	01253 879062
Fox's Marina & Boatyard	01473 689111
Foyle Port Marina	02871 860555
Galway Harbour Marina	+353 91 561874
Gillingham Marina	01634 280022
Glasson Waterside & Marina	01524 751491
Gosport Marina	023 9252 4811
Hafan Pwllheli	01758 701219
Hamble Point Marina	02380 452464
Harbour of Rye	01797 225225
Hartlepool Marina	01429 865744
Haslar Marina	023 9260 1201
Heybridge Basin	07712 079764
Holy Loch Marina	01369 701800
Holyhead Marina	01407 764242
Howth Marina	+353 1839 2777
Hull Waterside & Marina	01482 609960
Humber Cruising Association	01472 268424
Hythe Marina Village	02380 207073
Inverness Marina	01463 220501
Ipswich Haven Marina	01473 236644
Island Harbour Marina	01983 539994
James Watt Dock Marina	01475 729838
Kemps Quay	023 8063 2323
Kerrera Marina	01631 565333
Kilmore Quay Marina	+353 53 91 29955
Kilrush Marina	+353 65 9052072
Kinsale Yacht Club Marina	+353 876 787377
Kip Marina	01475 521485
Kirkcudbright Marina	01557 331135
Kirkwall Marina	07810 465835
Lady Bee Marina	01273 593801
Lake Yard Marina	01202 674531
Largs Yacht Haven	01475 675333
Lawrence Cove Marina	+353 27 75044
Limehouse Waterside & Marina	020 7308 9930
Littlehampton Marina	01903 713553
Liverpool Marina Bar & Grill	0151 707 6777
Lossiemouth Marina	01343 813066
Lowestoft Cruising Club	07810 522515
Lowestoft Haven Marina	01502 580300
Lymington Harbour Commission	01590 672014
Lymington Town Quay	01590 672014
Lymington Yacht Haven	01590 677071
Malahide Marina	+353 1 845 4129
Mallaig Marina	01687 462406
Maryport Harbour and Marina Ltd	01900 814431
Mayflower International Marina	01752 556633
Melfort Pier & Harbour	01852 200333
Mercury Yacht Harbour and Holiday Park	023 8045 5994
Milford Marina	01646 696312
Mylor Yacht Harbour	01326 372121
Nairn Marina	01667 456008
Neptune Marina Ltd	01473 215204
New Ross Marina	+353 86 3889652
Newhaven Marina	01273 513881
Neyland Yacht Haven	01646 601601
Northney Marina	02392 466321
Noss on Dart Marina	01803 839087
Ocean Village Marina	023 8022 9385
Padstow Harbour	01841 532239
Parkstone YC Haven	01202 738824
Peel Marina	01624 842338
Penarth Marina	02920 705021
Penton Hook	01932 568681
Peterhead Bay Marina	01779 477868
Plymouth Yacht Haven	01752 404231
Poole Quay Boat Haven	01202 649488
Port Bannatyne Marina	01700 503116
Port Edgar Marina	0131 331 3330
Port Ellen Marina	07464 151200
Port Hamble Marina	023 8045 2741
Port of Poole Marina	01202 649488
Port Pendennis Marina	01326 211211
Port Solent Marina	02392 210765
Port Werburgh	01634 252107
Portaferry Marina	07703 209780
Portavadie Marina	01700 811075
Portishead Marina	01275 841941
Portland Marina	01305 866190
Preston Marina	01772 733595
Queen Anne's Battery	01752 671142
Rhu Marina	01436 820238
Ridge Wharf Yacht Centre	01929 552650
Rossaveel Marina	+353 86 41813422
Royal Clarence Marina	02392 523523
Royal Cork Yacht Club Marina	+353 21 483 1023
Royal Harbour Marina, Ramsgate	01843 572100
Royal Harwich Yacht Club Marina	01473 780319
Royal Norfolk and Suffolk Yacht Club	01502 566726
Royal Northumberland Yacht Club	01670 353636
Royal Quays Marina	0191 272 8282
Ryde Leisure Harbour	01983 613879
Salterns Marina Ltd	01202 709971
Salve Engineering Marina	+353 21 483 1145
Sandpoint Marina (Dumbarton)	01389 762396
Saxon Wharf	023 8033 9490
Seaport Marina	01463 725500

Seaton's Marina   028 703 832086
Shamrock Quay   023 8022 9461
Shotley Marina   01473 788982
South Dock Marina   020 7252 2244
South Ferriby Marina   01652 635620
Southsea Marina   02392 822719
Sovereign Harbour Marina
    01323 470099
Sparkes Marina   023 92463572
St Helier Marina   01534 447708
St Katharine Docks Marina
    0207 264 5312
St Peter Port Marinas   01481 720229
St Peter's Marina   0191 265 4472
Stornoway Marina   01851 702688
Stranraer Marina   01776 706565
Stromness Marina   07483 366655
Suffolk Yacht Harbour Ltd
    01473 659240
Sunderland Marina   0191 514 4721
Sutton Harbour   01752 204702
Swansea Marina   01792 470310
Swanwick Marina   01489 884081
Tarbert Harbour   01880 820344
Titchmarsh Marina   01255 672185
Tobermory Harbour Authority
    01688 302876
Tollesbury Marina   01621 869202
Torquay Marina   01803 200210
Town Quay Marina   02380 234397
Troon Yacht Haven   01292 315553
Universal Marina   01489 574272
Victoria Marina   01481 725987
Walton & Frinton Yacht Trust Limited
    01255 675873
Waterford City Marina
    +353 87 2384944
Weymouth Harbour   01305 838423
Weymouth Marina   01305 767576
Whitby Marina   01947 602354
Whitehaven Marina   01946 692435
Whitehills Marina   01261 861291
Wick Marina   01955 602030
Wicor Marine Yacht Haven
    01329 237112
Windsor Marina   01753 853911
Wisbech Yacht Harbour   01945 588059
Woolverstone Marina and Lodge Park
    01473 780206
Yarmouth Harbour   01983 760321

MARINE ENGINEERS

AAS Marine
Aberystwyth   01970 631090

Allerton Engineering
Lowestoft   01502 537870
APAS Engineering Ltd
Southampton   023 8063 2558
Ardmair Boat Centre
Ullapool   01854 612054
Arisaig Marine
Inverness-shire   01687 450224
Arun Craft
Littlehampton   01903 723667
ASL Auto Services
Boston   01205 761560
Atlantis Marine Power Ltd
Plymouth   01752 208810
Attrill & Sons, H
Bembridge   01983 872319
Auto & Marine Services
Botley   07836 507000
Auto Marine
Southsea   023 9282 5601
Baker, Keith
Brentford   07792 937790
BJ Marine Ltd Bangor   028 9127 1434
Brevik Marine Service Ltd
Stornoway   07876 721154
Bristol Boat Ltd
Bristol   01225 872032
Browne, Jimmy
Tralee   +353 87 262 7158
Buccaneer Ltd
Macduff   01261 835199
Buzzard Marine Engineering
Yarmouth   01983 760707
C & B Marine Ltd
Chichester Marina   01243 511273
Caddy, Simon
Falmouth Marina
Falmouth   01326 372682
Caledonian Marine
Rhu Marina   01436 821184
Cardigan Outboards
Cardigan   01239 613966
Channel Islands Marine Ltd
Guernsey   01481 716880
Channel Islands Marine Ltd
Jersey   01534 767595
Cook's Diesel Service Ltd
Faversham   01795 538553
Cragie Engineering
Kirkwall   01856 874680
Crinan Boatyard Ltd
Crinan   01546 830232
Cronin Commercials
Dunmanway   +353 23 8845498

Cutler Marine Engineering, John
Emsworth   01243 375014
Dale Sailing Co Ltd
Milford Haven   01646 603110
Davis Marine Services
Ramsgate   01843 586172
Denney & Son, EL
Redcar   01642 483507
DH Marine (Shetland) Ltd
Shetland   01595 690618
Dobson, Chris
Whitehaven   07986 086641
Emark Marine Ltd
Emsworth   01243 375383
Evans, Lyndon
Brentford   07795 218704
Evans Marine Engineering, Tony
Pwllheli   01758 703070
Ferrypoint Boat Co
Youghal   +353 24 94232
Fettes & Rankine Engineering
Aberdeen   01224 573343
Floetree Ltd
Loch Lomond Marina
Balloch   01389 752069
Fowey Harbour Marine Engineers
Fowey   01726 832806
Fox Marine Services Ltd
Jersey   01534 721312
Fleetwood Marine
Fleetwood   07508 807290
Freeport Marine Jersey   01534 888100
French Marine Motors Ltd
Colchester   01206 302133
French Marine Motors Ltd
Titchmarsh Marina   01255 850303
GH Douglas Marine Services
Fleetwood Harbour Village Marina,
Fleetwood   01253 877200
Golden Arrow Marine
Southampton   023 8071 0371
Goodchild Marine Services
Great Yarmouth   01493 782301
Goodwick Marine
Fishguard   01348 873955
Gordon Diesel Services
Stornoway   01851 702122
Gosport Marina   023 9252 4811
Griffins Garage Dingle Marina,
Co Kerry   +353 66 91 51178
Hale Marine, Ron
Portsmouth   023 9273 2985
Hamilton Brothers
Campbeltown   01586 553031

Hamnavoe Engineering
Stromness   01856 850576

Harbour Engineering
Itchenor   01243 513454

Hartlepool Marine Engineering
Hartlepool   01429 867883

Hayles, Harold Yarmouth 01983 760373

Herm Seaway Marine Ltd
St Peter Port   01481 726829

HNP Engineers (Lerwick Ltd)
Lerwick   01595 692493

Hodges, T Coleraine   028 7035 6422

Home Marine Emsworth Yacht
Harbour, Emsworth   01243 374125

Hook Marine Ltd
Troon   01292 679500

Humphrey, Chris
Teignmouth   01626 772324

Instow Marine Services
Bideford   01271 861081

Jones (Boatbuilders), David
Chester   01244 390363

Keating Marine Engineering Ltd, Bill
Jersey   01534 733977

Kingston Marine Services
Cowes   01983 299385

Kippford Slipway Ltd
Dalbeattie   01556 620249

L&A Marine
Campbeltown   01586 554479

Lansdale Pannell Marine
Chichester   01243 550042

Lencraft Boats Ltd
Dungarvan   +353 58 68220

Llyn Marine Services
Pwllheli   01758 612606

Lynx Engineering
St Helens, Isle of Wight   01983 873711

M&G Marine Services
Mayflower International Marina,
Plymouth   01752 563345

MacDonald & Co Ltd, JN
Glasgow   0141 810 3400

Mackay Marine Services
Aberdeen   01224 575772

Macmillan Engineering Ltd
Goat Is, Stornoway   001851 704411

Mainbrayce Marine
Alderney   01481 722772

Malakoff and Moore
Lerwick   01595 695544

Marine Blast
Holy Loch   01369 705394

Mallaig Boat Building and Engineering
Mallaig   01687 462304

Marindus Engineering
Kilmore Quay   +353 53 29794

Marine Engineering Looe
Brixham   01803 844777

Marine Engineering Looe
    01503 263009

Marine Engineering Services
Port Dinorwic   01248 671215

Marine General Engineers Beaucette
Marina, Guernsey   01481 245808

Marine Propulsion
Hayling Island   07836 737488

Marine & General Engineers
St. Sampsons Harbour, Guernsey
    01481 245808

Marine Servicing
Eastbourne   07932 318414

Marine-Trak Engineering
Mylor Yacht Harbour   01326 376588

Marine Warehouse
Gosport   023 9258 0420

Marlec Marine
Ramsgate   01843 592176

Martin Outboards
Galgate   01524 751750

McKenzie, D
Campbeltown   07799 651637

McQueen, Michael
Kilrush   +35 87 2574623

Meiher, Denis
Fenit   +353 87 958 4744

MES Marine Greenock   01475 744655

MMS Ardrossan   01294 604831/
    07836 342332

Mobile Marine Engineering Liverpool
Marina, Liverpool   01565 733553

Mobile Marine Maintenance
Poole   07931 776482

Mount's Bay Engineering
Newlyn   01736 363095

MP Marine Maryport   01900 810299

Murphy Marine Services
Cahersiveen   +353 66 9476365

New World Yacht Care
Helensburgh   01436 820586

North Western Automarine Engineers
Largs   01475 687139

Noss Marine Services Dart Marina,
Dartmouth   01803 833343

Owen Marine, Robert
Porthmadog   01766 513435

Pace, Andy
Newhaven   01273 516010

**Penzance Dry Dock and Engineering
Co Ltd** Penzance   01736 363838

Pirie & Co, John S
Fraserburgh   01346 513314

Portavon Marine
Keynsham   01225 424301

Power Afloat, Elkins Boatyard
Christchurch   01202 489555

Powerplus Marine Cowes Yacht Haven,
Cowes   01983 290421

Pro-Marine Queen Anne's Battery
Marina, Plymouth   01752 267984

PT Marine Engineering
Hayling Island   023 9246 9332

R & M Marine
Portsmouth   023 9273 7555

R & S Engineering
Dingle Marina   +353 66 915 1189

Reddish Marine
Salcombe   01548 844094

RHP Marine Cowes   01983 290421

RK Marine Ltd Hamble   01489 583585

RK Marine Ltd
Swanwick   01489 583572

Rossiter Yachts Ltd
Christchurch   01202 483250

Ryan & Roberts Marine Services
Askeaton   +353 61 392198

Salve Marine Ltd
Crosshaven   +353 21 4831145

Seamark-Nunn & Co
Felixstowe   01394 275327

Seapower
Ipswich   01473 780090

Seaward Engineering
Glasgow   0141 632 4910

Seaway Marine
Gosport   023 9260 2722

Shearwater Engineering Services Ltd
Dunoon   01369 706666

Silvers Marina Ltd
Helensburgh   01436 831222

Starey Marine
Salcombe   01548 843655

Swordfish Marine Engineering
Holy Loch   01369 701905

Tarbert Marine
Arbroath   01241 872879

Thorne Boat Services
Thorne   01405 814197

Tollesbury Marine Engineering
Tollesbury Marina   01621 869919

Tony's Marine Services
Coleraine   07866 690436

TOR (Gerald Hales)
Stornoway   01851 871025

Vasey Marine Engineering, Gordon
Fareham   07798 638625

Volspec Ltd Tollesbury   01621 869756

Wallis, Peter Torquay Marina,
Torquay   01803 844777

Wartsila Havant   023 9240 0121

WB Marine Chichester   01243 512857

West Coast Marine
Troon   01292 318121

West Marine
Brighton   01273 626656

Weymouth Marina Mechanical Services
Weymouth   01305 779379

Whittington, G Lady Bee Marine,
Shoreham   01273 593801

Whitewater Marine
Malahide   +353 1 816 8473

Wigmore Wright Marine Services
Penarth Marina   029 2070 9983

Wright, M Manaccan   01326 231502

Wyko Industrial Services
Aberdeen   01224 246560

Ynys Marine
Cardigan   01239 613179

Youngboats
Faversham   01795 536176

1° West Marine Ltd
Portsmouth   023 9283 8335

MASTS, SPARS & RIGGING

JWS Marine Services
Portsmouth   02392 755155

A2 Rigging
Falmouth   01326 312209

Allspars Plymouth   01752 266766

Amble Boat Co Ltd
Morpeth   01665 710267

Arun Canvas & Rigging
Littlehampton   01903 732561

B+ St Peter Port   01481 726071

Briggs, Nick
Fleetwood   07513 403831

Buchanan, Keith
St Mary's   01720 422037

Bussell & Co, WL
Weymouth   01305 785633

Carbospars Ltd
Hamble   023 8045 6736

Cable & Rope Works
Bexhill-on-Sea   01424 220112

Clarke Rigging, Niall
Coleraine   07916 083858

Clyde Rigging
Ardrossan   07773 244821

Coates Marine Ltd
Whitby   01947 604486

Cunliffe, Alistair
Fleetwood   07555 798310

Dauntless Boatyard Ltd
Canvey Island   01268 793782

Davies Marine Services
Ramsgate   01843 586172

Eurospars Ltd
Plymouth   01752 550550

Exe Leisure
Exeter   01392 879055

Fox's Marine Ipswich Ltd
Ipswich   01473 689111

Freeland Yacht Spars Ltd
Dorchester on Thames   01865 341277

Gordon, AD Portland   01305 821569

Hamble Custom Rigging Centre
Hamble   023 8045 2000

Harris Rigging Totnes   01803 840160

Heyn Engineering
Belfast   028 9035 0022

Holman Rigging
Chichester   01243 514000

Irish Spars and Rigging
Malahide   +353 86 209 5996

JWS Marine Services
Portsmouth   02392 755155

Kildale Marine Hull   01482 227464

Kilrush Marina Boatyard
Kilrush   +35 87 7990091

Lowestoft Yacht Services
Lowestoft   01502 585535

Laverty, Billy Galway +353 86 3892614

Leitch, WB
Tarbert, Loch Fyne   01880 820287

Lewis, Harry
Kinsale   +353 87 266 7127

Marine Resource Centre
Oban   01631 720291

Martin Leaning Masts & Rigging
Hayling   023 9237 1157

Mast & Rigging
Crosshaven   +353 21 483 3878

Mast & Rigging Services
Largs   01475 670110

Mast & Rigging Services
Inverkip   01475 522700

MP Marine Maryport   01900 810299

Ocean Rigging
Lymington   01590 676292

Owen Sails Oban   01631 720485

Pro Rig S Ireland   +353 87 298 3333

Ratsey, Stephen
Milford Haven   01646 601561

Riglt Ardrossan   07593 220213

Rig Magic Ipswich   01473 655089

Rig Shop
Southampton   023 8033 8341

Ronstan Gosport   023 9252 5377

Salcombe Boatstore
Salcombe   01548 843708

Seldén Mast Ltd
Gosport   01329 504000

Silvers Marina Ltd
Helensburgh   01436 831222

Silverwood Yacht Services Ltd
Portsmouth   023 9232 7067

Spencer Rigging Cowes 01983 292022

Storrar Marine Store
Newcastle upon Tyne   0191 266 1037

Tedfords Rigging & Rafts
Belfast   028 9032 6763

TJ Rigging Conwy   07780 972411

TS Rigging Maldon   01621 874861

Windjammer Marine
Milford Marina   01646 699070

Yacht Rigging Services
Plymouth   01752 226609

Z Spars UK Hadleigh   01473 822130

NAVIGATION EQUIPMENT – GENERAL

Belson Design Ltd, Nick
Southampton   077 6835 1330

Brown Son & Ferguson Ltd
Glasgow   0141 429 1234

Cooke & Son Ltd, B
Hull   01482 223454

Diverse Yacht Services
Hamble   023 8045 3399

Dolphin Maritime Software Ltd
Lancaster   01524 841946

Dubois Phillips & McCallum Ltd
Liverpool   0151 236 2776

Garmin Southampton   02380 524000

Geonav UK Ltd
Poole   0870 240 4575

Imray Laurie Norie and Wilson Ltd
St Ives, Cambs   01480 462114

Kelvin Hughes
Southampton   023 8063 4911

Lilley & Gillie Ltd, John
North Shields   0191 257 2217

Marine Chart Services
Wellingborough   01933 441629

Navico UK Romsey   01794 510010

PC Maritime
Plymouth   01752 254205

Price & Co, WF Bristol   0117 929 2229

Raymarine Ltd
Portsmouth   023 9269 3611

Royal Institute of Navigation
London   020 7591 3130

Sea Chest Nautical Bookshop
Plymouth   01752 222012

Seath Instruments (1992) Ltd
Lowestoft   01502 573811

Smith (Marine) Ltd, AM
London   020 8529 6988

South Bank Marine Charts Ltd
Grimsby   01472 361137

Southcoasting Navigators
Devon   01626 335626

Stanford Charts
Bristol   0117 929 9966
London   020 7836 1321
Manchester   0870 890 3730

Todd Chart Agency Ltd
County Down   028 9146 6640

UK Hydrographic Office
Taunton   01823 337900

Warsash Nautical Bookshop
Warsash   01489 572384

Yachting Instruments Ltd
Sturminster Newton   01258 817662

PAINT & OSMOSIS

Advanced Blast Cleaning Paint
Tavistock   01822 617192
                07970 407911

Herm Seaway Marine Ltd
St Peter Port   01481 726829

Gillingham Marina   01634 280022

Hempel Paints
Southampton   02380 232000

International Coatings Ltd
Southampton   023 8022 6722

Marineware Ltd
Southampton   023 8033 0208

NLB Marine
Ardrossan   01563 521509

Pro-Boat Ltd
Burnham on Crouch   01621 785455

Rustbuster Ltd
Peterborough   01775 761222

SP Systems
Isle of Wight   01983 828000

PROPELLERS & STERGEAR/REPAIRS

CJR Propulsion Ltd
Southampton   023 8063 9366

Darglow Engineering Ltd
Wareham   01929 556512

Propeller Revolutions
Poole   01202 671226

Sillette – Sonic Ltd
Sutton   020 8337 7543

Vetus Den Ouden Ltd
Southampton   02380 454507

RADIO COURSES / SCHOOLS

**Bisham Abbey Sailing & Navigation
School** Bisham   01628 474960

**East Coast Offshore Yachting –
Les Rant** Perry   01480 861381

Hamble School of Yachting
Hamble   023 8045 6687

Pembrokeshire Cruising
Neyland   01646 602500

Plymouth Sailing School
Plymouth   01752 493377

Start Point Sailing
Kingsbridge   01548 810917

REEFING SYSTEMS

Atlantic Spars Ltd
Brixham   01803 843322

Calibra Marine International Ltd
Southampton   08702 400358

Eurospars Ltd
Plymouth   01752 550550

Holman Rigging
Chichester   01243 514000

Sea Teach Ltd
Emsworth   01243 375774

Southern Spar Services
Northam   023 8033 1714

Wragg, Chris
Lymington   01590 677052

Z Spars UK Hadleigh   01473 822130

REPAIR MATERIALS & ACCESSORIES

Akeron Ltd
Southend on Sea   01702 297101

Howells & Son, KJ Poole 01202 665724

JB Timber Ltd
North Ferriby   01482 631765

Robbins Timber Bristol 0117 9633136

Sika Ltd
Welwyn Garden City   01707 394444

Solent Composite Systems
East Cowes   01983 292602

Technix Rubber & Plastics Ltd
Southampton   01489 789944

Tiflex Liskeard   01579 320808

Timage & Co Ltd
Braintree   01376 343087

Trade Grade Products Ltd
Poole   01202 820177

Wessex Resins & Adhesives Ltd
Romsey   01794 521111

ROPE & WIRE

Cable & Rope Works
Bexhill-on-Sea   01424 220112

Euro Rope Ltd
Scunthorpe   01724 280480

Marlow Ropes
Hailsham   01323 444444

Mr Splice Leicester   0800 1697178

Spinlock Ltd Cowes   01983 295555

TJ Rigging Conwy   07780 972411

SAFETY EQUIPMENT

AB Marine Ltd
St Peter Port   01481 722378

Adec Marine Ltd
Croydon   020 8686 9717

Anchorwatch UK
Edinburgh   0131 447 5057

Avon Inflatables
Llanelli   01554 882000

Cosalt International Ltd
Aberdeen   01224 588327

Crewsaver Gosport   01329 820000

Glaslyn Marine Supplies Ltd
Porthmadog   01766 513545

Exposure Lights
Pulborough   01798 839300

Guardian Fire Protection
Manchester   0800 358 7522

Hale Marine, Ron
Portsmouth   023 9273 2985

Herm Seaway Marine Ltd
St Peter Port   01481 722838

KTS Seasafety Kilkeel   028 41762655

McMurdo Pains Wessex
Portsmouth   023 9262 3900

Met Office Exeter   0870 900 0100

Nationwide Marine Hire
Warrington   01925 245788

Norwest Marine Ltd
Liverpool   0151 207 2860

Ocean Safety
Southampton   023 8072 0800

Polymarine Ltd
Conwy   01492 583322

Premium Liferaft Services
Burnham-on-Crouch   0800 243673

Ribeye Dartmouth   01803 832060

South Eastern Marine Services Ltd
Basildon   01268 534427

Suffolk Sailing
Ipswich   01473 604678

Whitstable Marine
Whitstable   01227 262525

Winters Marine Ltd
Salcombe   01548 843580

SAILMAKERS & REPAIRS

Alsop Sailmakers, John
Salcombe   01548 843702

AM Trimming
Windsor   01932 821090

Arun Canvas & Rigging
Littlehampton   01903 732561

Barrett, Katy
St Peter Port   07781 404299

Batt Sails Bosham   01243 575505

Bissett and Ross
Aberdeen   01224 580659

Boatshed, The
Felinheli, Bangor   01248 679939

Breaksea Sails Barry   01446 730785

Bristol Sails Bristol   0117 922 5080

Buchanan, Keith
St Mary's   01720 422037

C&J Marine Ltd
Chichester   01243 785485

Calibra Sails Dartmouth 01803 833094

Clarke Rigging, Niall
Coleraine   07916 083858

Coastal Covers
Portsmouth   023 9252 0200

Covercare Fareham   01329 311878

Covers + Stuff
Douglas, Isle of Man   07624 400037

Crawford, Margaret
Kirkwall   01856 875692

Crusader Sails Poole   01202 670580

Crystal Covers
Portsmouth   023 9238 0143

Cullen Sailmakers
Galway   +353 91 771991

Dolphin Sails Harwich   01255 243366

Doyle Sails
Southampton   023 8033 2622

Downer International Sails & Chandlery
Dun Laoghaire   +353 1 280 0231

Duthie Marine Safety, Arthur
Glasgow   0141 429 4553

Dynamic Sails
Emsworth   01243 374495

Flew Sailmakers
Portchester   01329 822676

Fylde Coast Sailmaking Co
Fleetwood   01253 873476

Freeman Sails Padstow   07771 610053

Garland Sails Bristol   01275 393473

Goacher Sails
Bowness, Cumbria   01539 488686

Gowen Ocean Sailmakers
West Mersea   01206 384412

Green Sailmakers, Paul
Plymouth   01752 660317

Henderson Sails & Covers
Southsea   023 9229 4700

Hood Sailmakers UK
Wareham   0844 209 4789

Hooper, A Plymouth   01752 830411

Hyde Sails
Southampton   0845 543 8945

Jackson Yacht Services
Jersey   01534 743819

Jeckells and Son Ltd (Wroxham)
Wroxham   01603 782223

Jessail Ardrossan   01294 467311

JKA Sailmakers Pwllheli 01758 613266

Kemp Sails Ltd
Wareham   01929 554308/554378

Kildale Marine Hull   01482 227464

Lawrence Sailmakers, J
Brightlingsea   01206 302863

Leitch, WB
Tarbert, Loch Fyne   01880 820287

Leith UK
Berwick on Tweed   01289 307264

Le Monnier, Yannick
Galway   +353 87 628 9854

Lodey Sails
Newlyn   01736 719359

Lossie Sails
Lossiemouth   07989 956698

Lucas Sails Portchester 023 9237 3699

Malakoff and Moore
Lerwick   01595 695544

McCready and Co Ltd, J
Belfast   028 90232842

McKillop Sails, John
Kingsbridge   01548 852343

McNamara Sails, Michael
Great Yarmouth   01692 584186

McWilliam Sailmaker (Crosshaven)
Crosshaven   +353 21 4831505

Sail Shape
Fowey   01726 833731

Montrose Rope and Sails
Montrose   01674 672657

Mountfield Sails
Hayling Island   023 9246 3720

Mouse Sails Holyhead   01407 763636

Nicholson Hughes Sails
Rosneath   01436 831356

North Sea Sails
Tollesbury   01621 869367

North West Sails
Keighley   01535 652949

Northrop Sails Ramsgate 01843 851665

O'Mahony Sailmakers
Kinsale   +353 86 326 0018

O'Sullivans Marine Ltd
Tralee   +353 66 7129635

Owen Sails Benderloch   01631 720485

Parker & Kay Sailmakers –
East Ipswich   01473 659878

Parker & Kay Sailmakers –
South Hamble   023 8045 8213

Penrose Sailmakers
Falmouth   01326 312705

Pinnell & Bax
Northampton   01604 592808

Pollard Marine
Port St Mary   01624 835831

Quantum Sails
Ipswich Haven Marina   01473 659878

Quantum-Parker & Kay Sailmakers		
Hamble	023 8045 8213	
Quay Sails (Poole) Ltd		
Poole	01202 681128	
Ratsey & Lapthorn		
Isle of Wight	01983 294051	
Ratsey Sailmakers, Stephen		
Milford Haven	01646 601561	
Relling One Design		
Portland	01305 826555	
SO31 Bags		
Southampton	023 8045 5106	
Rig Shop, The		
Southampton	023 8033 8341	
Rockall Sails Chichester	01243 573185	
Sail Locker		
Woolverstone Marina	01473 780206	
Sail Style		
Hayling Island	023 9246 3720	
Sails & Canvas Exeter	01392 877527	
Sail Register Ulceby	01469 589444	
Saltern Sail Co		
West Cowes	01983 280014	
Saltern Sail Company		
Yarmouth	01983 760120	
Sanders Sails		
Lymington	01590 673981	
Saturn Sails Largs	01475 689933	
Scott & Co, Graham		
St Peter Port	01481 259380	
Shore Sailmakers		
Swanwick	01489 589450	
SKB Sails Falmouth	01326 372107	
Sketrick Sailmakers Ltd		
Killinchy	028 9754 1400	
Solo Sails Penzance	01736 366004	
Storrar Marine Store		
Newcastle upon Tyne	0191 266 1037	
Suffolk Sails		
Woodbridge	01394 386323	
Sunset Sails Sligo	+353 71 62792	
Torquay Marina Sails and Canvas		
Exeter	01392 877527	
Trident UK Gateshead	0191 490 1736	
Sailcare (UK) Ltd Cowes	01983 248589	
W Sails Leigh-on-Sea	01702 714550	
Warren Hall Beaucette	07781 444280	

Watson Sails Dublin   +353 1 846 2206

WB Leitch and Son
Tarbert   01880 820287

Westaway Sails
Plymouth Yacht Haven   01752 892560

Westsails.ie Kilrush   +35 876289854

Wilkinson Sails
Burnham-on-Crouch   01621 786770

Wilkinson Sails
Teynham   01795 521503

Yacht Shop, The
Fleetwood   01253 879238

SOLAR POWER

Ampair Ringwood   01425 480780

Barden UK Ltd Fareham   01489 570770

Marlec Engineering Co Ltd
Corby   01536 201588

SPRAYHOODS & DODGERS

A & B Textiles
Gillingham   01634 579686

Allison–Gray Dundee   01382 505888

Arton, Charles
Milford-on-Sea   01590 644682

Arun Canvas and Rigging Ltd
Littlehampton   01903 732561

Boatshed, The
Felinheli, Bangor   01248 679939

Buchanan, Keith
St Mary's   01720 422037

C & J Marine Textiles
Chichester   01243 785485

Covercare Fareham   01329 311878

Covercraft
Southampton   023 8033 8286

Crystal Covers
Portsmouth   023 9238 0143

Forth Marine Textiles
Holy Loch   01383 622444

Jeckells and Son Ltd
Wroxham   01603 782223

Jessail Ardrossan   01294 467311

Lomond Boat Covers
Alexandria   01389 602734

Lucas Sails
Portchester   023 9237 3699

Poole Canvas Co Ltd
Poole   01202 677477

Sail Register Ulceby   01469 589444

Saundersfoot Auto Marine
Saundersfoot   01834 812115

Trident UK Gateshead   0191 490 1736

SURVEYORS AND NAVAL ARCHITECTS

Amble Boat Company Ltd
Amble   01665 710267

Ark Surveys East Anglia/South Coast
01621 857065/01794 521957

Atkin & Associates
Lymington   01590 688633

Barbican Yacht Agency Ltd
Plymouth   01752 228855

Battick, Lee St Helier   01534 611143

Booth Marine Surveys, Graham
Birchington-on-Sea   01843 843793

Byrde & Associates
Kimmeridge   01929 480064

Bureau Maritime Ltd
Maldon   01621 859181

Byrde & Associates
Kimmeridge   01929 480064

Cannell & Associates, David M
Wivenhoe   01206 823337

Cardiff Commercial Boat Operators Ltd
Cardiff   029 2037 7872

Clarke Designs LLP, Owen
Dartmouth   01803 770495

Connor, Richard
Coleraine   07712 115751

Cox, David Penryn   01326 340808

Davies, Peter N
Wivenhoe   01206 823289

Down Marine Co Ltd
Belfast   028 90480247

Evans, Martin
Kirby le Soken   07887 724055

Goodall, JL Whitby   01947 604791

Green, James Plymouth   01752 660516

Greening Naval Architect Ltd, David
Salcombe   01548 842000

Hansing & Associates
North Wales/Midlands   01248 671291

JP Services – Marine Safety & Training
Chichester   01243 537552

MacGregor, WA
Felixstowe   01394 676034

Mahoney & Co, KPO
Co Cork   +353 21 477 6150

Marinte Surveys UK
Emsworth   07798 554535

Marintec Lymington   01590 683414

Norwood Marine
Margate   01843 835711

Quay Consultants Ltd
West Wittering   01243 673056

Scott Marine Surveyors & Consultants
Conwy   01492 573001

S Roberts Marine Ltd
Liverpool   0151 707 8300

Staton-Bevan, Tony
Lymington   01590 645755/
07850 315744

Thomas, Stephen
Southampton   023 8048 6273

Towler, Perrin
Lymington   01590 718087

Victoria Yacht Surveys   0800 083 2113

Ward & McKenzie
Woodbridge   01394 383222

Ward & McKenzie (North East)
Pocklington   01759 304322

YDSA Yacht Designers & Surveyors
Association Bordon   0845 0900162

TAPE TECHNOLOGY

CC Marine Services (Rubbaweld) Ltd
London   020 7402 4009

Trade Grade Products Ltd
Poole   01202 820177

UK Epoxy Resins
Burscough   01704 892364

3M United Kingdom plc
Bracknell   0870 5360036

TRANSPORT/YACHT DELIVERIES

Boat Shifters
07733 344018/01326 210548

Convoi Exceptionnel Ltd
Hamble   023 8045 3045

Debbage Yachting
Ipswich   01473 601169

East Coast Offshore Yachting
01480 861381

Hainsworth's UK and Continental
Bingley   01274 565925

Houghton Boat Transport
Tewkesbury   07831 486710

MCL Transboat   08455 201900

MJS Boat Transport
Alexandria, Scotland   01389 755047

Moonfleet Sailing
Poole   01202 682269

Performance Yachting
Plymouth   01752 565023

Peters & May Ltd
Southampton   023 8048 0480

Reeder School of Seamanship, Mike
Lymington   01590 674560

Seafix Boat Transfer   01766 514507

Sealand Boat Deliveries Ltd
Liverpool   01254 705225

Shearwater Sailing
Southampton   01962 775213

Southcoasting Navigators
Devon   01626 335626

West Country Boat Transport
01566 785651

Wolff, David   07659 550131

TUITION/SAILING SCHOOLS

Association of Scottish Yacht
Charterers Argyll   07787 363562
01852 200258

Bisham Abbey Sailing & Navigation
School Bisham   01628 474960

Blue Baker Yachts
Ipswich   01473 780008

British Offshore Sailing School
Hamble   023 8045 7733

Coastal Sea School
Weymouth   0870 321 3271

Dart Harbour Sea School
Dartmouth   01803 839339

Dartmouth Sailing
Dartmouth   01803 833399

Drake Sailing School
Plymouth   01635 253009

East Anglian Sea School
Ipswich   01473 659992

East Coast Offshore Yachting
– Les Rant Perry   01480 861381

Gibraltar Sailing Centre   +350 78554

Glenans Irish Sailing School
Baltimore   +353 28 20154

Hamble School of Yachting
Hamble   023 8045 6687

Haslar Sea School
Gosport   023 9260 2708

Hobo Yachting
Southampton   023 8033 4574

Hoylake Sailing School
Wirral   0151 632 4664

Ibiza Sailing School
07092 235 853

International Yachtmaster Academy
Southampton   0800 515439

JP Services – Marine Safety & Training
Chichester   01243 537552

Lymington Cruising School
Lymington   01590 677478

Marine Leisure Association (MLA)
Southampton   023 8029 3822

Menorca Cruising School
01995 679240

Moonfleet Sailing Poole 01202 682269

National Marine Correspondence
School Macclesfield   01625 262365

Pembrokeshire Cruising
Neyland   01646 602500

Performance Yachting & Chandlery
Plymouth   01752 565023

Plain Sailing
Dartmouth   01803 853843

Plymouth Sailing School
Plymouth   01752 493377

Port Edgar Marina & Sailing School
Port Edgar   0131 331 3330

Portsmouth Outdoor Centre
Portsmouth   023 9266 3873

Portugal Sail & Power   01473 833001

Safe Water Training Sea School Ltd
Wirral   0151 630 0466

Sail East Felixstowe   01255 502887

Sail East
River Crouch   07860 271954

Sail East
River Medway   07932 157027

Sail East Harwich   01473 689344

Sally Water Training
East Cowes   01983 299033

Sea-N-Shore
Salcombe   01548 842276

Seafever
East Grinstead   01342 316293

Solaris Mediterranean Sea School
01925 642909

Solent School of Yachting
Southampton   023 8045 7733

Southcoasting Navigators
Devon   01626 335626

Southern Sailing
Southampton   01489 575511

Start Point Sailing
Dartmouth   01548 810917

Sunsail
Port Solent/Largs   0870 770 6314

Team Sailing Gosport   023 9252 4370

WORLD
CLASS
SKIPPERS
WANTED

NO PRESSURE

Sir Robin Knox-Johnston
*Founder of the Clipper Round
the World Yacht Race*

**Join the elite and take on the
world's longest yacht race,
crewed exclusively by novice crew
embarking on the race of their lives.**

Clipper Race Skippers are exceptional.
These men and women have the fortitude to take
on the toughest of mental challenges, and the
physical endurance to successfully lead a team
through Mother Nature's extreme environments
on a 40,000 mile lap around the globe.

We are recruiting experienced professional
Skippers for the next edition of the Clipper Race.
To qualify you must hold a valid Yachtmaster
Ocean certificate [commercial endorsed] or
International Yacht Training Master of Yachts.

↘ **APPLY NOW**

clipperroundtheworld.com/careers
raceskipper@clipper-ventures.com
+44 (0) 2392 526000

CLIPPER | **ROUND THE WORLD**

Workman Marine School
Portishead   01275 845844

Wride School of Sailing, Bob
North Ferriby   01482 635623

WATERSIDE ACCOMMODATION & RESTAURANTS

51st State Bar & Grill
Dunoon   01369 703595

Abbey, The Penzance   01736 366906

Al Porto
Hull Marina   01482 238889

Arun View Inn, The
Littlehampton   01903 722335

Baywatch on the Beach
Bembridge   01983 873259

Beaucette Marina Restaurant
Guernsey   01481 247066

Bella Napoli
Brighton Marina   01273 818577

Bembridge Coast Hotel
Bembridge   01983 873931

Budock Vean Hotel
Porth Navas Creek   01326 252100

Café Mozart Cowes   01983 293681

Caffé Uno Port
Solent   023 9237 5227

Chandlers Bar & Bistro
Queen Anne's Battery Marina
Plymouth   01752 257772

Cruzzo Malahide Marina
Co Dublin   +353 1 845 0599

Cullins Yard Bistro
Dover   01304 211666

Custom House, The
Poole   01202 676767

Dart Marina River Lounge
Dartmouth   01803 832580

Doghouse Swanwick Marina,
Hamble   01489 571602

Dolphin Restaurant
Gorey   01534 853370

Doune Knoydart   01687 462667

El Puertos
Penarth Marina   029 2070 5551

Falmouth Marina
Marine Bar and Restaurant
Falmouth   01326 313481

Ferry Boat Inn West Wick Marina
Nr Chelmsford   01621 740208

Ferry Inn, The (restaurant)
Pembroke Dock   01646 682947

Fisherman's Wharf
Sandwich   01304 613636

Folly Inn Cowes   01983 297171

Gaffs Restaurant
Fenit, County Kerry   +353 66 71 36666

Godleys Hotel Fenit
County Kerry   +353 66 71 36108

Harbour Lights Restaurant
Walton on the Naze   01255 851887

Haven Bar and Bistro, The
Lymington Yacht Haven 01590 679971

Haven Hotel Poole   08453 371550

HMS Ganges Restaurant
Mylor Yacht Harbour   01326 374320

Holy Loch Inn
Holy Loch   01369 706903

Hunters Bar & Grill
Holy Loch   01369 707772

Jolly Sailor, The
Bursledon   023 8040 5557

Kames Hotel Argyll   01700 811489

Ketch Rigger, The Hamble Point
Marina Hamble   023 8045 5601

Kings Arms Stoborough 01929 552705

Kota Restaurant
Porthleven   01326 562407

La Cala Lady Bee Marina
Shoreham   01273 597422

La Cantina Restaurant
Dunoon   01369 703595

Lake Yard Ltd
Poole   01202 676953

Le Nautique
St Peter Port   01481 721714

Lighter Inn, The
Topsham   01392 875439

Mariners Bistro Sparkes Marina,
Hayling Island   023 9246 9459

Mary Mouse II Haslar Marina,
Gosport   023 9252 5200

Martha's Vineyard
Milford Haven   01646 697083

Master Builder's House Hotel
Buckler's Hard   01590 616253

Millstream Hotel
Bosham   01243 573234

Montagu Arms Hotel
Beaulieu   01590 612324

Oyster Quay
Mercury Yacht Harbour,
Hamble   023 8045 7220

Paris Hotel Coverack   01326 280258

Pebble Beach, The
Gosport   023 9251 0789

Philip Leisure Group
Dartmouth   01803 833351

Priory Bay Hotel
Seaview, Isle of Wight   01983 613146

QC's Cahersiveen   +353 66 9472244

Quay Bar
Galway   +353 91 568347

Quayside Hotel Brixham 01803 855751

Queen's Hotel Kirkwall 01856 872200

Sails Dartmouth   01803 839281

Shell Bay Seafood Restaurant
Poole Harbour   01929 450363

Simply Italian Sovereign Harbour,
Eastbourne   01323 470911

Spit Sand Fort
The Solent   01329 242077

Steamboat Inn
Lossiemouth   01343 812066

Tayvallich Inn, The
Argyll   01546 870282

Villa Adriana Newhaven Marina
Newhaven   01273 513976

Warehouse Brasserie, The
Poole   01202 677238

36 on the Quay
Emsworth   01243 375592

WEATHER INFORMATION

Met Office Exeter   0870 900 0100

WOOD FITTINGS

Howells & Son, KJ
Poole   01202 665724

Onward Trading Co Ltd
Southampton   01489 885250

Robbins Timber
Bristol   0117 963 3136

Sheraton Marine Cabinet
Witney   01993 868275

YACHT BROKERS

ABC Powermarine
Beaumaris   01248 811413

ABYA Association of
Brokers & Yacht Agents
Bordon   0845 0900162

Adur Boat Sales
Southwick   01273 596680

Ancasta International Boat Sales
Southampton   023 8045 0000

Anglia Yacht Brokerage
Bury St Edmunds   01359 271747

Ardmair Boat Centre
Ullapool   01854 612054

Barbican Yacht Agency, The
Plymouth   01752 228855

Bates Wharf Marine Sales Ltd
                          01932 571141

BJ Marine Bangor   028 9127 1434

Boatworks + Ltd
St Peter Port   01481 726071

Caley Marina Inverness 01463 236539

Calibra Marine International Ltd
Southampton   08702 400358

Camper & Nicholsons International
London   020 7009 1950

Clarke & Carter Interyacht Ltd
Ipswich/Burnham on Crouch
             01473 659681/01621 785600

Coastal Leisure Ltd
Southampton   023 8033 2222

Dale Sailing Brokerage
Neyland   01646 603105

Deacons Southampton   023 8040 2253

Exe Leisure Topsham   001392 879055

Ferrypoint Boat Co
Youghal   +353 24 94232

Gweek Quay Boatyard
Helston   01326 221657

International Barge & Yacht Brokers
Southampton   023 8045 5205

Iron Wharf Boatyard
Faversham   01795 536296

Jackson Yacht Services
Jersey   01534 743819

Kings Yacht Agency
Beaulieu   01590 616316

Kippford Slipway Ltd
Dalbeattie   01556 620249

Lencraft Boats Ltd
Dungarvan   +353 58 68220

Liberty Yachts Ltd
Plymouth   01752 227911

Lucas Yachting, Mike
Torquay   01803 212840

Network Yacht Brokers
Dartmouth   01803 834864

Network Yacht Brokers
Plymouth   01752 605377

New Horizon Yacht Agency
Guernsey   01481 726335

Oyster Brokerage Ltd
Southampton   02380 831011

Pearn and Co, Norman
(Looe Boatyard) Looe   01503 262244

Performance Boat Company
Maidenhead   07768 464717

Peters Chandlery
Chichester   01243 511033

Portavon Marina
Keynsham   0117 986 1626

Retreat BY Topsham   01392 874720

SD Marine Ltd
Southampton   023 8045 7278

Sea & Shore Ship Chandler
Dundee   01382 202666

South Pier Shipyard
St Helier   01534 711000

South West Yacht Brokers Group
Plymouth   01752 401421

Sunbird Marine Services
Fareham   01329 842613

Swordfish Marine Brokerage
Holy Loch   01369 701905

Trafalgar Yacht Services
Fareham   01329 823577

Transworld Yachts
Hamble   023 8045 7704

Walker Boat Sales
Deganwy   01492 555706

Walton Marine Sales
Brighton   01273 670707
Portishead   01275 840132
Wroxham   01603 781178

Watson Marine, Charles
Hamble   023 8045 6505

Western Marine
Dublin   +353 1280 0321

Woodrolfe Brokerage
Maldon   01621 868494

Youngboats Faversham   01795 536176

YACHT CHARTERS & HOLIDAYS

Ardmair Boat Centre
Ullapool   01854 612054

Association of Scottish Yacht Charterers Argyll   01880 820012

Camper & Nicholsons International
London   020 7009 1950

Coastal Leisure Ltd
Southampton   023 8033 2222

Crusader Yachting
Turkey   01732 867321

Dartmouth Sailing
Dartmouth   01803 833399

Dartmouth Yacht Charters
Kingswear   01803 883501

Doune Marine Mallaig   01687 462667

Four Seasons Yacht Charter
Gosport   023 9251 1789

Golden Black Sailing
Cornwall   01209 715757

Hamble Point Yacht Charters
Hamble   023 8045 7110

Haslar Marina & Victory Yacht Charters
Gosport   023 9252 0099

Indulgence Yacht Charters
Padstow   01841 719090

Liberty Yachts West Country, Greece,
Mallorca & Italy   01752 227911

Nautilus Yachting
Mediterranean & Caribbean
                       01732 867445

On Deck Sailing
Southampton   023 8063 9997

Patriot Charters & Sail School
Milford Haven   01437 741202

West Country Yachts
Plymouth   01752 606999
Falmouth   01326 212320

Puffin Yachts Port Solent 01483 420728

Sailing Holidays Ltd
Mediterranean   020 8459 8787

Sailing Holidays in Ireland
Kinsale   +353 21 477 2927

Setsail Holidays
Greece, Turkey,
Croatia, Majorca   01787 310445

Shannon Sailing Ltd
Tipperary   +353 67 24499

Sleat Marine Services
Isle of Skye   01471 844216

Smart Yachts
Mediterranean   01425 614804

South West Marine Training
Dartmouth   01803 853843

Sovereign Sailingl
Kinsale   +353 87 6172555

Sunsail
Worldwide   0870 770 0102

Templecraft Yacht Charters
Lewes   01273 812333

TJ Sailing
Gosport   07803 499691

Top Yacht Sailing Ltd
Havant   02392 347655

Victory Yacht Charters
Gosport   023 9252 0099

West Wales Yacht Charter
Pwllheli   07748 634869

39 North (Mediterranean)
Kingskerwell   07071 393939

YACHT CLUBS

Aberaeron YC
Aberdovey   01545 570077

Aberdeen and Stonehaven SC
Nr Inverurie   01569 764006

Aberdour BC   01383 860029

Abersoch Power BC
Abersoch   01758 712027

Aberystwyth BC
Aberystwyth   01970 624575

Aldeburgh YC   01728 452562

Alderney SC   01481 822959

Alexandra YC
Southend-on-Sea   01702 340363

Arklow SC   +353 402 33100

Arun YC
Littlehampton   01903 716016

Axe YC Axemouth   01297 20043

Ayr Yacht and CC   01292 476034

Ballyholme YC
Bangor   028 91271467

Baltimore SC   +353 28 20426

Banff SC	01464 820308	**Castlegate Marine Club**		**Essex YC** Southend	01702 478404	
Bantry Bay SC	+353 27 51724	Stockton on Tees	01642 583299	**Exe SC (River Exe)**		
Barry YC	01446 735511	**Chanonry SC** Fortrose	01463 221415	Exmouth	01395 264607	
Beaulieu River SC		**Chichester Cruiser and Racing Club**		**Eyott SC** Mayland	01245 320703	
Brockenhurst	01590 616273		01483 770391	**Fairlie YC**	01294 213940	
Bembridge SC		**Chichester YC**	01243 512918	**Falmouth Town SC**	01326 373915	
Isle of Wight	01983 872237	**Christchurch SC**	01202 483150	**Falmouth Watersports Association**		
Benfleet YC		**Clyde CC** Glasgow	0141 221 2774	Falmouth	01326 211223	
Canvey Island	01268 792278	**Co Antrim YC**		**Fareham Sailing & Motor BC**		
Blackpool and		Carrickfergus	028 9337 2322	Fareham	01329 280738	
Fleetwood YC	01253 884205	**Cobnor Activities Centre Trust**		**Felixstowe Ferry SC**	01394 283785	
Blackwater SC Maldon	01621 853923		01243 572791	**Findhorn YC** Findhorn	01309 690247	
Blundellsands SC	0151 929 2101	**Coleraine YC**	028 703 44503	**Fishguard Bay YC**		
Bosham SC Chichester		**Colne YC** Brightlingsea	01206 302594	Lower Fishguard	01348 872866	
	01243 572341	**Conwy YC** Deganwy	01492 583690	**Flushing SC** Falmouth	01326 374043	
Brading Haven YC		**Coquet YC**	01665 710367	**Folkestone Yacht and Motor BC**		
Isle of Wight	01983 872289	**Corrib Rowing & YC**		Folkestone	01303 251574	
Bradwell CC	01621 892970	Galway City	+353 91 564560	**Forth Corinthian YC**		
Bradwell Quay YC		**Cowes Combined Clubs**		Haddington	0131 552 5939	
Wickford	01268 890173		01983 295744	**Forth YCs Association**		
Brancaster Staithe SC	01485 210249	**Cowes Corinthian YC**		Edinburgh	0131 552 3006	
Brandy Hole YC		Isle of Wight	01983 296333	**Fowey Gallants SC**	01726 832335	
Hullbridge	01702 230320	**Cowes Yachting**	01983 280770	**Foynes YC** Foynes	+353 69 91201	
Brightlingsea SC	01206 303275	**Cramond BC**	0131 336 1356	**Galway Bay SC**	+353 91 794527	
Brighton Marina YC		**Creeksea SC**		**Glasson SC** Lancaster	01524 751089	
Peacehaven	01273 818711	Burnham-on-Crouch	01245 320578	**Gosport CC** Gosport	02392 586838	
Bristol Avon SC	01225 873472	**Crookhaven SC**	+353 87 2379997	**Gravesend SC**	07538 326623	
Bristol Channel YC		**Crouch YC**		**Greenwich YC** London	020 8858 7339	
Swansea	01792 366000	Burnham-on-Crouch	01621 782252	**Grimsby and Cleethorpes YC**		
Bristol Corinthian YC		**Dale YC**	01646 636362	Grimsby	01472 356678	
Axbridge	01934 732033	**Dartmouth YC**	01803 832305	**Guernsey YC**		
Brixham YC	01803 853332	**Deben YC** Woodbridge	01394 384440	St Peter Port	01481 725342	
Burnham Overy		**Dell Quay SC** Chichester	01243 514639	**Hamble River SC**		
Staithe SC	01328 730961	**Dingle SC**	+353 66 51984	Southampton	023 80452070	
Burnham-on-Crouch SC		**Douglas Bay YC**	01624 673965	**Hampton Pier YC**		
	01621 782812	**Dovey YC**		Herne Bay	01227 364749	
Burnham-on-Sea SC		Aberdovey	01213 600008	**Hardway SC** Gosport	023 9258 1875	
Bridgwater	01278 792911	**Dun Laoghaire MYC**	+353 1 288 938	**Hartlepool YC**	01429 233423	
Burry Port YC	01554 833635	**Dunbar SC**		**Harwich Town SC**	01255 503200	
Cabot CC	01275 855207	Cockburnspath	01368 86287	**Hastings and St Leonards YC**		
Caernarfon SC (Menai Strait)		**East Antrim BC**	028 28 277204	Hastings	01424 420656	
Caernarfon	01286 672861	**East Belfast YC**	028 9065 6283	**Haven Ports YC**		
Campbeltown SC	01586 552488	**East Cowes SC**	01983 531687	Woodbridge	01473 659658	
Island YC Canvey Island	01702 510360	**East Dorset SC** Poole	01202 706111	**Hayling Ferry SC; Locks SC**		
Cardiff YC	029 2046 3697	**East Lothian YC**	01620 892698	Hayling Island	07870 367571	
Cardiff Bay YC	029 20226575	**Eastney Cruising Association**		**Hayling Island SC**	023 92463768	
Carlingford Lough YC		Portsmouth	023 92734103	**Helensburgh SC** Rhu	01436 672778	
Rostrevor	028 4173 8604	**Eling SC**	023 80863987	Helensburgh	01436 821234	
Carrickfergus SC		**Emsworth SC**	01243 372850	**Helford River SC**		
Whitehead	028 93 351402	**Emsworth Slipper SC**	01243 372523	Helston	01326 231006	
Castle Cove SC				**Herne Bay SC**	01227 375650	
Weymouth	01305 783708			**Highcliffe SC**		
				Christchurch	01425 274874	

Holyhead SC	01407 762526
Holywood YC	028 90423355
Hoo Ness YC Sidcup	01634 250052
Hornet SC Gosport	023 9258 0403
Howth YC	+353 1 832 2141
Hoylake SC Wirral	0151 632 2616
Hullbridge YC	01702 231797
Humber Yawl Club	01482 667224
Hundred of Hoo SC	01634 250102
Hurlingham YC	
London	020 8788 5547
Hurst Castle SC	01590 645589
Hythe SC	
Southampton	02380 846563
Hythe & Saltwood SC	01303 265178
Ilfracombe YC	01271 863969
Iniscealtra SC	
Limerick	+353 61 338347
Invergordon BC	01349 893772
Irish CC	+353 214870031
Island CC Salcombe	01548 844631
Island SC Isle of Wight	01983 296621
Island YC Canvey Island	01268 510360
Isle of Bute SC	
Rothesay	01700 502819
Isle of Man YC	
Port St Mary	01624 832088
Itchenor SC Chichester	01243 512400
Keyhaven YC	01590 642165
Killyleagh YC	028 4482 8250
Kircubbin SC	028 4273 8422
Kirkcudbright SC	01557 331727
Langstone SC Havant	023 9248 4577
Largs SC Largs	01475 670000
Larne Rowing & SC	028 2827 4573
Lawrenny YC	01646 651212
Leigh-on-Sea SC	01702 476788
Lerwick BC	01595 696954
Lilliput SC Poole	01202 740319
Littlehampton Yacht Club	
Littlehampton	01903 713990
Loch Ryan SC Stranraer	01776 706322
Lochaber YC	
Fort William	01397 772361
Locks SC Portsmouth	07980 856267
Looe SC	01503 262559
Lossiemouth CC	
Fochabers	01348 812121
Lough Swilly YC Fahn	+353 74 22377
Lowestoft CC	07810 522515

Lyme Regis Power BC	01297 443788
Lyme Regis SC	01297 442373
Lymington Town SC	0159 674514
Lympstone SC Exeter	01395 278792
Madoc YC Porthmadog	01766 512976
Malahide YC	+353 1 845 3372
Maldon Little Ship Club	01621 854139
Manx Sailing & CC	
Ramsey	01624 813494
Marchwood YC	023 80666141
Margate YC	01843 292602
Marina BC Pwllheli	01758 612271
Maryport YC	01228 560865
Mayflower SC Plymouth	01752 662526
Mayo SC (Rosmoney)	
Rosmoney	+353 98 27772
Medway YC Rochester	01634 718399
Menai Bridge BC	
Beaumaris	01248 810583
Mengham Rythe SC	
Hayling Island	023 92463337
Merioneth YC	
Barmouth	01341 280000
Monkstone Cruising and SC	
Swansea	01792 812229
Montrose SC Montrose	01674 672554
Mumbles YC Swansea	01792 369321
Mylor YC Falmouth	01326 374391
Nairn SC	01667 453897
National YC	
Dun Laoghaire	+353 1 280 5725
Netley SC Netley	023 80454272
New Quay YC	
Aberdovey	01545 560516
Newhaven & Seaford SC	
Seaford	01323 890077
Newport and Uskmouth SC	
Cardiff	01633 271417
Newtownards SC	028 9181 3426
Neyland YC	01646 600267
North Devon YC	
Bideford	01271 861390
North Fambridge Yacht Centre	
	01621 740370
North Haven YC Poole	01202 708830
North of England Yachting Association	
Kirkwall	01856 872331
North Sunderland Marine Club	
Sunderland	01665 721231
North Wales CC Conwy	01492 593481
North West Venturers YC (Beaumaris)	
Beaumaris	0161 2921943

Oban SC Ledaig by Oban	
	01631 563999
Orford SC Woodbridge	01394 450997
Orkney SC Kirkwall	01856 872331
Orwell YC Ipswich	01473 602288
Oulton Broad Yacht Station	
	01502 574946
Ouse Amateur SC	
Kings Lynn	01553 772239
Paignton SC Paignton	01803 525817
Parkstone YC Poole	01202 743610
Peel Sailing and CC Peel	01624 842390
Pembroke Haven YC	01646 684403
Pembrokeshire YC	
Milford Haven	01646 692799
Penarth YC	029 20708196
Pentland Firth YC	
Thurso	01847 891803
Penzance YC	01736 364989
Peterhead SC Ellon	01779 75527
Pin Mill SC	
Woodbridge	01394 780271
Plym YC Plymouth	01752 404991
Poolbeg YC	+353 1 660 4681
Poole YC	01202 672687
Porlock Weir SC	
Watchet	01643 862702
Port Edgar YC Penicuik	0131 657 2854
Port Navas YC Falmouth	
	01326 340065
Port of Falmouth Sailing Association	
Falmouth	01326 372927
Portchester SC	
Portchester	023 9237 6375
Porthcawl Harbour BC	
Swansea	01656 655935
Porthmadog SC	
Porthmadog	01766 513546
Portrush YC Portrush	028 7082 3932
Portsmouth SC	02392 820596
Prestwick SC Prestwick	01292 671117
Pwllheli SC Pwllheli	01758 613343
Queenborough YC	
Queenborough	01795 663955
Quoile YC	
Downpatrick	028 44 612266
River Towy BC Tenby	01267 241755
RAFYC	023 80452208
Redclyffe YC Poole	01929 557227
Restronguet SC	
Falmouth	01326 374536

Ribble CC
Lytham St Anne's 01253 739983

River Wyre YC 01253 811948

RNSA (Plymouth) 01752 55123/83

Rochester CC 01634 841350

Rock Sailing and Water Ski Club
Wadebridge 01208 862431

Royal Dart YC
Dartmouth 01803 752496

Royal Motor YC Poole 01202 707227

Royal Anglesey YC (Beaumaris)
Anglesey 01248 810295

Royal Burnham YC
Burnham-on-Crouch 01621 782044

Royal Channel Islands YC (Jersey)
St Aubin 01534 745783

Royal Cinque Ports YC
Dover 01304 206262

**Royal Corinthian YC
(Burnham-on-Crouch)**
Burnham-on-Crouch 01621 782105

Royal Corinthian YC (Cowes)
Cowes 01983 293581

Royal Cork YC
Crosshaven +353 214 831023

Royal Cornwall YC (RCYC)
Falmouth 01326 312126

Royal Dorset YC
Weymouth 01305 786258

Royal Forth YC
Edinburgh 0131 552 3006

Royal Fowey YC Fowey 01726 833573

Royal Gourock YC 01475 632983

Royal Highland YC
Nairn 01667 493855

Royal Irish YC
Dun Laoghaire +353 1 280 9452

Royal London YC
Isle of Wight 019 83299727

Royal Lymington YC 01590 672677

Royal Mersey YC
Birkenhead 0151 645 3204

Royal Motor YC Poole 01202 707227

Royal Naval Club and Royal Albert YC
Portsmouth 023 9282 5924

Royal Naval Sailing Association
Gosport 023 9252 1100

Royal Norfolk & Suffolk YC
Lowestoft 01502 566726

Royal North of Ireland YC
028 90 428041

Royal Northern and Clyde YC
Rhu 01436 820322

Royal Northumberland YC
Blyth 01670 353636

Royal Plymouth Corinthian YC
Plymouth 01752 664327

Royal Scottish Motor YC
0141 881 1024

Royal Solent YC
Yarmouth 01983 760256

Royal Southampton YC
Southampton 023 8022 3352

Royal Southern YC
Southampton 023 8045 0300

Royal St George YC
Dun Laoghaire +353 1 280 1811

Royal Tay YC Dundee 01382 477133

Royal Temple YC
Ramsgate 01843 591766

Royal Torbay YC
Torquay 01803 292006

Royal Ulster YC
Bangor 028 91 270568

Royal Victoria YC
Fishbourne 01983 882325

Royal Welsh YC (Caernarfon)
Caernarfon 01286 672599

Royal Welsh YC
Aernarfon 01286 672599

Royal Western YC
Plymouth 01752 226299

Royal Yacht Squadron
Isle of Wight 01983 292191

Royal Yorkshire YC
Bridlington 01262 672041

Rye Harbour SC 01797 223136

Salcombe YC 01548 842593

Saltash SC 01752 845988

Scalloway BC Lerwick 01595 880409

Scarborough YC 01723 373821

Schull SC +353 28 37352

Scillonian Sailing and BC
St Mary's 01720 277229

Seasalter SC Whitstable 07773 189943

Seaview YC
Isle of Wight 01983 613268

Shoreham SC Henfield 01273 453078

Skerries SC +353 1 849 1233

Slaughden SC
Duxford 01728 689036

Sligo YC Sligo +353 71 77168

Solva Boat Owners Association
Fishguard 01437 721538

Solway YC
Kirkdudbright 01556 620312

South Caernavonshire YC
Abersoch 01758 712338

South Cork SC +353 28 36383

South Devon Sailing School
Newton Abbot 01626 52352

South Gare Marine Club - Sail Section
Middlesbrough 01642 505630

South Shields SC 0191 456 5821

South Woodham Ferrers YC
Chelmsford 01245 325391

Southampton SC 023 8044 6575

Southwold SC 01986 784225

Sovereign Harbour YC
Eastbourne 01323 470888

St Helier YC 01534 721307/32229

St Mawes SC 01326 270686

Starcross Fishing & CC (River Exe)
Starcross 01626 891996

Starcross YC Exeter 01626 890470

Stoke SC Ipswich 01473 624989

Stornoway SC 01851 705412

Stour SC 01206 393924

Strangford Lough YC
Newtownards 028 97 541202

Strangford SC
Downpatrick 028 4488 1404

Strood YC
Aylesford 01634 718261

Sunderland YC 0191 567 5133

Sunsail Portsmouth 023 92222224

Sussex YC
Shoreham-by-Sea 01273 464868

Swanage SC 01929 422987

Swansea Yacht & Sub-Aqua Club
Swansea 01792 469096

Tamar River SC
Plymouth 01752 362741

Tarbert Lochfyne YC 01880 820376

Tay Corinthian BC
Dundee 01382 553534

Tay YCs Association 01738 621860

Tees & Hartlepool YC 01429 233423

Tees SC
Aycliffe Village 01429 265400

Teifi BC - Cardigan Bay
Fishguard 01239 613846

Teign Corinthian YC
Teignmouth 01626 777699

Tenby SC 01834 842762

Tenby YC 01834 842762

Thames Estuary YC 01702 345967

Thorney Island SC 01243 371731

Thorpe Bay YC	01702 587563
Thurrock YC Grays	01375 373720
Tollesbury CC	01621 869561
Topsham SC	01392 877524
Torpoint Mosquito SC - Plymouth	01752 812508
Tralee SC	+353 66 7136119
Troon CC	01292 311190
Troon YC	01292 315315
Tudor SC Portsmouth	02392 662002
Tynemouth SC Newcastle upon Tyne	0191 2572167
Up River YC Hullbridge	01702 231654
Upnor SC	01634 718043
Vanguard SC Workington	01228 674238
Wakering YC Rochford	01702 530926
Waldringfield SC Woodbridge	01394 283347
Walls Regatta Club Lerwick	01595 809273
Walton & Frinton YC Walton-on-the-Naze	01255 675526
Warrenpoint BC	028 4175 2137
Warsash SC Soton	01489 583575
Watchet Boat Owner Association Watchet	01984 633736
Waterford Harbour SC Dunmore East	+353 51 383389
Watermouth YC Watchet	01271 865048

Wear Boating Association	0191 567 5313
Wells SC Wells-next-the-sea	01328 711190
West Kirby SC	0151 625 5579
West Mersea YC Colchester	01206 382947
Western Isles YC	01688 302371
Western YC Kilrush	+353 87 2262885
Weston Bay YC Portishead	07867 966429
Weston CC Soton	02380 466790
Weston SC Soton	02380 452527
Wexford HBC	+353 53 22039
Weymouth SC	01305 785481
Whitby YC	07786 289393
Whitstable YC	01227 272942
Wicklow SC	+353 404 67526
Witham SC Boston	01205 363598
Wivenhoe SC Colchester	01206 822132
Woodbridge CC	01394 386737
Wormit BC	01382 553878
Yarmouth SC	01983 760270
Yealm YC Newton Ferrers	01752 872291
Youghal Sailing Club	+353 24 92447

YACHT DESIGNERS

Cannell & Associates, David M Wivenhoe	01206 823337
Clarke Designs LLP, Owen Dartmouth	01803 770495
Giles Naval Architects, Laurent Lymington	01590 641777
Harvey Design, Ray Barton on Sea	01425 613492
Jones Yacht Design, Stephen Warsash	01489 576439
Wharram Designs, James Truro	01872 864792
Wolstenholme Yacht Design Coltishall	01603 737024

YACHT MANAGEMENT

Barbican Yacht Agency Ltd Plymouth	01752 228855
Coastal Leisure Ltd Southampton	023 8033 2222
O'Sullivan Boat Management Dun Laoghaire	+353 86 829 6625
Swanwick Yacht Surveyors Swanwick	01489 564822
Amble Boat Company Ltd Amble	01665 710267

YACHT VALETING

Autogleam Lymington	0800 074 4672
Blackwell, Craig Co Meath	+353 87 677 9605
Bright 'N' Clean South Coast	01273 604080
Clean It All Nr Brixham	01803 844564
Kip Marina Inverkip	01475 521485
Mainstay Yacht Maintenance Dartmouth	01803 839076
Mobile Yacht Maintenance	07900 148806
Shipshape Hayling Is	023 9232 4500